THE HIDDEN MOD IN MODERN ART

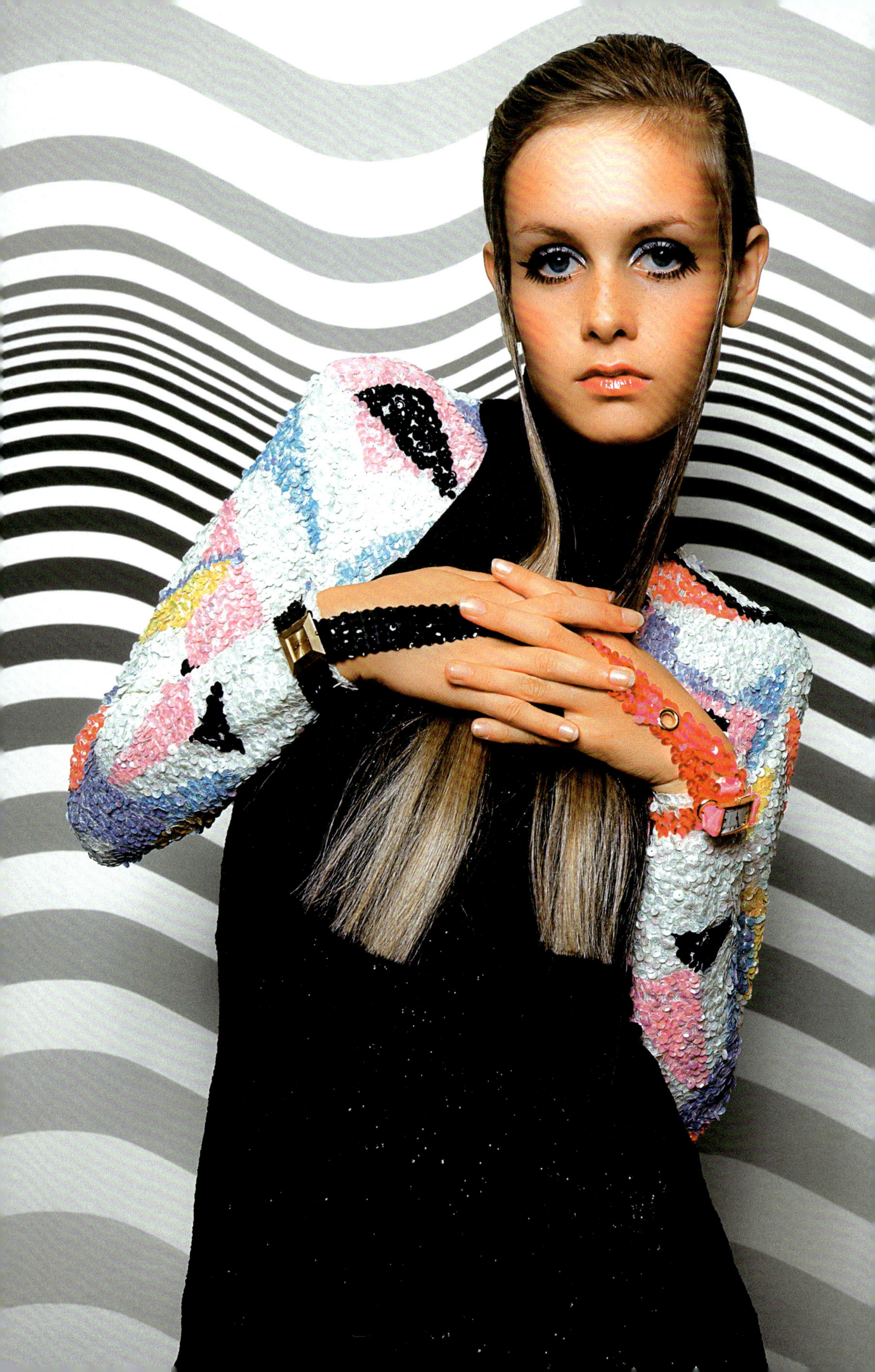

THOMAS CROW

THE HIDDEN MOD IN MODERN ART: LONDON 1957–1969

Paul Mellon Centre for Studies in British Art
Distributed by Yale University Press
New Haven and London

FOR ANDREW HOLMES
AND DAVID ALAN MELLOR

First published in 2020 by the
Paul Mellon Centre for Studies in British Art
16 Bedford Square, London, WC1B 3JA

paul-mellon-centre.ac.uk

ISBN 978-1-913107-13-0 HB

Library of Congress Control Number: 2020935731

British Library Cataloguing-in-Publication Data
A catalogue record for this book is available from the British Library

Designed by Dalrymple
Typeset in Sentinel and Bureau Grotesque
Origination by Evergreen Colour Management Ltd
Printed in Italy by Conti Tipocolor

FSC www.fsc.org MIX Paper from responsible sources FSC® C016114

Frontispiece Twiggy in a sequined jumpsuit by Gene Shelley, photographed by Bert Stern, *Vogue*, 1967 (detail of fig. 91)

CONTENTS

ACKNOWLEDGMENTS

I owe this book primarily to one person: Mark Hallett, Director of Studies at the Paul Mellon Centre for Studies in British Art. His counter-intuitive idea that I might deliver the Paul Mellon Lectures stemmed from some pages on London embedded in my 2015 book *The Long March of Pop*. By no means enough to qualify me as a specialist in the art of the United Kingdom, they nonetheless sparked in him the leap of faith that this seed could flower into the requisite five talks at the National Gallery, London, and subsequently at the Yale Center for British Art. So it did, with a commensurable debt owed to my old colleague and friend David Alan Mellor, whose foundational *The Sixties Art Scene in London* contained the key apperceptions on young artists and Mod style from which the talks were built. In a wider sense, during the years when David and I taught together at the University of Sussex, he was my Virgil where the intricacies of British art, society, and postwar culture were concerned. Londoner Andrew Holmes, master over all that is deep, distinguished, and soulful in the popular cultures of both the US and UK, offered his wise, steadying hand while the lectures unfolded from week to week.

Presuming to speak of times and events in which certain members of the audience had participated, my trepidation was allayed by the generous attention of the National Gallery audiences. As Mark had sensed, Londoners were more than ready to encourage this art-historical institution to extend itself further toward the present and deeper into the culture of the young, which we all occupy at one point in our lives. The Paul Mellon Centre, with Sarah Turner presiding, imaginatively convened occasions around the lectures, where an inter-generational group of scholars was generous enough to expand the dialogue with their own insights and research. These supportive colleagues included Kate Aspinall, Helena Bonett, Chris Breward, Becky Conekin, Elena Crippa, Anne Massey, Alex Massouras, Lynda Nead, Alex Seago, Catherine Spencer, and Lisa Tickner. The welcome faces I saw at the talks included Jo Applin, Jon Bird, Cathy Courtney, Michael Craig-Martin, Emily Crow, Jeremy Deller, Briony Fer, Gabriele Finaldi, Hannah Freedberg, Paul Gilroy, Cora Gilroy-Ware, Martin Hammer, Maureen Hedges, Bernice Holmes, Catherine Lampert, Tom Perchard, George Shaw, David Solkin, Chris Stevens, and Sue Tate. John Kasmin was warmly forthcoming with his time, photographs, and fund of stories, while I like to think that I felt Terry Atkinson's guiding presence from afar. Some time later, a glorious day with Billy Apple and Mary Morrison in Auckland greatly enlarged my fund of knowledge and filled a crucial portion of the story, an occasion I owe to Julia Waite.

My time in London was smoothed and enriched by the members of staff at the Mellon Centre: along with Mark and Sarah, Baillie Card, Ella Fleming, Martin Postle, Maisoon Rehani, and Sarah Ruddick. Turning toward this published version, Emily Lees, Tom Powell, and Katharine Ridler kept it all on track. In the warm surroundings of the Yale Center for British Art, Director Amy Meyers welcomed the lectures and events with all her customary graciousness, sustained by the understanding oversight of Martina Droth and Jane Nowosadko. Steady support in the audience came from Tim Barringer, Jules Prown, Jonathan Weinberg, Bryan Wolf, and Mimi Yiengpruksawan. Close to home in Old Saybrook, these friends were joined by my wife Catherine Phillips, whose presence always means more to me than I can express.

Music runs through all these chapters, as it did in the lectures. But it was never obvious how to present this aural dimension in a compressed visual lecture. I elected to play some relevant tracks over the PA each week as the audience assembled. And one of the best moments in London came before the last talk. As Desmond Dekker's "You Can Get It If You Really Want" kicked things off, the young ushers at the back of the hall began to dance. That was my kind of art history.

PROLOGUE
THE HIDDEN MOD IN THE NEW ART HISTORY

WHEN, DURING THE 1970s, IT BECAME POSSIBLE to talk about a New Art History, the term carried an implicit allusion to art of a particular place and time. The place was Paris; the time was the second half of the nineteenth century; the art in question represented the data of contemporary life to the exclusion of older subjects like myth and religion. The city exerted a spell, making the urban transformations of its core and periphery somehow exemplary as to how modern life was to be lived. By extension, art that qualified as modern needed to have drawn both its subject matter and its sensibility from the same phenomena.[1]

Older distinctions between Realism, Impressionism, and Post-Impressionism in nineteenth-century French art became less salient, the rubric "Modern-Life" encompassing their shared territory. That usurpation entailed a shift in definition from particulars of painterly style to what older art historians had sequestered in their discipline under the heading of "iconography," in other words, characteristic subject matter bearing coded cultural meaning. So it was more than a matter of opulent boulevards or weekend leisure as objects of description; it was a different way of life betokened by such innovative urban and suburban pastimes.

For guidance to the coded meanings of the modernizing city, certain period commentators, often dyspeptic ones, offered eloquent testimony. Especially favored were the writers Edmond and Jules Goncourt, who opined in their singular voice about the disquiet they experienced at the changes around them. In one passage from their journal (18 November

1860), they reacted with almost apocalyptic alarm at the colonization of central public thoroughfares by open-air cafés and the lingering, loitering crowds they attracted:

> *I am going this evening to the Eldorado, a café-concert on the Boulevard de Strasbourg, a room with columns and very luxurious decor and paintings ... Social life is beginning a grand evolution. I see women, children, households, families in this café. The interior is about to die. Life threatens to become public ... I am a stranger to what is coming to what exists now, as I am to these new boulevards without turnings, without adventures of perspective, implacably enforcing the straight line, which carry no more any feeling of Balzac's world, which carry one's thoughts to some American Babylon of the future.*[2]

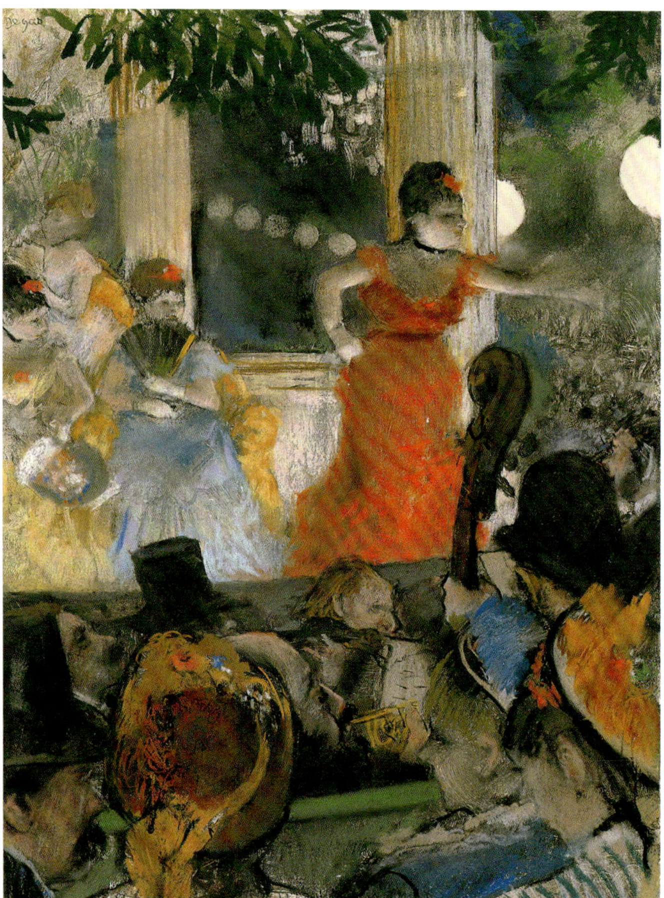

1 Edgar Degas, *Café-concert aux Ambassadeurs*, 1876–7
Pastel over paper, 37 × 26 cm
Musée des Beaux-Arts, Lyon

The particular objects of their diatribe were the *cafés-concerts* or *cafés-chantants*, establishments open to the street in milder weather that offered musical performances by popular singers performing the latest, most topical songs – along with the favorites with which a particular entertainer was identified. To sit down close to the performers required ordering a fairly pricey drink and keeping the glass filled. But it was common for contemporary observers to note the existence of another audience circulating just beyond the perimeter, "which gives itself the pleasure, free of charge, of seizing the new songs on the wing," said one: "They are Parisians, listening naïvely to the inept refrains they so much want to learn by heart."[3]

No artist left more eloquent portrayals of these venues than did Edgar Degas (fig. 1), and the following passage might well have been written with precisely such pictures by Degas in mind:

> *As life moved increasingly from the inside to the outside, as it flowed more and more along public channels or stood in public places, so the aesthete, the artist followed it out into its new setting and caught it there ... The subject matter of the Impressionists, or at any rate the subject matter that is peculiar to them, could be characterized as life modified in accordance with the Goncourts' prophecy.*

The sentiment is entirely consistent with the New-Art-History moment of the 1980s, but the date of its publication is 1962. Its author is the philosopher Richard Wollheim, who titled his essay "Babylon, Babylone" and pursued this insight to the point of adumbrating virtually the entire intellectual project to come two decades later:

> *whereas the Goncourts had predicted that the general engulfment of private life in the public existence of the city would mean the extinction of taste and sensibility, it seemed at first as though Impressionism had refuted this by showing how the city could become the focus of a kind of taste and sensibility as fine and rich as any of an older, pre-industrial age ... a passion for the total panorama of urban life in its high color, its stridency, its complexity, upon which the sensitive eye or ear could impose its own particular aesthetic pattern* (fig. 2).[4]

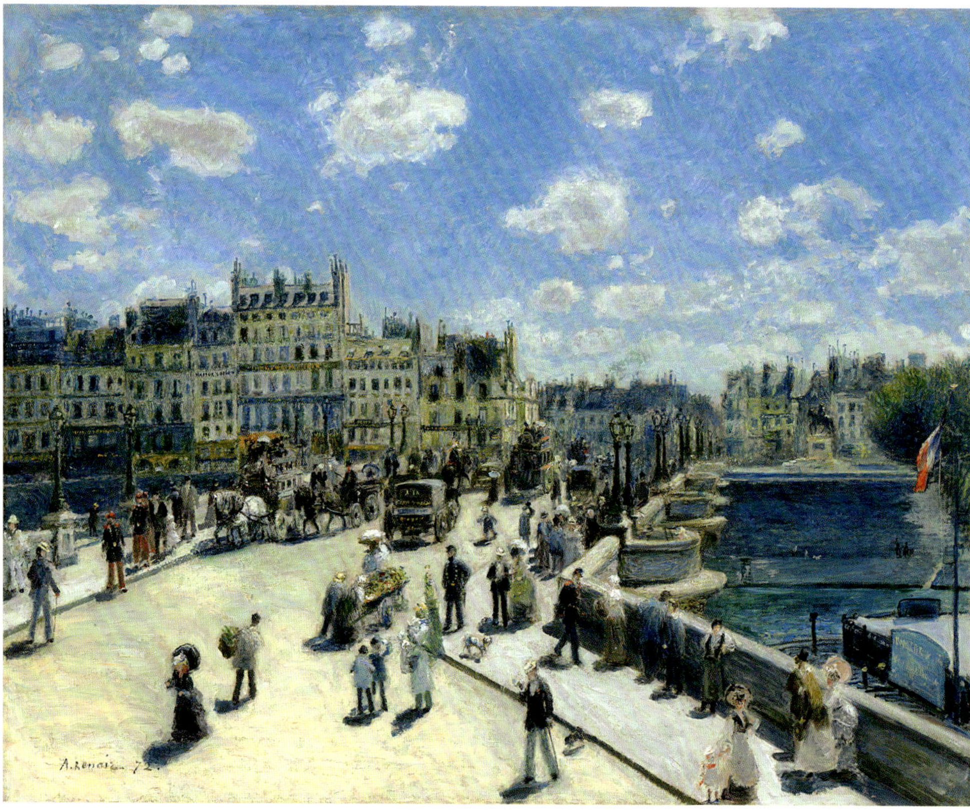

2 Pierre-Auguste Renoir, *Le Pont Neuf*, 1872

Oil on canvas, 75.3 × 93.7 cm
National Gallery of Art, Washington DC

He is quick to add: "But now it seems that the Impressionists achieved this only by suppressing many of the special characteristics of the city," chiefly the human and environmental costs of the new industries that made possible all the captivating prosperity on its surface.[5] The phrase "now it seems," however, sounds an over-optimistic note, as these recognitions had then struck few besides himself, the chief exception being his friend the American art historian Meyer Schapiro, who had advanced a similar view as early as 1936.[6] When their common outlook returned to visibility around 1980, this time with a certain academic imprimatur, it could still provoke and even scandalize the guardians of received ideas, its sin being to interpret the sunny visions of Impressionism (of all things) as bespeaking sordid matters of social class and labor exploitation. Schapiro had by then received a certain retroactive acknowledgment as father of these ideas, but next to no one remembered that Wollheim had presciently reiterated them with greater scope and sharper rhetoric:

the creators of the industrial nightmare emerge from the canvases of Impressionism credited with having been so many theatrical designers or landscape gardeners of genius (fig. 3) ... *there is no recognition in this art of the terrible price that in reality has to be paid, in terms of human suffering and deprivation, for these effects and impressions. Indeed, it is this that gives the painting, for all its fine sensibility, a kind of cold inhumanity.*[7]

Where Schapiro had written that Impressionism "had a moral aspect," Wollheim's forgotten contribution was considerably more forthright in pointing toward the door at which the moral reckoning should be laid: "the changes that the Goncourts deplored and the Impressionists celebrated were brought about by the vast organised conventional sections of Parisian society. It was the *bourgeoisie* that thought of them, it was the *bourgeoisie* that enjoyed them, it was the *bourgeoisie* that subsidised them, and it was the *bourgeoisie* that grew rich on them."[8]

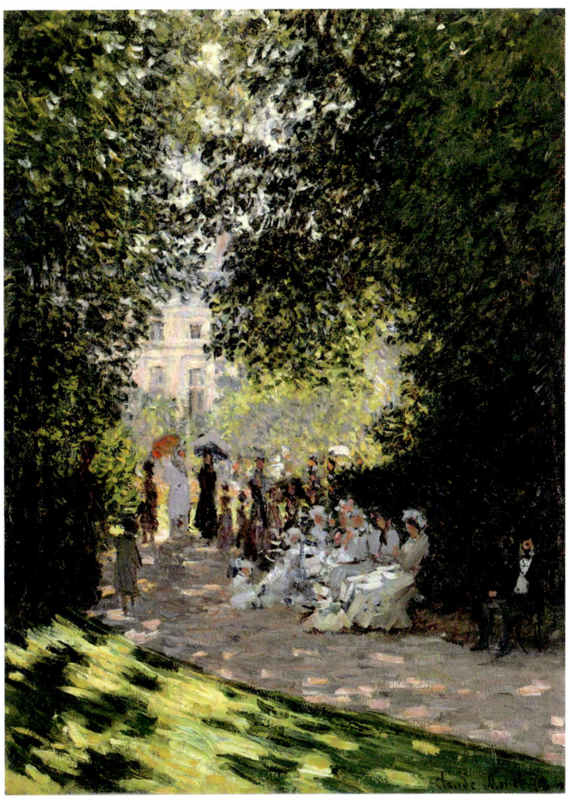

3 Claude Monet, *Le Parc Monceau*, 1878
Oil on canvas, 72.7 × 54.3 cm
Metropolitan Museum of Art, New York

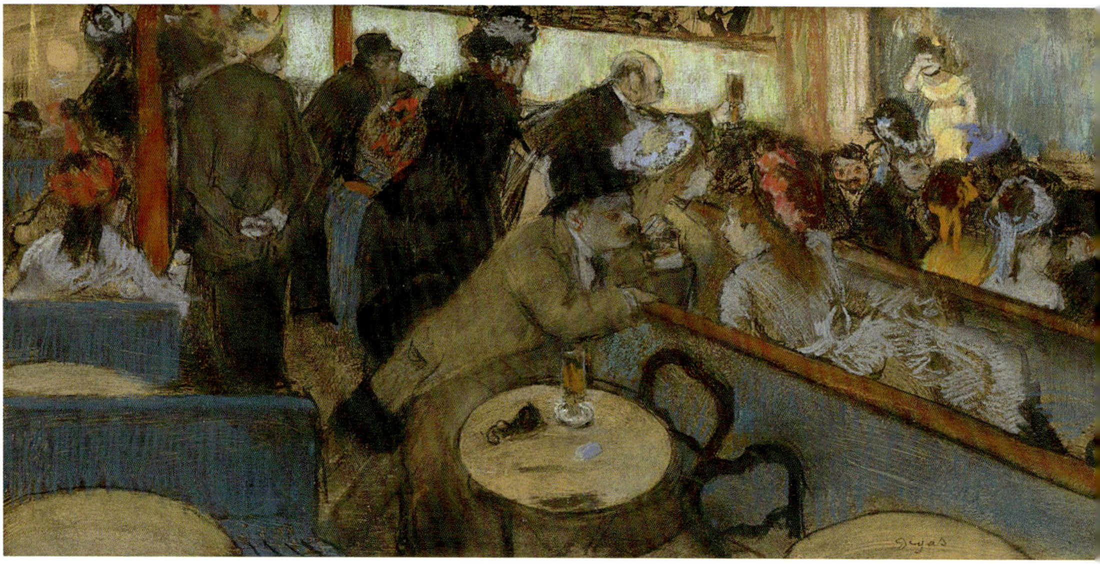

4 Edgar Degas, *Le Café-concert (Les Spectateurs)*, 1876–7

Pastel over monotype on buff wove paper, laid down on tan card, 20.1 × 41.5 cm
Art Institute of Chicago

It was curious, however, that this clarity failed to survive in the New Art History to come, as exemplified by T. J. Clark's highly influential study of 1984, *The Painting of Modern Life*. Addressing the same phenomena as Wollheim, keying on the same quotation by the Goncourts, Clark turned his fire on another social type altogether: not the *grand bourgeois* who engineered and stood to profit from a city made over in the interests of commerce, manufacturing, transport, and entertainment; instead it was a distinctive figure from the working class, but one who pretended to be bourgeois. Various period terms, chiefly *calicot* (after the kind of cloth), designate the shop assistant or clerical apprentice who could afford to dress up and frequent the café-concert, either from the tables (fig. 4) or the fringe on the street. The *calicots* seemed to personify these venues in all their novelty and raucous allure. They could shout along with the songs in their rough humor and slangy diction with language they would never venture in the presence of their customers or superiors, as if, according to Clark, "the clerks and shop assistants are required to admit their cultural and material links to the working class even as they deny them: they define themselves by their difference from the popular, *but also their possession of it* [emphasis in original] ... They are the connoisseurs of popular culture, its experts, its aestheticians."[9]

Wollheim too brings to the fore a type that fits this description, though without the edge of reproach and in a different time and place, as he makes the transition from his prescient account of Parisan modern-life painting to the real business of his essay: a review of recent writings by the novelist and essayist Colin MacInnes and the implicit account of postwar London conveyed by them. His central exhibit is *Absolute Beginners*, MacInnes's 1959 novel acerbically narrated by a nameless sixteen-year-old school-leaver and freelance photographer. Style merchant and connoisseur of the popular if ever there was one, this character plies the London streets on an Italian scooter in pursuit of both his next gig and his beloved but elusive Suzette. Wollheim had for some years been friendly with MacInnes as well as with Schapiro, and his essay offered him the occasion to link their shared urban preoccupations.[10] Via the former's lens on London, it became possible to draw a parallel between the transformations in the city during the 1950s and "the social change that the Goncourts saw with such horror creeping over the Paris of their day: the turning inside-out of life."[11]

A century on, as Wolleim saw it, somber, damp, and sooty London found itself opened to the same phenomenon, with performers and consumers silhouetted against proliferating, brightly illuminated places of amusement. But the agents of such changes were not the moneyed industrialists and real-estate speculators who drove the nineteenth-century changes to Paris; it was rather, Wollheim argues, the powerless themselves, chiefly adventurous English teenagers and migrants from Africa and the Caribbean, who refused to let the existing facades of the built environment determine how life in the city must be lived: "Habitations are altered beyond recognition, or put to uses for which they were never intended. A cellar becomes a club; a non-conformist chapel is turned into an all-night café; a sordid shop-front is decorated with record sleeves; streets that used to sleep quiet at night are filled with blaring music; pubs are given strip lighting and jukeboxes."[12]

Barely was the garish paint dry on these bottom-up renovations than MacInnes came along to give it an exemplary actor, one who leads the reader on a tour from one hip circle to the next, concluding with a Dante-esque descent into the 1958 riots in Notting Dale (the narrator's beloved "Napoli"), when

African and Caribbean migrants (the narrator's allies) are set upon by gangs of white nationalist thugs. This character, the archetypal Teenager in Wollheim's retelling, "rejected the conception of the city as a solid three-dimensional environment that shapes and enfolds his life, and instead regards it as a kind of highly coloured backcloth against which he acts out, and upon which he projects his fantasies."[13]

Although Wollheim never utters it, the name in actual use for such a protagonist was Modernist. Most often shortened to just Mod, the word signified a young man, sharply dressed in a narrow, Italian-style suit, mobile and independent on a likewise Italian Vespa or Lambretta. Devoted on a nearly full-time basis to fastidious discrimination in the styling of the self, the Mod's templates were largely imported: Italian, American, and an amalgam of the two. The Hollywood tailoring of Cy Devore, who dressed the likes of Bogart and the Sinatra-centric Rat Pack, offered a template from American movies. But the deeper emotional urgency came from music, from bebop, from the more propulsive hard bop that gained wider popularity among black audiences toward the end of the 1950s and from the more restrained style associated with Miles Davis (fig. 5). Renowned for the "cool" in both his clear, measured playing and in the understated elegance he cultivated in his dress, Davis contained inward rage by playing down rather than acting out. In the summer of 1959, fresh from the triumph of his watershed album *Kind of Blue,* he had walked a white woman to a cab from the entrance of Birdland, the famous Manhattan club where he was headlining, only to find himself savagely beaten to the ground by two lurking policemen: "Blood was running down the khaki suit I had on," he later recounted.[14] The Mod chronicler Paolo Hewitt puts it well: "By dressing in the clothing of those who fiercely resent their culture, their music, the color of their skin, Miles and his peers are playing the enemy beautifully, walking amongst them whilst changing the landscape forever. You think he's a bank manager, in fact Miles is a revolutionary in silk and mohair."[15]

The Birdland incident showed that the disguise had its limits, but the strategy was understood in London and emulated by self-conscious, minority devotees of modern jazz as a wordless form of defiance against the subservience expected of Secondary Modern products. The reliable observer Richard Barnes, who shared a flat with the young Pete Townshend, sums it up: “It was from their Modern Jazz tastes that they named themselves. They called themselves Modernists.”[16]

As the emergent Mods first began to manifest themselves in Soho, central London, where their favored clubs and coffee bars were concentrated, they could often be identified by a talismanic long-playing record (LP) carried under one arm. If a Blue Note title, the artist’s image would appear in the decisive black-and-white photography of Francis Wolff (co-owner of the label), set off by the spare, crisp design of the young Reid Miles (fig. 6). This team synthesized visual urbanity in both photographic images and quality of modern design, providing young London consumers with a portable template for their minority taste and sense of misunderstood apartness so well

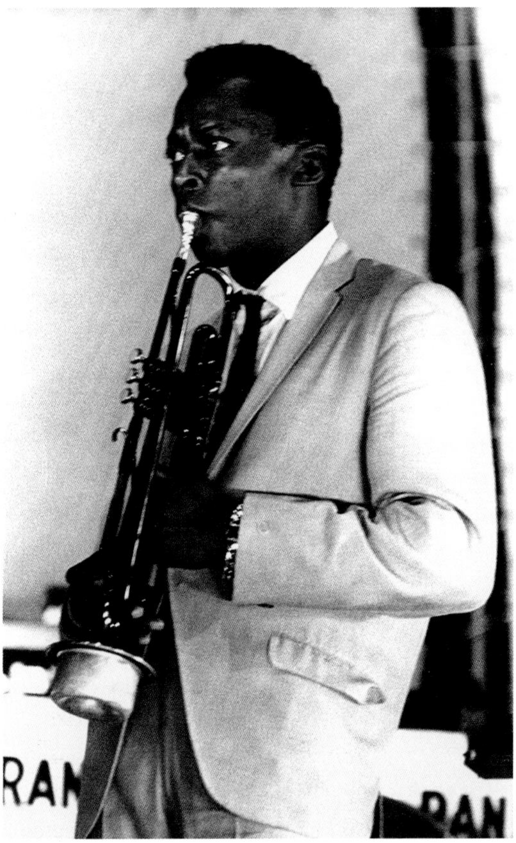

5 Miles Davis, 1960

expressed by MacInnes's acerbic, jazz-loving narrator. And the bearer would be doing his best to keep up the standard in dress set by the black American performers so depicted. One can imagine the impact made by both the content and photograph on the sleeve of Lee Morgan's eponymous Blue Note album from 1956 (fig. 7).[17] The fact that the mercurial trumpeter was only eighteen years old at the time could only have reinforced the magnetism in his amalgam of style and cultivated outsiderdom (without knowing Morgan's later reputation for epitomizing "the moody arrogant hipster," as one jazz writer puts it, or that his fate was to be fatally shot aged thirty-three by his common-law wife in a Lower East Side club).[18]

What the Mods knew, in their discerning fandom, was that a fine suit on an American jazz musician escaped local, literal-minded reading of class signifiers. A top Mod was not putting on a disguise as middle class; he understood a certain kind of suit as already a disguise. At the beginning, no more than a few hundred fans in the most discerning clubs opted for this multifaceted style – in the face of relative mobs packing the venues devoted to the revivalist repackaging of pre-war

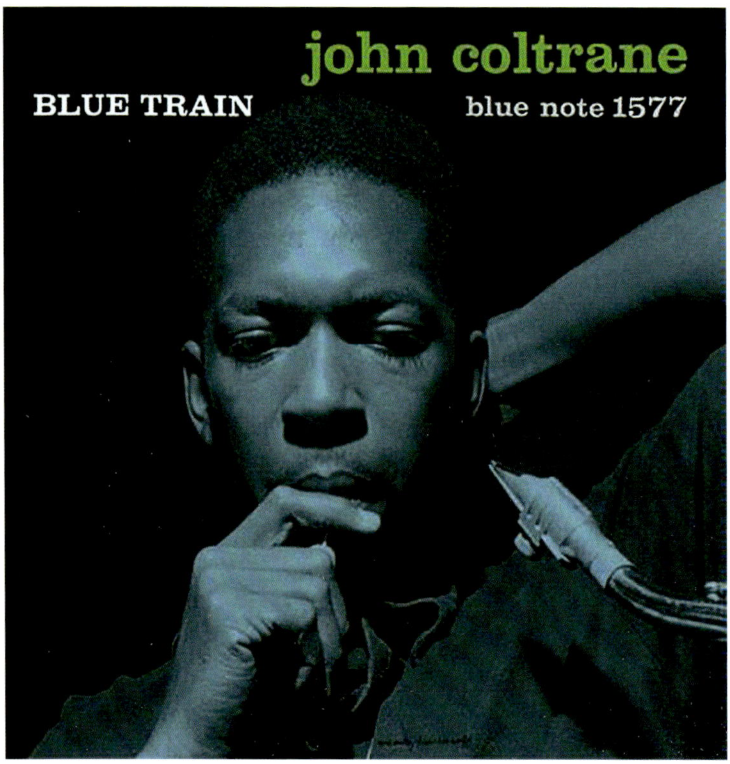

6 Francis Wolff and Reid Miles, *John Coltrane: Blue Train*, LP record cover, 1958

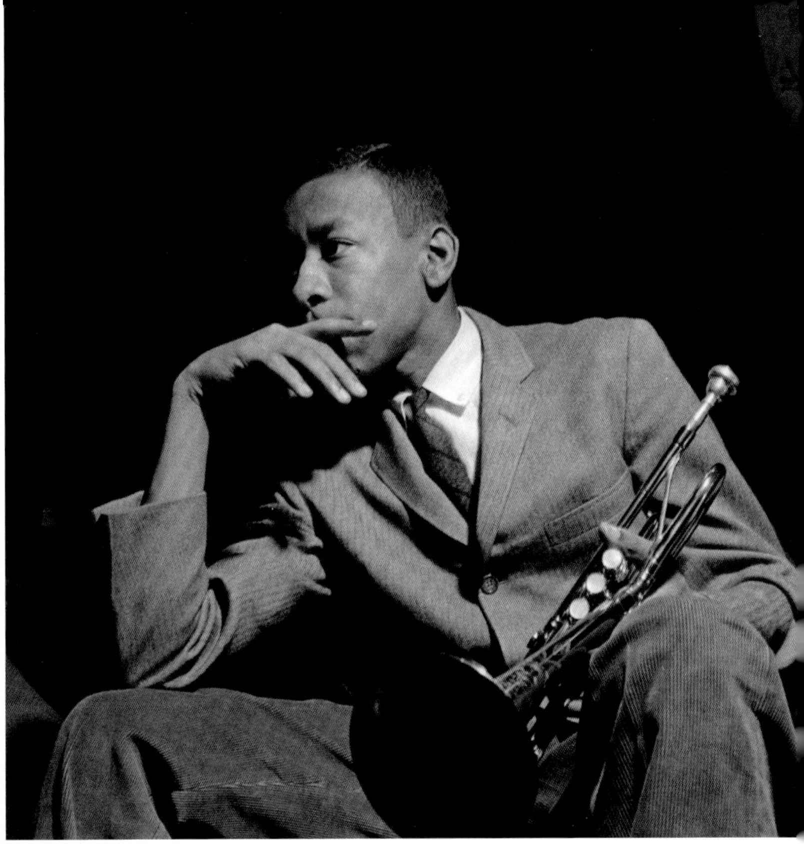

7 Lee Morgan, photographed by Francis Wolff, 1956

New Orleans, the so called Trads (naturally despised by the Mods). Against the very English baggy sweaters, hand-rolled cigarettes, and real ale favored in Trad circles, the Mods transformed their discerning consumption of advanced jazz into their own brand of performance, infused with an equal measure of continental flair, played out against the lurid illuminations of nocturnal Soho, the city's traditional quarter for louche amusements.[19]

MacInnes offers a ground-level, eyewitness snapshot from 1958 of the two types side by side in the 2 I's coffee bar in Old Compton Street, invidiously rendered by the teenage narrator of *Absolute Beginners*:

> *Though both are friends of mine, and, in a way, even friends of each other, these two don't mix in public, on account of the Dean being a sharp modern jazz creation and the Kid just a skiffle survival, with horrible leanings to the trad. thing ... i.e., combos of booking-office clerks and quantity-surveyor's assistants who've handed in their cards, and dedicated themselves to blowing what they believe to be the same note as the wonderful Creoles who invented the whole thing ...*

The Dean character went even further in his emulation of the American jazz modernist, having acquired a heroin habit to go with his impeccable turn out, inventoried by the narrator: "College-boy smooth crop hair with burned-in parting, neat white Italian round-collared shirt, short Roman jacket *very* tailored (two little vents, three-buttoned), no-turn-up narrow trousers with 17-inch bottoms absolute maximum, pointed-toed shoes ... One 'a bum and a bohemian'; the other a 'sharp modernist number': 'Compare them,' he triumphantly concludes, 'and take your pick!'"[20]

In London around 1960, the capitalized terms "Modernist" and "Modernism" barely registered as aesthetic categories in the fine arts, but had become strong identifiers claimed by actual individuals and explicitly ascribed to them by others. That is to say, there were individuals on the streets, in the shops and clubs, toward whom one could point and say, "There goes a Modernist": one style setter of the period even took "Modern" as his surname.[21] His type arrived on the London scene under the auspices of popular music, of race, youth, and a consequent obligation to cultivate an exquisite style of dress. Origins in the appearances of American jazz stars confound the common sociological presupposition, fostered by the subsequent advent of Cultural Studies as an academic discipline, that Modernist styles betokened an imaginary upward mobility and false consciousness about social class.[22] And there are ample indications that this take on the London Mod colors Clark's rendering of the Parisian *calicot* as exemplary denizen of that city's consumer phantasmagoria in the later nineteenth century. When he asserts that *calicot* "posited his class position – opened a distance between himself and his inferiors – in terms of preferred representations, in terms of sheer style," those who know the vocabulary of Cultural Studies will recognize the transposition of its idiom into Clark's way of describing the clerks and shop assistants in the audience at the El Dorado or Alcazar.[23]

Alongside that anachronism, there were the already archaic connotations of the term *calicot* by the 1870s and 1880s, its moment of fresh currency having been in the later 1810s, during the immediate aftermath of France's defeat

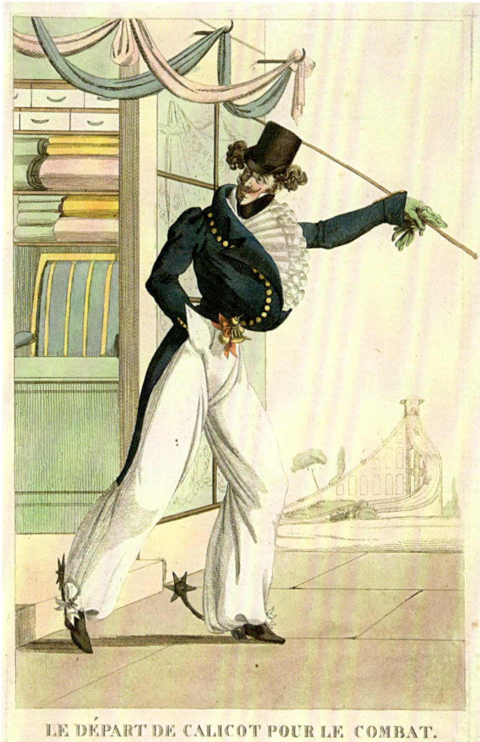

8 Anonymous, "Le Départ de Calicot pour le Combat," 1817–18
Hand-colored etching, 38.2 × 25.5
Metropolitan Museum of Art, New York

in the Napoleonic Wars. The lifting of the Allies' blockade reinvigorated commerce, which in turn called forth a new population of male shop assistants expected to cut fine figures for their female clients. Eager to borrow the social and sexual cachet of officers returned from the field, these civilian *calicots*, carrying the taint of conscription avoidance, affected an exaggerated mimicry of military dash, down to the wearing of spurs as an everyday accessory (fig. 8). Their drapers' implements replacing lances and sabers, these poseurs naturally became the objects of caustic satire in print and on stage.[24]

A half-century later, the stereotype had aged to the point that it becomes difficult to tell whether a given commentator is offering anything in the way of fresh observation or is instead relying on a received image still being refurbished as satirical comedy. Despite these ambiguities, Clark assigns a salient ideological function to the Parisian *calicot* of the early Third Republic. The qualities that fired the hit songs of the cafés-concerts came from a place alien to their commercially packaged pleasures, from, as he puts it, the "collective vehemence" of the outlying proletarian districts, their ferocity feared by the authorities but usefully domesticated and defused by the machinery of entertainment in order to flatter the complicit *calicots*.

The introduction of the key term "collective vehemence" is followed by an endnote that begins as follows:

> *For the petit-bourgeois consumer of culture in the twentieth century, the available form of popular art has been black American music, and that is where my notion of collective vehemence was picked up – from kinds of blues singing and shouting, from improvised ensemble playing, from Charlie Parker's way with the themes and harmonies of white popular music, from Little Richard and Fats Domino.*[25]

There is in this passage a disarming confession that scant evidence survives for the authentic underclass expression fundamental to the analysis; so Clark adduces instead the signature enthusiasms of the London Mods, his exact English contemporaries, which extended from advanced jazz to the finer examples of American Rhythm and Blues. The trans-historical parallel forthrightly posited by Wollheim twenty years before thus reappears, but almost surreptitiously and with great ambivalence. Giving with one hand and taking away with the other, Clark imposes onto these Mod passions the heavily qualifying terms popular and petit-bourgeois. While not appearing to denigrate the music itself, this move places its consumption under two negative signs. The "popular" signifies for him the opposite of truth in underclass expression; thus the Mod style of "petit-bourgeois" expertise and connoisseurship effects a Midas touch in reverse, turning the authentic into the duplicitous, just what the putative *calicots* had visited, he posits, on the unheard and unknowably authentic refrains of the revolutionary *quartiers populaires*.

In a surprising way, then, a major, formative episode in the maturation of art history as an intellectual discipline emerged under the auspices of the teenage London Modernist around 1960. As might be expected, Wollheim's forgotten version is gentler with the Mods' necessary limitations in the political sphere. In the end, "the base upon which the Absolute Beginner stands as he hurls his message of scorn at society is too narrow for us to hope for too much from his gesture."[26] But there is no tortured ambivalence in the affirmative way that Wollheim regards, as he describes them, the "'kiddos' who get their clothes from Cecil Gee's [Charing Cross men's clothier] or hang around Ronnie Scott's [jazz club], who go jiving up at the Manor House [dance hall], who buy LPs and go abroad for their holidays, who are the great consumers in the Common Market of juvenile taste ... "[27] Relatively few in number these Mods might be (fig. 9), "but they fulfill an exemplary role within the society of their contemporaries."[28]

In this category of contemporaries, Wollheim casts his net far beyond those of similar social origin, but posits that the Mods' superiority, "their habits, their tastes, their pleasures, their attitudes are something to be admired and even, within

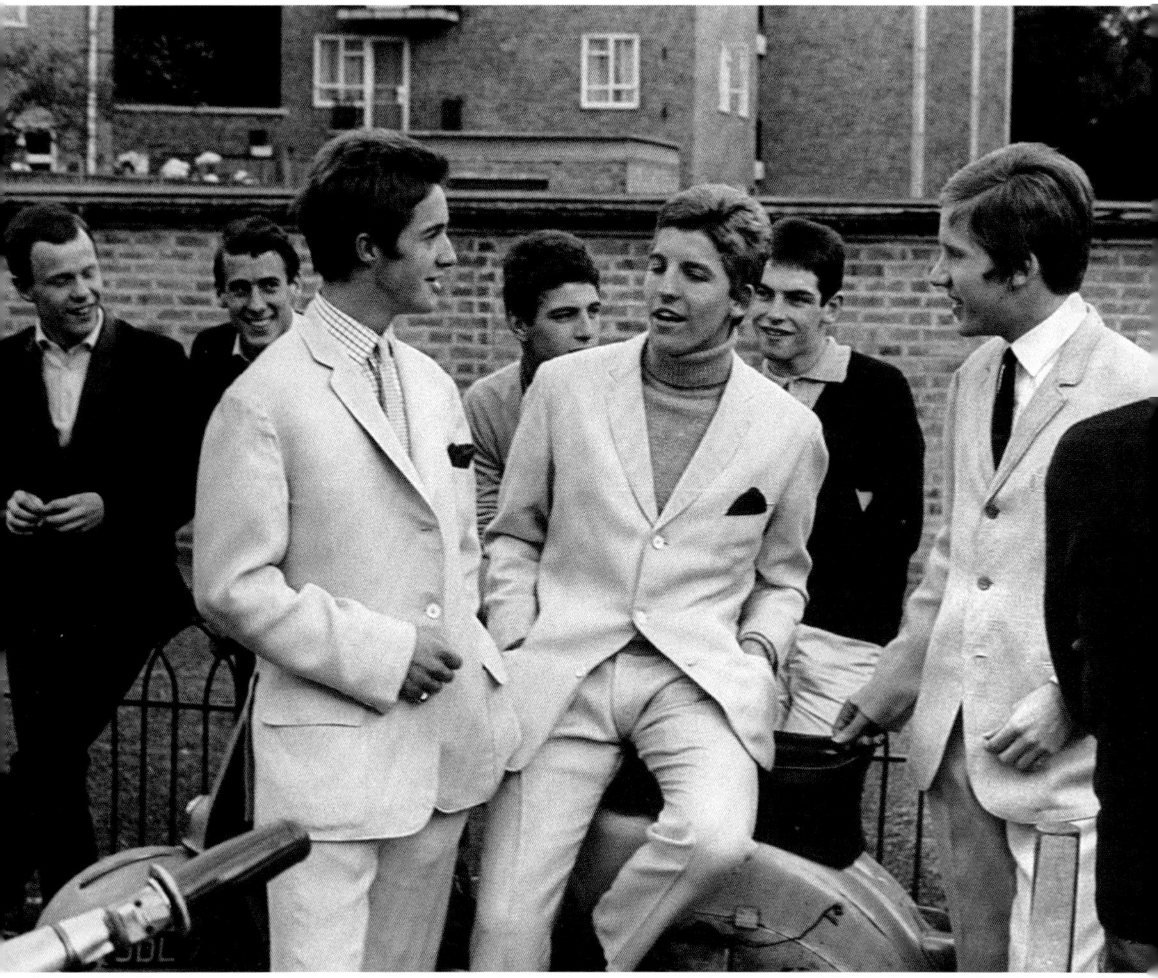

9 Trio of Mods (Barry Hall, Ken Todd and Brian Hemmings), photographed by Terence Spencer, 1964

certain limits, to be copied" widely across the social spectrum: "The Absolute Beginner bids fair to be the hero not only of the Non-starter but also of the High Flyer."[29] Ample evidence for this thesis might have been gleaned – as Wollheim had ample opportunity to observe – from the leading figures in London contemporary art of the later 1950s. The chapter to follow takes this confluence as its subject.

CHAPTER ONE
MODERNIST FACES: HARD BOP AND CLEAN DESIGN

IT IS OFTEN USEFUL TO LAUNCH AN INVESTIGATION into any artistic episode from an apparently marginal and inauspicious point of entry. The candidate in this instance is an advertisement from 1957 (fig. 10) that would not rank high among examples of British art in its period – or in any

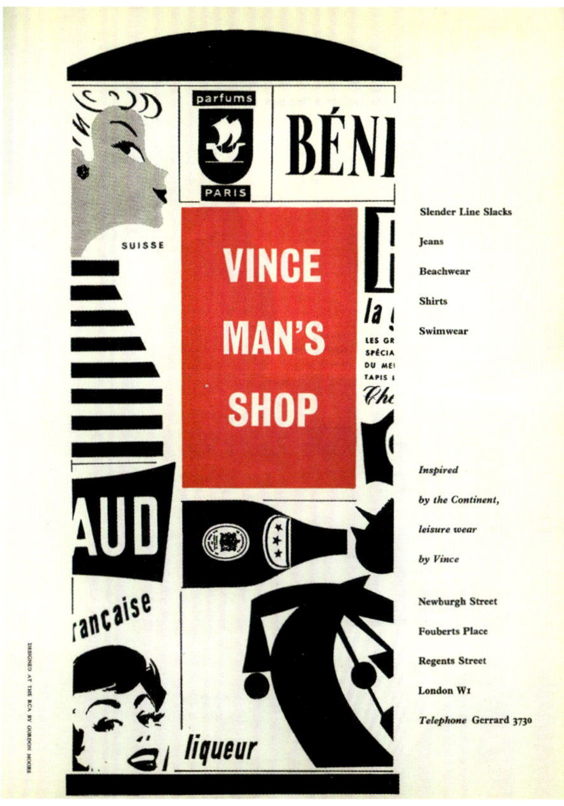

10 Advertisement for Vince Man's Shop, *Ark* 19, Journal of the Royal College of Art (Spring 1957), designed by Gordon Moore

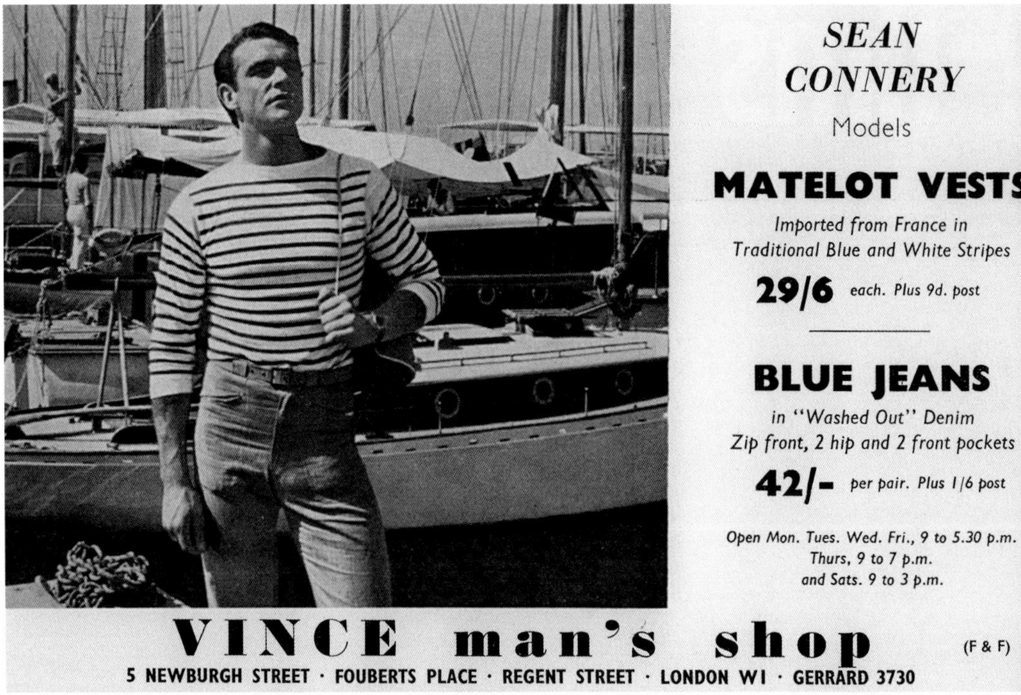

11 Advertisement for Vince Man's Shop featuring Sean Connery, 1956

other. But one can well ask, where and what was Vince? Where did this item appear? And who designed it?

Firstly, the address: Newburgh Street comprises a couple of blocks in Soho, one over from Carnaby Street – though in 1957 that more famous counterpart was still an unknown and unprepossessing alleyway dominated by the blank brick wall of a power station. The location of Vince Man's Shop placed it around the corner from the Palladium, providing a ready clientele from music and theater, which Vince supplied with continental European items otherwise unavailable in a London retail landscape just emerging from conformist austerity. The advertisement arranges its copy into a schematic Parisian kiosk, the theme in keeping with its list of items: "slender line slacks, jeans, beachwear, shirts, swimwear inspired by the Continent." Jeans, the next item, were a rarity in London shops at that date, and firmly identified with American Levi 501s, but Vince offered French varieties in washed-out blue and black.

Any knowing reader would therefore expect some fusion of imported American and European styles – one in keeping with another advertisement (fig. 11) for the shop that deployed the young, slim-line Sean Connery to play up the matelot and denim combination, the French-American signature of the shop. Vince was the pseudonym of Bill Green, one he had adopted when setting up as a photographer after the war, specializing in bodybuilders and selling to male physique magazines. Having started a line in posing briefs for his models, he expanded to a general clothing business in 1954. The attractions of the down-at-heel precinct around Newburgh and Carnaby Streets were simple, as the pop-culture sage Nik Cohn relates: "the rents were cheap and Newburgh Street was just next to Marshall Street baths, where all the muscle boys and butch trade trained. As they came out, they were confronted by a dazzle of hipster pants, expensive tight sweaters (about 7 pounds), briefs and shirts in bright reds, yellows, and purples."[1]

In 1957, Green commissioned a quasi-magazine feature showing a pretend couple on an inspiring visit to Vince (fig. 12). The woman and respectable-looking gent seem intended to counter the gay stereotype that surrounded the shop, but the sequence offers a rare glimpse of what it looked like and what it stocked, while advertising its powers to melt away stuffy conformity. Cohn speaks to the shop's genuine appeal across varied client types, saying: "At a time when men's shops were almost all pompous," he notes, "it was fun and so were its clothes: lurid and sometimes badly made but, at least, never boring."[2] That observation is seconded by the recollections of the punk impresario Malcolm McLaren, then the young Malcolm Edwards, who said of his hated adolescence in the suburb of Hendon, "as you looked like a peacock, you became a member of a surrogate club of outsiders and rebels. As a teenager, I scoured every shop on the way home from school studying details of scarves, shoes, socks in the window displays. Then I would go to Vince's ... "[3]

The ad raises the question: to which of Green's client types was it addressed? The readers in this case would first have been attracted by a magazine about art rather than one about bodybuilding or fashion per se: the magazine being *Ark*, the student-edited and designed publication of the Royal College of Art. The Vince design, which takes up the whole of the issue's unmissable first page, is credited in a discreet byline to Gordon Moore, one of the leading RCA design students active

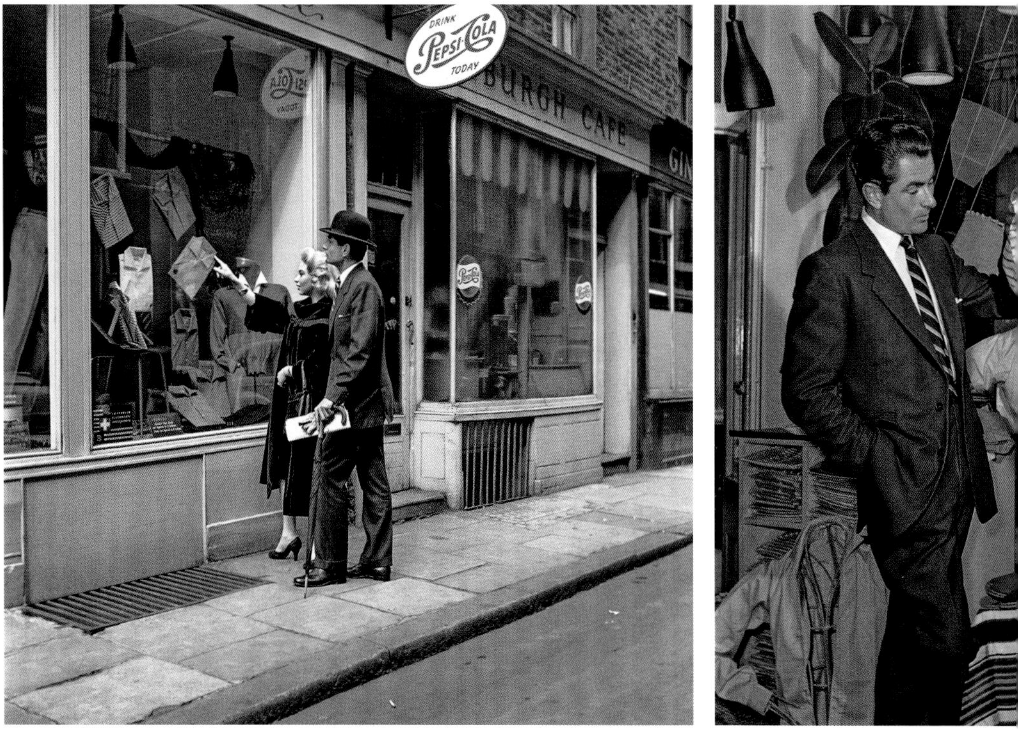

12a–c Promotional photographs for Vince Man's Shop, 1957

in *Ark*'s production (who by the early 1960s had become the art director of *Queen*). Moore had likewise been responsible for the startling cover (fig. 13) with its dot-screen Mona Lisa, conveyed via his pastiche of Marcel Duchamp's parodic assisted readymade, *L.H.O.O.Q.*, a found color reproduction with its phonetic ascription of sexual arousal to the icon. Taking up a prototype that already mocked the "fine-art" aspiration of a reproductive print, Moore subjected the Duchamp to another round of reproductive technology, sending it through a further dot-screen processing in black and white, then enlarging the results so that the abstracting simplification becomes the foreground visual event. The fact that Moore's much earlier example has largely been lost from art history should not diminish its standing vis-à-vis the triumphant and enduring re-invention of the same operation by Andy Warhol – a reminder that analogous artistic innovations can arise from distinctly different genealogies.

In this earlier instance, the fine-art authority of the original takes a back seat to the charisma of Italy, bannered in the colors of its national flag. Gaggia espresso machines,

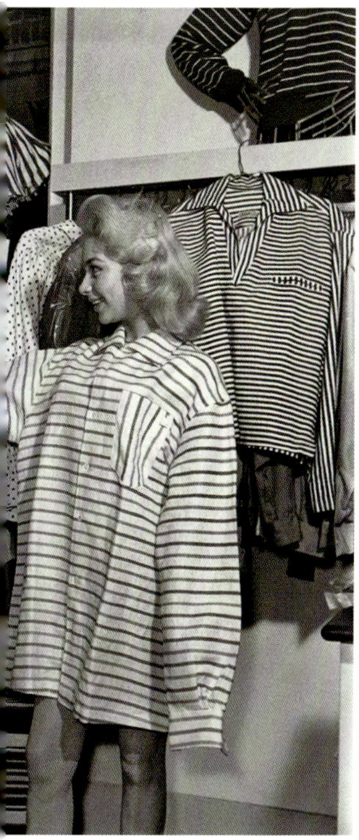

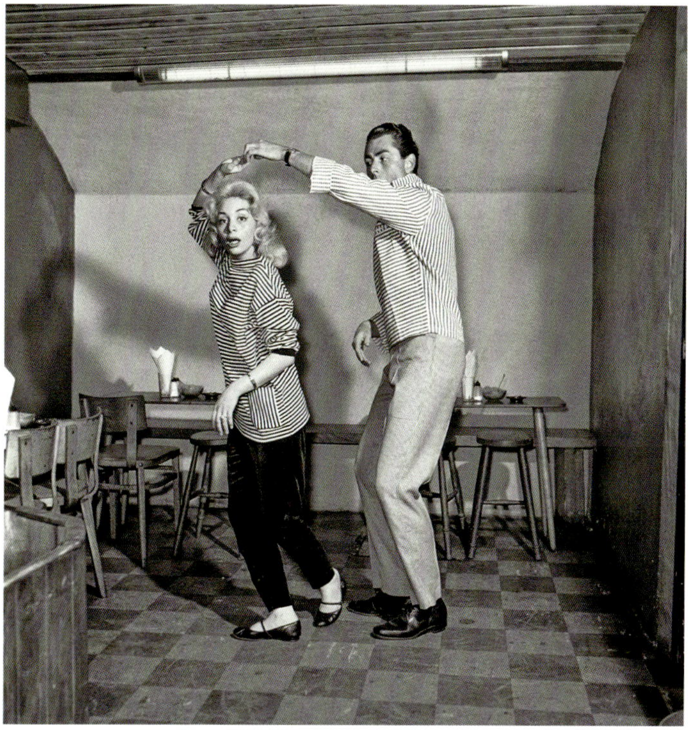

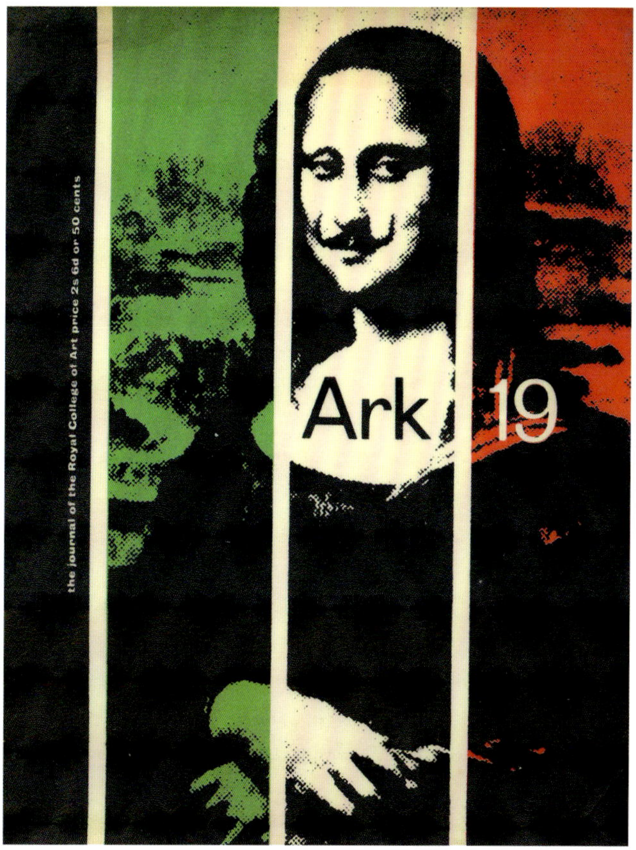

13 Cover of *Ark* 19, Journal of the Royal College of Art (Spring 1957), designed by Gordon Moore

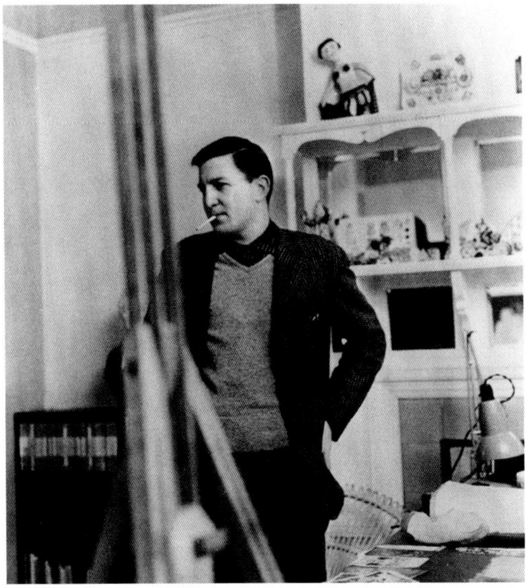

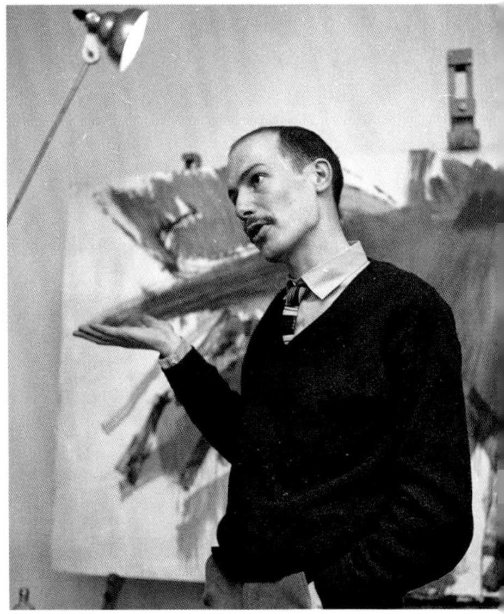

14 Roger Coleman, 1959

15 Richard Smith, photographed by Ken Harding, 1958

Lambretta scooters, and Roman tailoring carried talismanic status in the Mod life, and *Ark*'s student editor, Roger Coleman (fig. 14), shared the same preoccupations. The son of a Leicestershire factory worker, Coleman carried the right class credentials for a London Modernist, as he did in his musical preferences (in 1959 he tried to explain to a public audience the clear superiority of the saxophonist Gerry Mulligan over Elvis Presley).[4] And he sported a sharp Italian line in his clothes and barbering, as he appears in a period photograph, affirming on behalf of himself and his artist friends a conscious attachment to the Mod standard in outward appearance: "Italian gear was very in then ... What was interesting is that we all tended to have our hair cut rather short at that time in the Perry Como 'college boy' hairstyle," instancing his artist-contemporaries "Dick Smith (fig. 15), Robyn Denny, and Peter Blake ... "[5]

Another member of the cohort, the designer and painter Gordon House, testified in his customary staccato style with a rapid-fire litany of the passions he shared with his school friend Smith and their typical itineraries on visits to Soho:

> *A teenage enthusiasm for local jazz, movies, plastic discs and radio; the recording of international musicians of the time; Kenton's Bebop, Brubeck and the* MJQ, *with cool urban interpretations fired our weekend visits from out of town art*

school, by train to the City – London: Dankworth's Club 11, Windmill Street, The Florida, Leicester Square and on to Oxford Street 100 Club. Then it seemed our need for sounds linked with contemporary style.[6]

Nor did these enthusiasms abate as these artists left their teenage years behind. In 1959 Robyn Denny (aged twenty-nine) produced one eye-filling example of what this ethos might mean for art in the shape of a quasi-mural, titled *Great, Big, Wide, Biggest* but dominated by the word London (fig. 16). The skill that Denny had been developing in his abstract studio practice is evident, as is his ability to execute his ideas

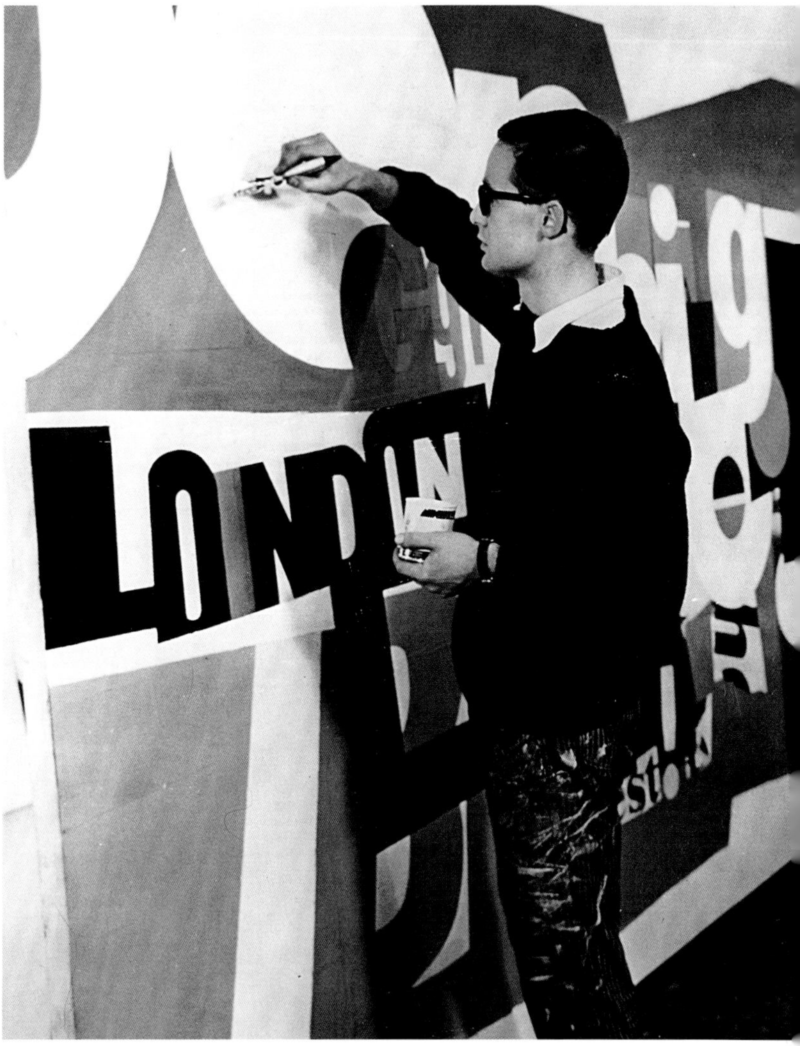

16 Robyn Denny finishing *Great, Big, Wide, Biggest* (Austin Reed Mural), photographed by Tony Messenger, 1959

on the wall-filling scale that had become newly salient in London following the contemporary exhibitions of Jackson Pollock and other Americans of the New York School. The change lay in channeling those abilities via the energized cacophony of street hoardings and commercial signs.

By almost any measure, Denny had lent the emerging English Pop aesthetic its most successful painted expression to date (fig. 17). But if one counts as Pop Art a work that takes some fine-art distance from the work of commercial advertising Denny's painting might fall outside of the category, as it functionally was an advertisement – albeit a unique, hand-made example rendered in pigment with collage – commissioned by a clothier in the same tight area around Soho, Austin Reed in Regent Street. Indeed, the management kept it in place long enough for another musical genre to begin supplanting jazz among youthful consumers: the Beatles posed for photographs in front of it in 1961 (fig. 18). Exposure of the Liverpool band to the metropolitan Modernist sensibility offered a template for the outward transformations crucial to their move from the seedy Hamburg waterfront to the wide fame envisioned by their manager, Brian Epstein.

Local Mods even took them in hand: Jeff Dexter, the young club DJ, describes first meeting the Beatles at a Soho café in 1962, "and then Epstein gave them some money to give them the chance to buy some decent clothes. We got the Beatles along to Dougie Millings and they got their first bunch of clobber there. They didn't look too bright at the time so Dougie asked me to take them to my shirtmaker ... "[7] On their first visit, the two owners anxiously took Dexter to one side and asked if the lads could afford the merchandise and whether they might rob them. Even in Liverpool the Beatles had stood out as rough and incorrigible, and it had required as perspicacious a manager as Epstein even to take them on.[8] The Austin Reed photograph charts the transformation from George Harrison's stubbornly provincial, leather-clad Rocker tendency at the far left to something approaching a Modernist sensibility in Paul McCartney's put-together outfit at the opposite end of the lineup.

The late-coming Liverpudlians remained reluctant converts, at least by the testimony a few years later of John Lennon, who made it clear that he had never seen the subtle

17 Robyn Denny, *Great, Big, Wide, Biggest* (Austin Reed Mural), 1959
Oil, collage and mixed media on panel, 188 × 305 cm
Austin Reed, London

18 The Beatles at Austin Reed in front of Robyn Denny's *Great, Big, Wide, Biggest*, photographed by Mark and Colleen Hayward, 1963

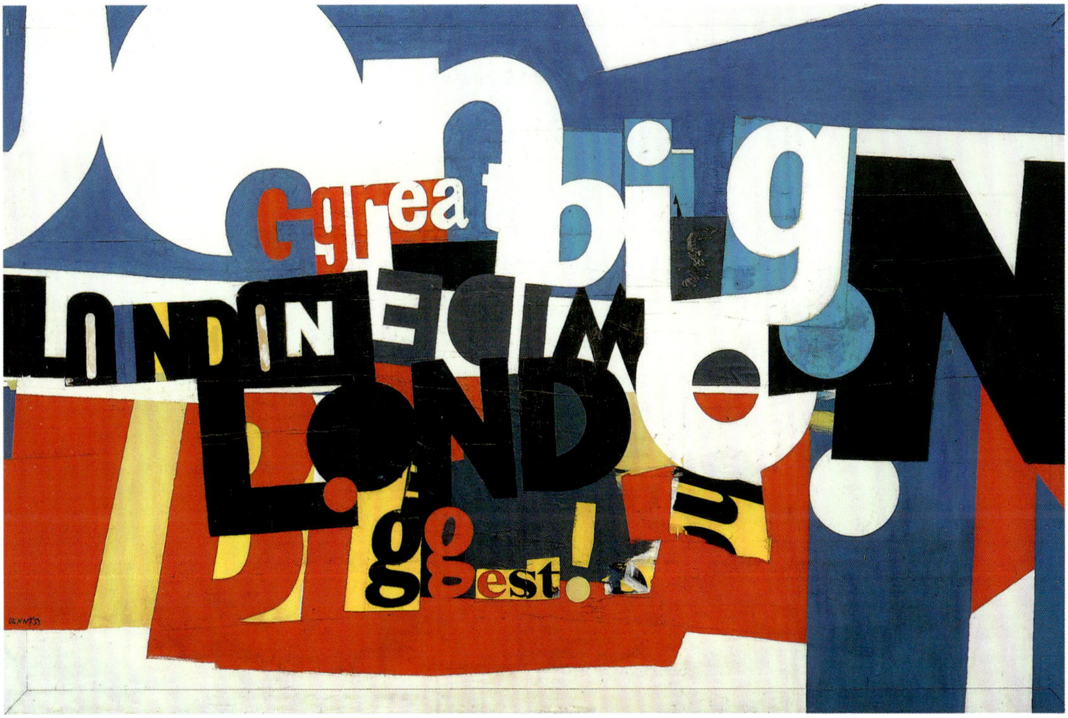
big
LONDON
LOND
ggest!

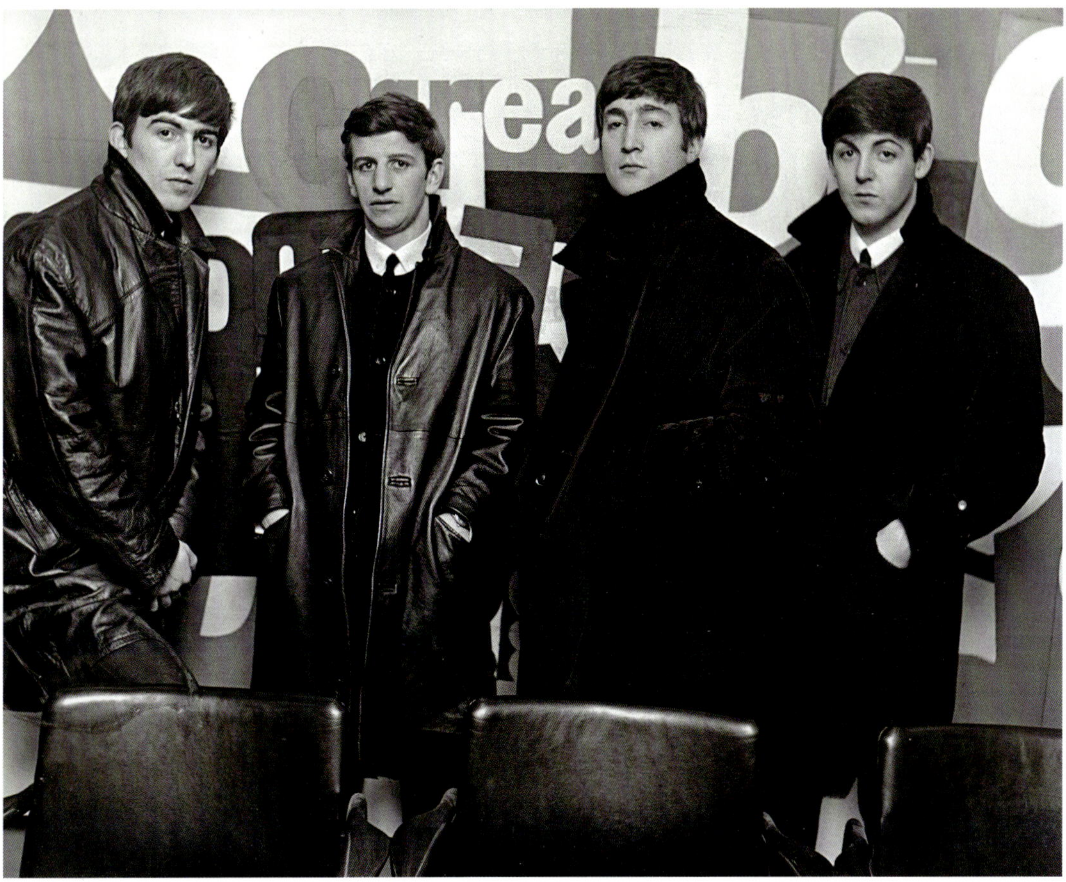

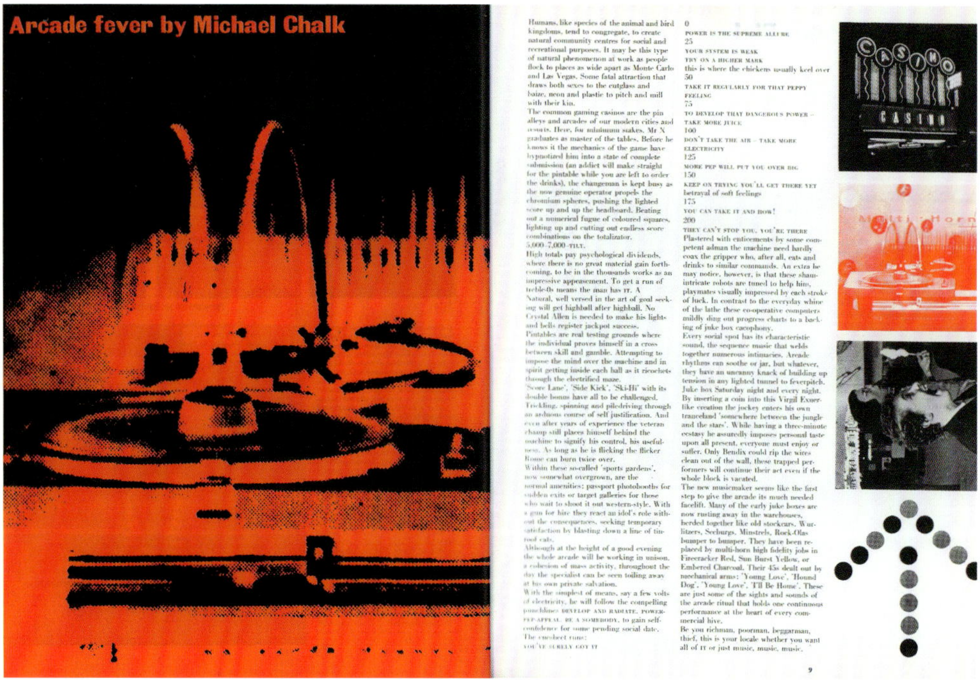

Arcade fever by Michael Chalk

Humans, like species of the animal and bird kingdoms, tend to congregate, to create natural community centres for social and recreational purposes. It may be this type of natural phenomenon at work as people flock to places as wide apart as Monte Carlo and Las Vegas. Some fatal attraction that draws both sexes to the cutglass and baize, neon and plastic to pitch and mill with their kin.

The common gaming casinos are the pin alleys and arcades of our modern cities and resorts. Here, for minimum stakes, Mr X graduates as master of the tables. Before he knows it the mechanics of the game have hypnotized him into a state of complete submission (an addict will make straight for the pintable while you are left to order the drinks), the changeman is kept busy as the now genuine operator propels the chromium spheres, pushing the lighted score up and up the headboard. Beating out a numerical fugue of coloured squares, lighting up and cutting out endless score combinations on the totalizator.

5,000–7,000–TILT.

High totals pay psychological dividends, where there is no great material gain forthcoming, to be in the thousands works as an impressive appeasement. To get a run of treble-0s means the man has IT. A Natural, well versed in the art of goal seeking will get highball after highball. No Crystal Allen is needed to make his lights and bells register jackpot success.

Pintables are real testing grounds where the individual proves himself in a cross between skill and gamble. Attempting to impose the mind over the machine and in spirit getting inside each ball as it ricochets through the electrified maze.

'Score Lane', 'Side Kick', 'Ski-Hi' with its double bonus have all to be challenged. Trickling, spinning and piledriving through an arduous course of self justification. And even after years of experience the veteran champ still places himself behind the machine to signify his control, his usefulness. As long as he is flicking the flicker Rome can burn twice over.

Within these so-called 'sports gardens', now somewhat overgrown, are the normal amenities: passport photobooths for sudden exits or target galleries for those who wait to shoot it out western-style. With a gun for hire they react an idol's role without the consequences, seeking temporary satisfaction by blasting down a line of tin-foil cats.

Although at the height of a good evening the whole arcade will be working in unison, a cohesion of mass activity, throughout the day the specialist can be seen toiling away at his own private salvation.

With the simplest of means, say a few volts of electricity, he will follow the compelling punchlines DEVELOP AND RADIATE, POWER-PEP-APPEAL, BE A SOMEBODY, to gain self-confidence for some pending social date. The cheekiest tone:

YOU'VE SURELY GOT IT

0

POWER IS THE SUPREME ALLURE

25

YOUR SYSTEM IS WEAK

TRY ON A HIGHER MARK

this is where the chickens usually keel over

50

TAKE IT REGULARLY FOR THAT PEPPY FEELING

75

TO DEVELOP THAT DANGEROUS POWER – TAKE MORE JUICE

100

DON'T TAKE THE AIR – TAKE MORE ELECTRICITY

125

MORE PEP WILL PUT YOU OVER BIG

150

KEEP ON TRYING YOU'LL GET THERE YET

betrayal of soft feelings

175

YOU CAN TAKE IT AND HOW!

200

THEY CAN'T STOP YOU, YOU'RE THERE

Plastered with enticements by some competent adman the machine need hardly coax the gripper who, after all, eats and drinks to similar commands. An extra he may notice, however, is that these sham-intricate robots are tuned to help him, playmates visually impressed by each stroke of luck. In contrast to the everyday whine of the lathe these co-operative computers mildly ding out progress charts to a backing of juke box cacophony.

Every social spot has its characteristic sound, the sequence music that welds together numerous intimacies. Arcade rhythms can soothe or jar, but whatever, they have an uncanny knack of building up tension in any lighted tunnel to feverpitch. Juke box Saturday night and every night. By inserting a coin into this Virgil Exner-like creation the jockey enters his own tranceland 'somewhere between the jungle and the stars'. While having a three-minute ecstasy he assuredly imposes personal taste upon all present, everyone must enjoy or suffer. Only Bendix could rip the wires clean out of the wall, these trapped performers will continue their act even if the whole block is vacated.

The new musicmaker seems like the first step to give the arcade its much needed facelift. Many of the early juke boxes are now rusting away in the warehouses, herded together like old stockcars. Wurlitzers, Seeburgs, Minstrels, Rock-Olas bumper to bumper. They have been replaced by multi-horn high fidelity jobs in Firecracker Red, Sun Burst Yellow, or Embered Charcoal. Their 45s dealt out by mechanical arms: 'Young Love', 'Hound Dog', 'Young Love', 'I'll Be Home'. These are just some of the sights and sounds of the arcade ritual that holds one continuous performance at the heart of every commercial hive.

Be you richman, poorman, beggarman, thief, this is your locale whether you want all of IT or just music, music, music.

9

subversions entailed in the Mod ethos for what they were, understanding them only as betrayals of the Beatles' formerly rough-hewn selves: "We weren't as open and truthful when we didn't have the power to be. We had to take it easy. We had to shorten our hair to leave Liverpool and get jobs in London. We had to wear suits to get on TV ... We had to falsify ..."[9] The kind of refinement that Coleman had laid out in the 1957 numbers of *Ark* was largely lost on them. His most decisive commissions had illuminated an interlocked realm of cafés, clubs, music, and clothes. Take an ecstatic prose-poem devoted to pinball arcades and jukeboxes composed by a painting student named Michael Chalk (fig. 19). The designer David Collins set a photograph of a jukebox's record-spinning mechanism in a low-resolution dot screen against a solid background of vivid red-orange.[10] As Warhol was to discover some years later, no artist could vie directly with the slick mass artifact, but it could be surpassed by means of extracting and re-presenting its codes in a stripped-down translation. Collins and the other designers working with Coleman were competing with the high-quality, four-color printing they saw in the imported American glossies. Vividness had to be attained some other

19 Michael Chalk, "Arcade Fever," *Ark* 20, Journal of the Royal College of Art (Autumn 1957)

way. The technically straightforward, two-color device brings a fine-artist's economy and directness to the business of editorial design.

That same device announces an article by Richard Smith on the core Modernist preoccupation of men's clothing (fig. 20). On the opening page, a photograph glows obscurely against the same electric red-orange used behind Chalk's jukebox, but instead of an up-to-date, youthful motif, Smith and Collins insert an old-school clothier's shop window as a benchmark of obsolete conformity. The background of the next page is plain white, but the daring economy of its imagery jumps like nothing else in the issue, indeed like little else in contemporary design. A young, top-hatted English gent strides in from the left, seemingly from the Royal Enclosure at Ascot, his rolled umbrella pointing like a sword through the legs of a small grinning Gene Autry, the American singing cowboy, in his full regalia. The costumed comic-book Superman occupies the upper left in charging airborne pose, while the right half of the page is dominated by an inspired overlay of three frontal poses by the actor Glenn Ford in a gun-slinging role, two of them in blue, the only color on the

20 Richard Smith, "Man and He-man," *Ark* 20, Journal of the Royal College of Art (Autumn 1957), designed by David Collins, Alan Bartram, and Richard Smith

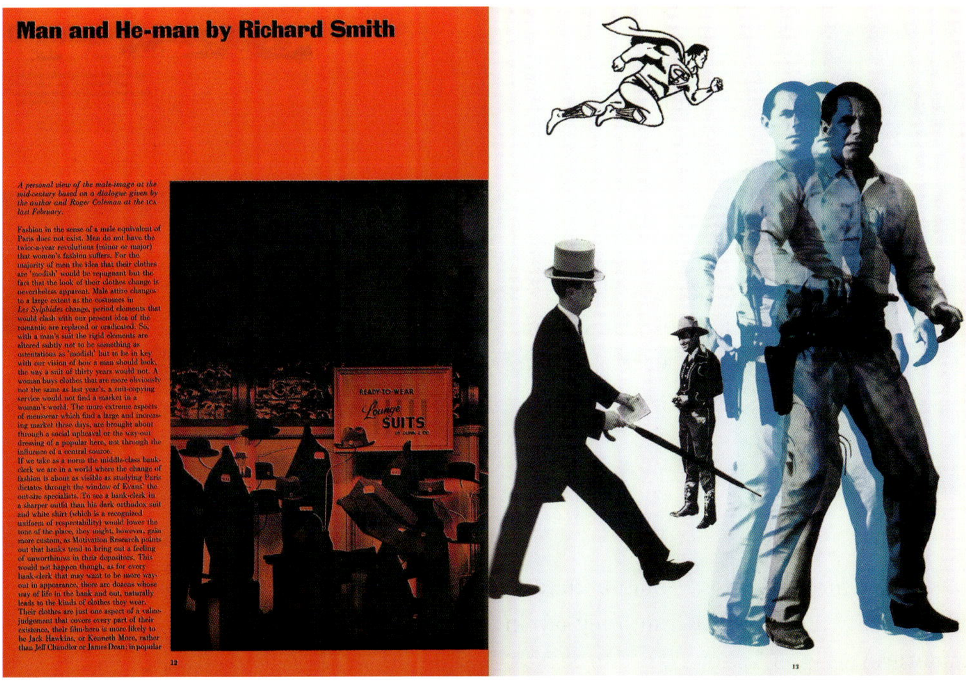

Man and He-man by Richard Smith

A personal view of the male-image at the mid-century based on a dialogue given by the author and Roger Coleman at the ICA last February.

Fashion in the sense of a male equivalent of Paris does not exist. Men do not have the twice-a-year revolutions (minor or major) that women's fashion suffers. For the majority of men the idea that their clothes are 'modish' would be repugnant but the fact that the look of their clothes change is nevertheless apparent. Male attire changes to a large extent as the costumes in *Les Sylphides* change, period elements that would clash with our present idea of the romantic are replaced or eradicated. So, with a man's suit the rigid elements are altered subtly not to be something as ostentatious as 'modish' but to be in key with our vision of how a man should look, the way a suit of thirty years would not. A woman buys clothes that are more obviously not the same as last year's, a suit-copying service would not find a market in a woman's world. The more extreme aspects of menswear which find a large and increasing market these days, are brought about through a social upheaval or the way-out dressing of a popular hero, not through the influence of a central source.
If we take as a norm the middle-class bank-clerk we are in a world where the change of fashion is about as visible as studying Paris dictates through the window of Evans' the out-size specialists. To see a bank-clerk in a sharper outfit than his dark orthodox suit and white shirt (which is a recognized uniform of respectability) would lower the tone of the place, they might, however, gain more custom, as Motivation Research points out that banks tend to bring out a feeling of unworthiness in their depositors. This would not happen though, as for every bank-clerk that may want to be more way-out in appearance, there are dozens whose way of life in the bank and out, naturally leads to the kinds of clothes they wear. Their clothes are just one aspect of a value-judgement that covers every part of their existence, their film-hero is more likely to be Jack Hawkins, or Kenneth More, rather than Jeff Chandler or James Dean; in popular

12

13

otherwise black and white page. The three silhouettes of Ford are parallel but not identical – like a short cinematic sequence, he clears his gun from the holster – but the effect, it need hardly be stated, forecasts the stuttering repetition of Warhol's immense 1963 canvases derived from Elvis Presley as gun fighter in the film vehicle *Flaming Star*.

This prescient Pop exercise expresses better than the text the underlying argument that outward appearance is now as malleable a repertoire as any other set of artistic materials. Its argument against inherited conformity takes even more

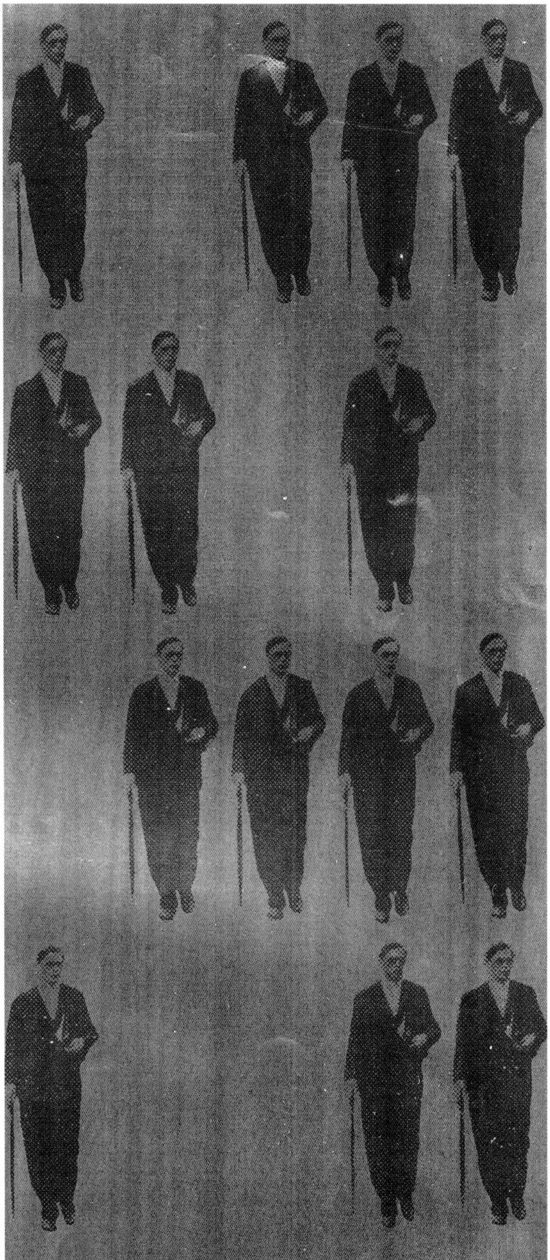

21 Richard Smith, "Man and He-man," *Ark* 20, Journal of the Royal College of Art (Autumn 1957), designed by David Collins, Alan Bartram, and Richard Smith

extraordinary form one page over, where the topic of compulsive invariance yields a new aesthetic landscape (fig. 21). The twilight of English hierarchical costume takes shape in fourteen identical full-figure images of an Eton College master in his archaic uniform, rolled umbrella to his side, shifting in and out of visibility against the muted reflective ink that covers the sheet from edge to edge, in contrast to the hot vibrancy with which the piece opened. Present here are the salient features of what will years later be identified with Warhol: use of found images, black photo-screen reproduction, grid-determined placement, serial repetition, monochrome fields. This long-overlooked, uncanny anticipation of a world-conquering Pop manner arose from an outlook that abjured distinctions between fine art, graphic design, and everyday fashion decisions by a host of anonymous actors.

The following year, 1958, Lawrence Alloway, the leading-edge critic and curator of the moment, published a short but landmark essay, "The Arts and the Mass Media," where he opposed the "urban and democratic" character of "the mass arts" to the "upper-class and pastoral ideas" that Smith and Collins had skewered in their brash *Ark* layout.[11] The issues of the journal overseen by Coleman represented an experiment in what the mass arts could achieve via democratization of technical means alongside self-consciously streetwise subject matter. The force of Alloway's cognate polemic was reinforced by his having proven himself as capable and imaginative a critic of traditional and avant-garde art as anyone in the country. But there were countervailing reasons why Alloway might have identified with the much younger Mods, much as Coleman and the younger Royal College artists were doing. His early education having been interrupted and curtailed by chronic illness, Alloway had garnered prodigious intellectual attainments without ever attending university. Beginning in 1949, he had mastered the history of art through assiduous application to his reviewer's duties at the fortnightly *Art News and Review*, then coming to figure in the discussions at the Institute of Contemporary Arts (ICA) by the so-called Independent Group (IG), where artists, architects, and designers first addressed with curiosity and sympathy the products of postwar, American-driven consumer culture. But Alloway then went further than his IG contemporaries in fashioning a historical and aesthetic rationale for incorporating "the long front of culture," to cite his famous phrase, into any adequate understanding of art.[12] That front, in his influential view, linked fine art to the vernacular and popular realms of film, genre fiction, music, and design.

Alloway's combined investigation and participation in these realms entailed sympathy with Mod enthusiasms, while his exclusion from a university-based cultural hierarchy prompted similar defenses to theirs as far as defiant outward style was concerned. His old IG colleague Reyner Banham, making a plain allusion to the Modernist-favored clothier Cecil Gee, called Alloway "a phenomenon, sawed-off, dapper (in the Charing Cross mode), with his ginger nut cropped close to the bone" (fig. 22).[13] A trim haircut and Italian-style suit signaled a contrary professional savvy and currency in the American style, and Alloway was referring as much to himself as he was to his younger allies in writing that they "try not to separate their work and their leisure: there is only what they do. The goods they use, the movies they see, the pulp fiction they read, are not 'relaxation', sealed off on a non-serious level from their 'life-work', but part of their life."[14]

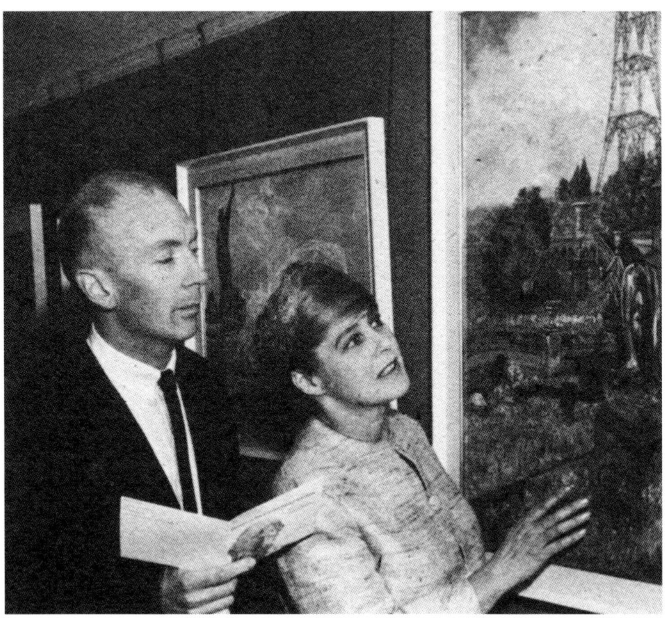

22 Lawrence Alloway and Sylvia Sleigh, 1958

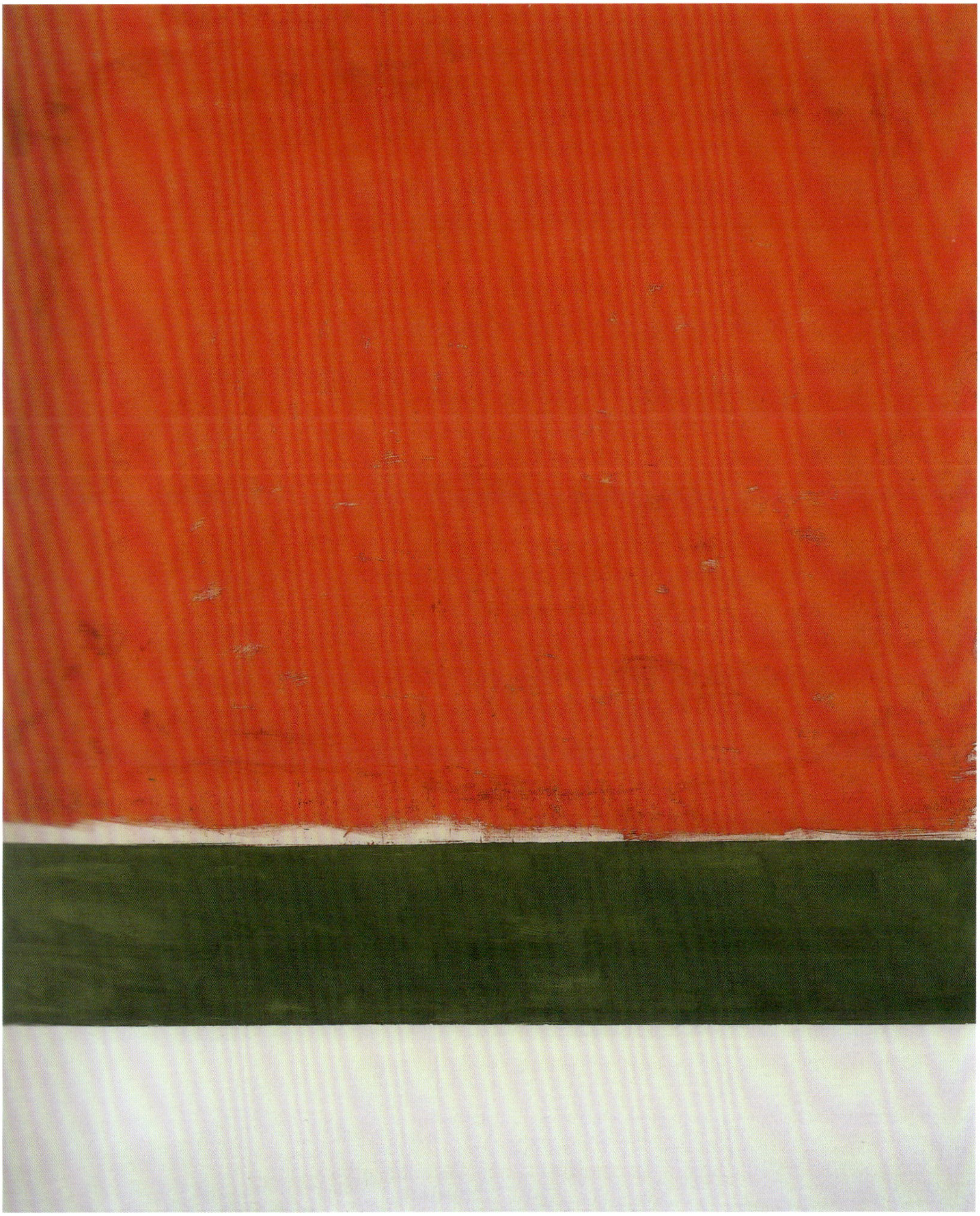

23 Robyn Denny,
Place Painting 6, 1959
Oil on canvas, 213.4 × 182.9 cm
Private collection

By 1958 Alloway had advanced to the position of Deputy Director for Exhibitions at the ICA. Once in his new position, he lost little time recruiting to his exhibitions sub-committee the young Roger Coleman, just graduated from the Royal College of Art and therefore finished with his editorship of *Ark*. In tandem, they turned their attention away from the realm of commercial entertainments toward large-scale abstract painting. Alloway had recently returned from a head-turning visit to New York, where the sharpness of critical dialogue had impressed him as much as his encounters with the decisively wall-filling canvases of the New York School.[15] Examples of the latter, as noted earlier, had come to London in a cycle of landmark exhibitions at the Tate and Whitechapel Galleries beginning in 1957, which presented an unavoidable challenge to Alloway and Coleman: how to match the Americans but couch the painting in an intellectual framework distinct to London.

By September 1959, the two curators had formulated their answer. They called the exhibition *Place*, and limited participation to a trio of younger artists – Denny and Smith, naturally enough, augmented by their age-contemporary Ralph Rumney. All joined in the agreement that each participant restrict himself to just two formats (widths of either four or six feet with heights well over seven) in just two combinations of colors: black and white and the complementary pair of red and green (fig. 23).[16] No individual labels would be found within the installation, each artist being identifiable in the program (fig. 24) by the angle and direction of his paintings, as well as by the personal style that each was encouraged as far as possible to retain. The experience for the viewer, faced with this environment made of paintings, would be gradually to sort out its logic by moving through it and absorbing its visual cues. The rules and arrangement of *Place* were to work against prolonged fixation on any one canvas, encouraging instead views past, through, to the sides, and all around. As Mods aimed to cut a figure against the streetscapes of London, it could be said that the aim of *Place* was to envelop visitors inside a canvas enclosure (fig. 25) in which onlookers appear simultaneously as performers against temporary backdrops.

Overtones in that last sentence recall the nineteenth-century street entertainments of Paris that Richard Wollheim, as

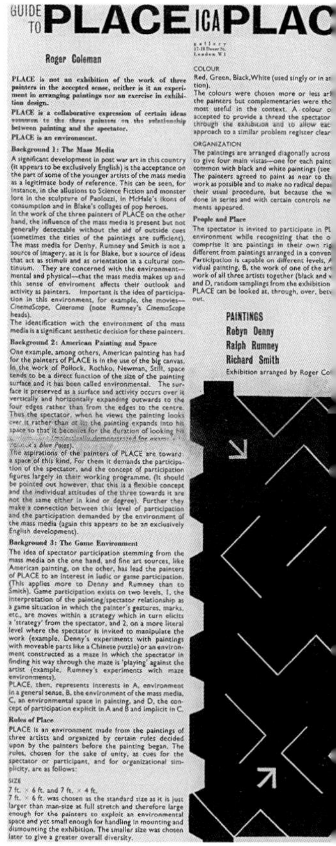

GUIDE TO PLACE ICA PLAC

gallery
17-18 Dover St.
London W1

Roger Coleman

PLACE is not an exhibition of the work of three painters in the accepted sense, neither is it an experiment in arranging paintings nor an exercise in exhibition design.

PLACE is a collaborative expression of certain ideas common to the three painters on the relationship between painting and the spectator.

PLACE is an environment.

Background 1: The Mass Media

A significant development in post war art in this country (it appears to be exclusively English) is the acceptance on the part of some of the younger artists of the mass media as a legitimate body of reference. This can be seen, for instance, in the allusions to Science Fiction and monster lore in the sculpture of Paolozzi, in McHale's ikons of consumption and in Blake's collages of pop heroes.

In the work of the three painters of PLACE on the other hand, the influence of the mass media is present but not generally detectable without the aid of outside cues (sometimes the titles of the paintings are sufficient). The mass media for Denny, Rumney and Smith is not a source of imagery, as it is for Blake, but a source of ideas that act as stimuli and as orientation in a cultural continuum. They are concerned with the environment—mental and physical—that the mass media makes up and this sense of enviroment affects their outlook and activity as painters. Important is the idea of participation in this environment, for example, the movies—*CinemaScope*, *Cinerama* (note Rumney's *CinemaScope heads*).

The identification with the environment of the mass media is a significant aesthetic decision for these painters.

Background 2: American Painting and Space

One example, among others, American painting has had for the painters of PLACE is in the use of the big canvas. In the work of Pollock, Rothko, Newman, Still, space tends to be a direct function of the size of the painting surface and it has been called environmental. The surface it preserved as a surface and activity occurs over it vertically and horizontally expanding outwards to the four edges rather than from the edges to the centre. Thus the spectator, when he views the painting looks over it rather than at it; the painting expands into his space so that it becomes for the duration of looking his [illegible] demonstrated for example [illegible] Pollock's *Blue Poles*).

The aspirations of the painters of PLACE are toward a space of this kind. For them it demands the participation of the spectator, and the concept of participation figures largely in their working programme. (It should be pointed out however, that this is a flexible concept and the individual attitudes of the three towards it are not the same either in kind or degree). Further they make a connection between this level of participation and the participation demanded by the environment of the mass media (again this appears to be an exclusively English development).

Background 3: The Game Environment

The idea of spectator participation stemming from the mass media on the one hand, and fine art sources, like American painting, on the other, has lead the painters of PLACE to an interest in ludic or game participation. (This applies more to Denny and Rumney than to Smith). Game participation exists on two levels, 1, the interpretation of the painting/spectator relationship as a game situation in which the painter's gestures, marks, etc., are moves within a strategy which in turn elicits a 'strategy' from the spectator, and 2, on a more literal level where the spectator is invited to manipulate the work (example, Denny's experiments with paintings with moveable parts like a Chinese puzzle) or an environment constructed as a maze in which the spectator in finding his way through the maze is 'playing' against the artist (example, Rumney's experiments with maze environments).

PLACE, then, represents interests in A, environment in a general sense, B, the environment of the mass media, C, an environmental space in painting, and D, the concept of participation explicit in A and B and implicit in C.

Rules of Place

PLACE is an environment made from the paintings of three artists and organized by certain rules decided upon by the painters before the painting began. The rules, chosen for the sake of unity, as cues for the spectator or participant, and for organizational simplicity, are as follows:

SIZE

7 ft. × 6 ft. and 7 ft. × 4 ft.

7 ft. × 6 ft. was chosen as the standard size as it is just larger than man-size at full stretch and therefore large enough for the painters to exploit an environmental space and yet small enough for handling in mounting and dismounting the exhibition. The smaller size was chosen later to give a greater overall diversity.

COLOUR

Red, Green, Black, White (used singly or in ar
tion).
The colours were chosen more or less ar
the painters but complementaries were the
most useful in the context. A colour c
accepted to provide a thread the spectator
through the exhibition and to allow eac
approach to a similar problem register clear

ORGANIZATION

The paintings are arranged diagonally across
to give four main vistas—one for each paint
common with black and white paintings (see
The painters agreed to paint as near to th
work as possible and to make no radical depa
their usual procedure, but because the w
done in series and with certain controls ne
ments appeared.

People and Place

The spectator is invited to participate in PL
environment while recognizing that the o
comprise it are paintings in their own rig
different from paintings arranged in a conven
Participation is capable on different levels, A
vidual painting, B, the work of one of the ar
work of all three artists together (black and v
and D, random samplings from the exhibition
PLACE can be looked at, through, over, betv
out.

PAINTINGS
Robyn Denny
Ralph Rumney
Richard Smith
Exhibition arranged by Roger Co

24 Roger Coleman, program for *Place*, Institute of Contemporary Arts, London, 1959

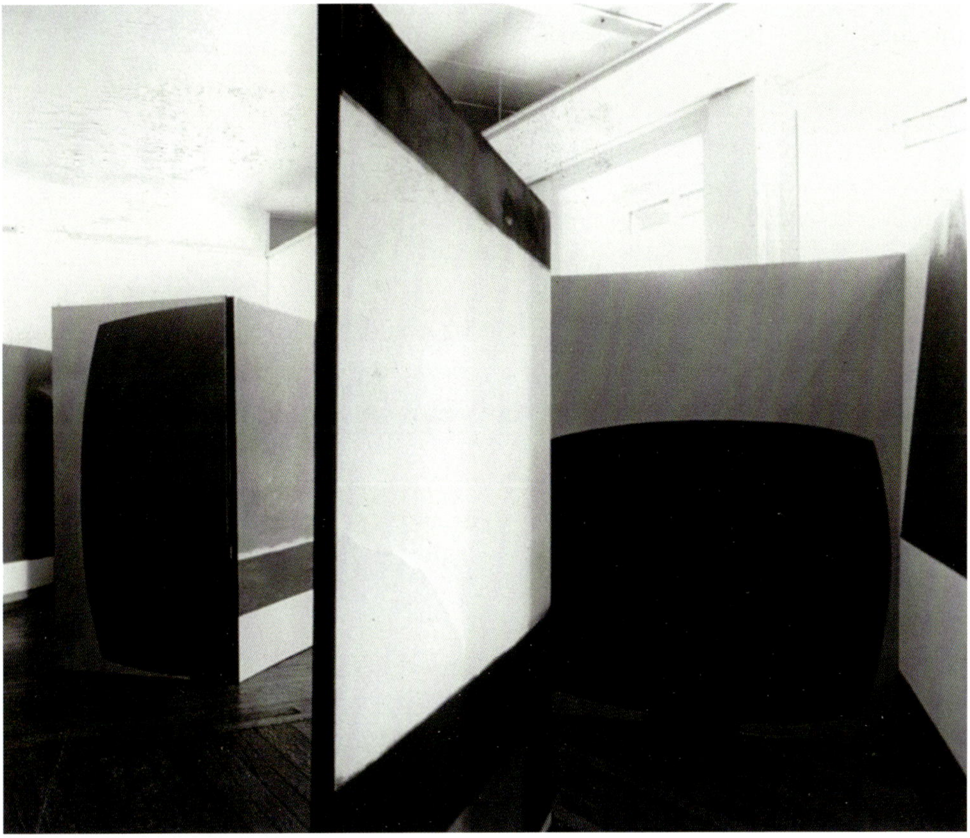

25 Installation view of *Place* (Robyn Denny, Ralph Rumney, Richard Smith), Institute of Contemporary Arts, London, 1959

noted in the Prologue, linked to the London Mod life. There was moreover a more active and immediate link to Paris in the making of the exhibition via the under-investigated contribution of Rumney, who could also claim membership in a self-elected cult of dissident youth, one less conspicuous than the Mods, to be sure, but one that would nonetheless exert a similarly outsized influence on the ways in which urban existence could be re-imagined.

In 1952, Rumney (fig. 26), aged eighteen and on the run from military conscription, had absconded across the Channel, where he fell in with a polyglot collection of young fugitives, undesirables, and unemployables living hand-to-mouth in the Paris quarter of Saint Germain des Près. "I and the rest of the tribe," he relates, "were extremely disreputable, scruffy, scurrilous, and penniless ... Our social exclusion made us into

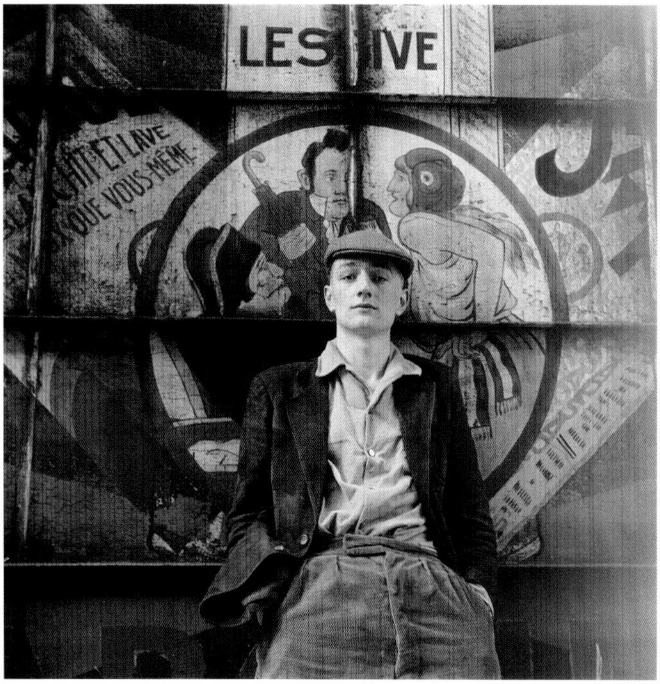

26 Ralph Rumney, photographed by John Deakin, mid-1950s

a closed group ... We wandered from café to café – we went where our feet and our inclinations carried us."[17] The Dutch photographer Ed van der Elsken, then in his late twenties, followed the group (fig. 27), paying a pittance to its most charismatic member, the Australian dancer and artist Vali Meyers, for posing as "Ann," muse and diva of the scene. He published the results in 1954 as the photo-book *Love on the Left Bank*, ever after talismanic for wide-eyed fledgling bohemians like the young Patti Smith, who wrote of Meyers: "With her wild hair, kohl-rimmed eyes, loose raincoat, and cigarette, she offered herself with abandon and self-containment. She mirrored what I aspired to aesthetically – to be unconscious of style, yet style itself. Her subterranean world seemed emblematic of all I hoped to attain."[18]

At the time, however, the group drew other eyes and companions antagonistic to all such romanticism. Rumney's hand-to-mouth troupe shared space in the same café, Chez Moineau, frequented by members of a radical micro-sect, the Lettrist International, among them its ringleader Guy-Ernest (later just Guy) Debord. Refusing all work, continually inebriated, and therefore nearly as derelict as Rumney and

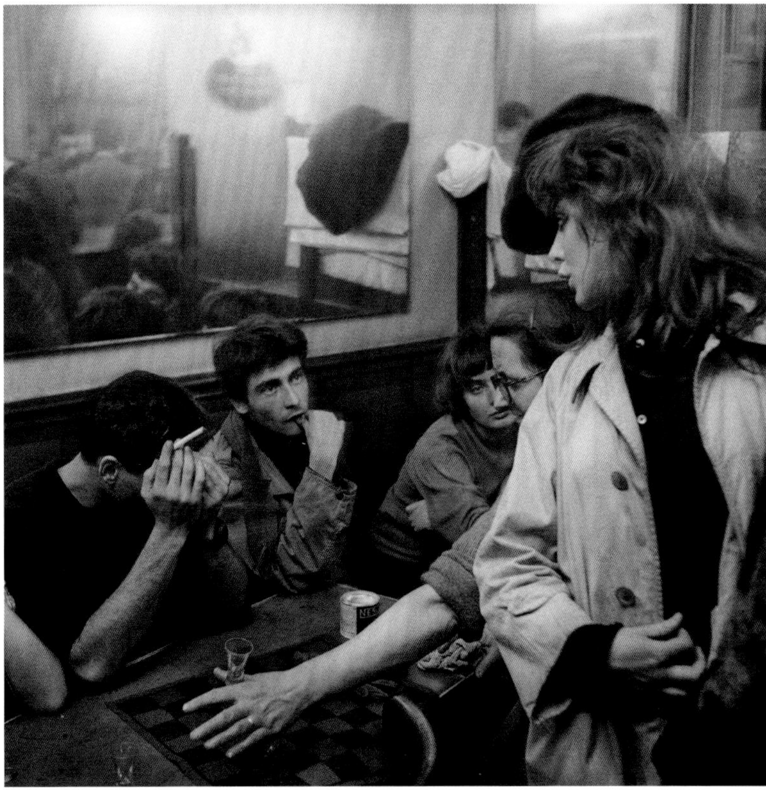

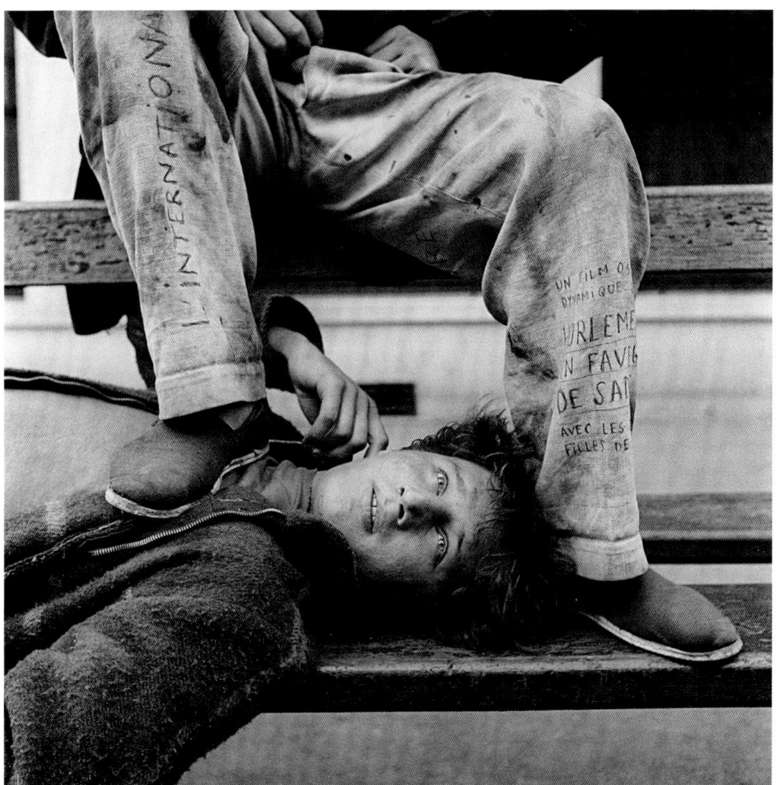

27 Bohemians in Café Chez Moineau, Paris, photographed by Ed van der Elsken, from *Love on the Left Bank* (London: Andre Deutsch, 1954)

28 Jean-Michel Mension and Auguste Hommel, photographed by Ed van der Elsken, Paris, 1953 his friends, Debord saw in them an anthropological model for the condition of total revolt he was seeking to articulate. One young dropout, Jean-Michel Mension, frequently arrested for petty crime and disorderly behavior, attracted Debord on account of his time spent inside a juvenile reformatory: "In a way," as Mension recounts it, "I was the existential principle and he was the theoretician; he must have been searching in me for the kind of trigger that causes someone to snap one day and begin living without rules."[19] That rapport prompted Mension to cross over from mere delinquent to recognized Lettrist, joining a dozen or so others as they drifted through the alleys between the dive bars of the Left Bank. Amid the group's intentionally bizarre dress and untamed hairstyles, Mension played the sandwich man in their perpetual *parade*, habitually wearing white painter's trousers with Lettrist slogans and advertisements scrawled on them (fig. 28).[20]

One of these advertised Debord's 1952 cinematic *Hurlements en faveur de Sade* (*Howls on Behalf of Sade*), which Rumney, having graduated himself from the delinquent brigade, arranged to screen back in London at the ICA in 1955, its maker in attendance. This "film" consists in fact only of alternating blank screens – white when one of the five voices on the soundtrack is speaking, black when silent. The script is a montage of borrowed legal statutes juxtaposed with personal banter and snippets of absolutist polemic against all the existing conventions of cinema and the bourgeois order they presumably support. Absolute incomprehension ensued, much to the satisfaction of Debord and his disciple.[21] Two years later, Rumney was likewise on hand in the tiny Italian town of Cosio d'Arroscia when Debord and the Lettrists joined forces with a handful of like-minded ultra-leftists to create the Situationist International (SI).[22] Styling himself as the delegate from the London Psychogeographical Committee – a self-invented entity of which he was the only member – Rumney played a significant role in the program and deliberations of the conference, though it was not long before he suffered "exclusion" at the hands of Debord, a soon-to-be routine event that eventually overtook nearly every member of the SI.[23]

Rumney nonetheless remained unwavering in his loyalty to Debord's core ideas and the centrality of drifting (*la dérive*) to any concept of emancipated existence. He brought to the *Place* exhibition a working familiarity with key terms in the Situationists' theoretical vocabulary, chief of which was "constructed situation" as the group's titular mission: creating, in Debord's semi-opaque language, "a moment of life concretely and deliberately constructed by the collective organization of a unitary ambiance and a game of events."[24] Rumney had signed on to *Place* in the expectation that the installation would introduce into an English art space some such game of events, an environment designed to disrupt its visitors' ingrained expectations of passive contemplation. But he almost failed to participate at all. Married since 1958 to Pegeen Guggenheim, the daughter of the heiress and collector Peggy (who vehemently opposed the match), Rumney was keeping largely to their residences in Paris and Peggy's home base of Venice. He had returned to London with only days to spare before the opening, but nonetheless fulfilled his quota of canvases.

In both its personnel and its conceptual gestation, *Place* was thus drawing on two models of how an unsanctioned, youthful cult might claim possession of the city: the Paris "Tribe" (Mension's coinage) of the early 1950s and the London "Modernists" of the end of the decade. On the home ground of the latter, it comes as no surprise that Rumney's Lettrist/Situationist component took a back seat to the Mod.[25] The liberatory *dérive,* derangement of the senses inspired by Rimbaud and fueled with alcohol, gave way to the acuity and focus of the Mod's Dexedrine alertness or jazzer's marijuana reverie. Alloway wrote on the occasion of the exhibition opening that the 1955 ICA performance of Debord's *Hurlements* had been "the only 'constructed situation' in England," which was to say that *Place* had not been so conceived. While he accorded the Situationists the status of "Paris's only living *avant-garde,*" this was in fact a term of abuse among them. He then compounded the insult by referring to Debord as "the Dr Mabuse of the group," thus equating him with the fictional arch-villain made famous in the 1922 film by Fritz Lang, who spreads his criminal web via the mind control he exerts over his henchmen.[26] Addressing Rumney's implied protestations of fealty, Alloway counters that Debord "has no use for painting," as "it's not socially real enough for him." Thus the young painter had been left on his own in more than one sense, and his stubborn effort to invent that impossible thing, Situationist painting, could be only realized, as Alloway put it, "by sharing the influences and interests of his collaborators (mass media, spectator participation, US art)."[27]

Coleman underscored that transformation in the notes he supplied for the visitor program:

> *A significant development in post war art in this country (it appears to be exclusively English) is the acceptance on the part of some of the younger artists of the mass media as a legitimate body of reference ... The mass media for Denny, Rumney, and Smith is not a source of imagery, as it is for [Peter] Blake, but a source of ideas that act as stimuli and as orientation in a cultural continuum."*[28]

Alongside "drifting" and "constructed situations," no term defines the Situationist project more than "the Spectacle," the defining condition of modern life under capitalism, by which all possibility of direct experience is sucked from the lives of passive consumers and sold back to them as enervating, imagistic entertainments.[29] Thus there would have been no mental state more likely to provoke Debord's expletive-laden contempt – and Rumney's dissent – than "identification with the environment of the mass media," still less the discriminating consumption at the core of a Soho Modernist's sensibility.

Alloway and Coleman, for all their evocation of the mass media, offered little further guidance as to where such correspondences might lie. Having adopted the restrained, put-together Modernist look in one's personal style, then having stripped one's painting down to match, the next question became: could the main protagonists of *Place* possibly take the materials of visual art further into the structural core of jazz, their great and longstanding inspiration? And did they? For an answer to this speculative question, one could start by asking how a small-group jazz performance comes about. The players agree on a basic melody, often a popular Broadway tune with some interesting chord changes, then a key, then a tempo, then modulation possibilities: in short a set of basic parameters from which the players proceed to improvise, contributing to the whole based on the capacities of one's instrument and individual sensibility. While the singularity of jazz giants is such that it can often be encapsulated in a single resonant syllable (Bird, Monk, Miles, 'Trane, Newk), none can function individually or dictate precisely what the accompanying musicians will play. On a given date, a leader might work in a supporting role, with a less heralded musician coming to the fore. Collective authorship is the norm; unaccompanied performance the rare exception. Disillusioned with public performance, Sonny Rollins ("Newk") may have blown his horn alone atop the Williamsburg Bridge for hours on end between 1959 and 1962 (fig. 29), but such isolation is so exceptional as to become the stuff of legend. And when Rollins returned to the studio, he did so with a tight quartet that counterposed the breathy heft of his tenor against the pixilated precision of Jim Hall's guitar.

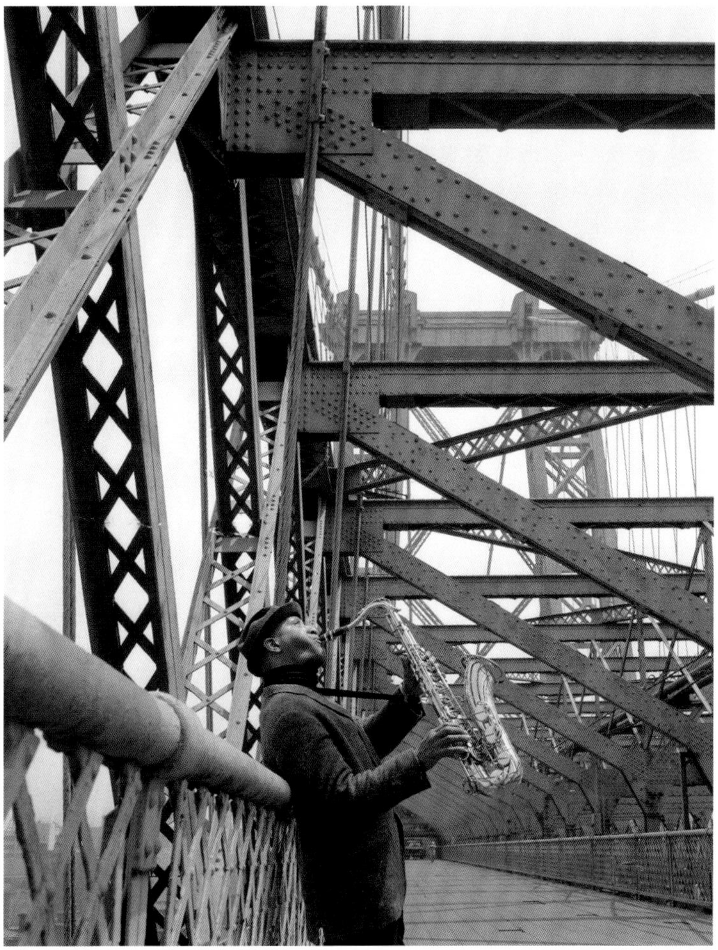

29 Sonny Rollins playing his saxophone on the Williamsburg Bridge, photographed by David McLane, *New York Daily News*, 19 June, 1966

However unheralded by comparison, *Place* took the idea of a similarly distributed authorship as its starting premise. Within its stated stipulations, each artist was enjoined to preserve his own personal manner, so the broad bands of Denny's canvases interacted with the distended rectangles in Rumney's and both with Smith's broad passages of translucent touches, all operating under rules, as with musicians' choices of key and chord changes, that set out permitted sizes, viewing angles, and colors. Then improvisation took hold. The fact that the prescribed sizes for *Place* were so large necessitated rapidity of execution reminiscent of on-the-spot improvisation. Rumney, because he arrived in London only four days before the opening, made all of his paintings in that interval, while Denny and Smith had executed their dozen or so large canvases in a matter of months. Their common size (such that one could not see over them) combined with their contiguous arrangement (such that one could not see around them) meant that some painting or combination of paintings would always be in the visitor's field of vision (fig. 30). Rumney attested to their intention that the visitor "should see pictures on the margins of his perception all the time without ever being forced to look directly at them unless he so desires."[30] Normally one has the option of looking away from a work of art; amid the *Place* installation that option was closed; wherever you looked you were seeing it, just as sound in a room is pervasive, allowing no way for the listener to avoid hearing it, nor imposing any obligation to focus directly on the playing of any individual musician.

The usual analogy of jazz to art is seen to lie in the improvisation inherent in the technique of a Jackson Pollock or Willem de Kooning. But that analogy quickly runs out of room on two grounds: firstly, those painters were not themselves enthusiasts for the advanced jazz of their own time (one would need the proto-Pop Larry Rivers for that); secondly, they were not painting with anybody else, thus had no need to adjust their performances to regulating patterns agreed on with any partners ahead of time. *Place*, by contrast, proceeded both from a shared enthusiasm for advanced jazz and from a willingness to cede a good portion of one's individual prerogatives to the demands of the ensemble. Its filtered component of Situationist thinking would probably be most evident in

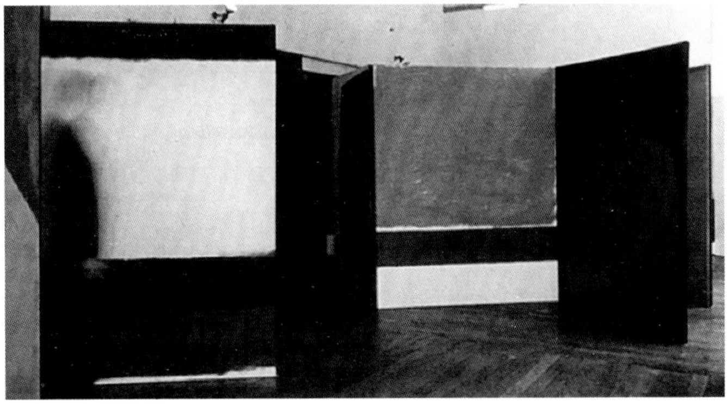

30 Installation view of *Place* (Robyn Denny, Ralph Rumney, Richard Smith), Institute of Contemporary Arts, London, 1959

this suspension of individualistic subjectivity. Left Bank intellectuals had of course been as fascinated by American jazz as the Soho Modernists would be: Vali Meyers danced to the African drummers in the same club, Le Tabou, where Miles Davis romanced the *chanteuse extraordinaire* Juliette Greco – and where the old Lettrists had staged performances. Even if the dyspeptic Debord doubtless excoriated jazz as just another enticement of the Spectacle, its proximity to the life of "the Tribe" arguably remained a latency that resonated with the jazz correspondences of *Place*.

Such dispersion of authorship collided in London with a brick wall of normative expectations concerning proper hanging of pictures and the sanctity of unmediated visual contact with the singular work. Witheringly dismissive reviews followed, the critic for *The Observer* pronouncing it "the silliest exhibition I have ever seen in my life."[31] General incomprehension ensured that this experiment with group improvisation was unlikely to be repeated by either its authors or its sponsoring institution – thus proving even shorter lived than the flare-up of *Ark* design under Coleman in 1957. It may well be that painting as a medium is structurally unsuited to the demands of collective invention that jazz musicians take for granted on a nightly basis. If it could, though, if painting could measure up to the charismatic exemplars encased in those Blue Note discs, if its authors could fully acknowledge the life-transforming power of those models, then *Place* was probably what the effort would have needed to look like.

To the extent that this jazz model reveals some of the Mod vitality in *Place*, its importance extends beyond the analogy with one musical idiom to the potential priority of collective over individual authorship in the city turned inside out. Colin MacInnes in *Absolute Beginners* and Richard Wollheim in "Babylon, Babylone" implicitly addressed the possible supersession of the singular object as it bore on the latter's philosophical subdiscipline in aesthetics, fixated as it was on individuated objects of art. Once Paris had undergone the transformations that unsettled the Goncourts, concluded Wollheim, the "aesthete's province was no longer merely the museum ... it now included in its domain the great thoroughfares and meeting-places of the modern city, the avenues, the cafés, the music-halls, the public gardens, the railway stations, where the flood of contemporary life swirled and raced at its highest mark." But he did not go so far as to posit a form of art making as part and parcel of this turbulent flux; instead, the modern artist, preeminently the Impressionist painters, found in these public spaces "positions of vantage from which the raw material of art could be extracted."[32]

Wollheim saw in this self-removal to the customary comfort of singular subjectivity, however, a high price paid in diminished scope and veracity of the art. "Modern urban life," in his view, "seems to have been freed of its attendant strains and anxieties, and presented as though it were a feast of assorted and subtle sensations." He implies but does not fully articulate the thesis that this deficiency follows from the individual artist acting on the city as "raw material" from which exquisite, "*travaillé*" objects continued to be fashioned, their destiny being to hang on museum walls. His account of the Absolute Beginner, as he refers to MacInnes's protagonist of 1959, offers another model of aesthetic activity, one through which authentic "strains and anxieties" make themselves abundantly felt. The Teenager, whom this character represents, is a composite identity, implicitly collective in character. His aesthetic endeavor lies in the improbable life he manages to lead, one that wrests the artistic values of "energy, spontaneity, and excitement" from the deadening determinations of the old, buttoned-up city. "As an extreme measure,"

Wollheim writes admiringly, "what he can do is try to create for himself a life ... for which there is no physical analogue in the lay-out of the city, for which there is no façade behind which it can properly occur." This is his art form, not sampled from the urban swirl at a safe distance but made in and of it: life as a creative act of adroit improvisation maintaining "a precarious balance poised on the 'dubious' fringe of society."[33]

The "he" in Wollheim's account functions as the personification of a shifting population: new recruits joining, style leaders ("Faces") innovating, older veterans falling away from youthful exactitude and back into more conventionally compromised life. The Modernist mode of life takes collective authorship – dispersed agency and distributed intelligence – to a level beyond any self-consciously artistic pursuit, processing by its own lights possible furnishings of life and definitions of self in the city conceived as theatrical backdrop. Decoding such moments of style-creation can become more than clinical exercises by according the cults the same assumptions of intention, intelligence, fine intuition, and self-critique that one would bestow on any certified fine art – but spread across a network far more extensive and democratic than even the most capacious avant-garde collective ever occupied.

CHAPTER TWO
GALLERY ONE AND THE ABSOLUTE BEGINNER

IN THE SOHO OF 1956, AN UP-TO DATE OBSERVER ON the lookout for the elusive Mods might, on sighting the young John Kasmin, have been confident that the quarry had been spotted. Older at twenty-two than the teenage norm, the slightly built Kasmin looked younger than his years. Dressed in tailored suits, neatly barbered, lover of modern jazz, the young art dealer could have blended into any gathering of neighborhood Modernists. Having spent his early life in an affluent Oxford household and private day school, Kasmin had been thrown on his own resources by family financial reverses while still a teenager. In 1951, at seventeen, he had made his way to New Zealand and re-invented himself as a poet (an ambitious calling in the country of Allen Curnow and James K. Baxter). And it was as a poet that he sought to establish himself on returning to London in 1956. On an impulse, mainly looking for excitement and intellectual connections, Kasmin was drawn to Gallery One in Soho, then both an outpost for advanced art on a Parisian model and a social nexus for the sort of people he wished to meet in pursuit of his literary calling. In the hope of a job, he presented himself to its owner, Victor Musgrave. For a pittance, on the condition that he look after the cooking for Musgrave's resident ménage, he became an apprentice art dealer.[1]

One could have walked in ten minutes from the upscale galleries of Mayfair to the premises of Gallery One on the ground floor of an unassuming house in D'Arblay Street, but its scruffy Soho milieu would have seemed a world away from Bond Street. To call it a shoestring operation would be to overstate its resources, which were so tight that Kasmin, living on the premises, slept for a time on a platform over the bathtub. Musgrave occupied one room, off limits to everyone else, while his wife, the Egyptian-born photographer Ida Kar, maintained her studio on the top floor. Room was even found for a paying lodger, none other than Colin MacInnes, then at work – in between stints as a BBC broadcaster and jobbing essayist – on his predecessor to *Absolute Beginners*, *City of Spades*, which took its subject from the nascent African and Afro-Caribbean migration to London. In Kasmin's recollection, the conflicted homosexual MacInnes "wanted to be a manly man amongst manly blacks and he had already acquired a great deal of the lingo, but with his accent and manner – he was tall, good looking, close-cropped hair, wonderful smile, rather military bearing – he was such an unlikely character to be speaking in the West Indian jargon, but he did … "[2] On the floor above Gallery One, the author lived austerely in a barely furnished room, while Kasmin had begun, at Musgrave's request, sharing a room with Kar on the top floor, acting as both her agent and lover, thereby relieving her husband of unwanted conjugal responsibilities.

Kar had struggled both to assert her photography as a genuine artistic pursuit and her place as a woman artist in the face of the period's withering sexism. In order to validate and publicize her standing as a portraitist, she had already sought out artists in London and Paris as subjects, mounting forty of the resulting prints in a 1954 exhibition at Gallery One. Kasmin undertook to build on this initiative by approaching creative celebrities of every kind as potential subjects: "I would telephone and say I'd been commissioned by a newspaper to interview them and photograph them. I'd just bluff it. Whether it was Tennessee Williams or T. S. Eliot, I'd just telephone and with most of the calls I would arrange visits. We collected authors and artists."[3] They would sell them via an agency "to newspapers all over the world." Hovering over the sessions, Kasmin could smooth over awkwardness like the moment

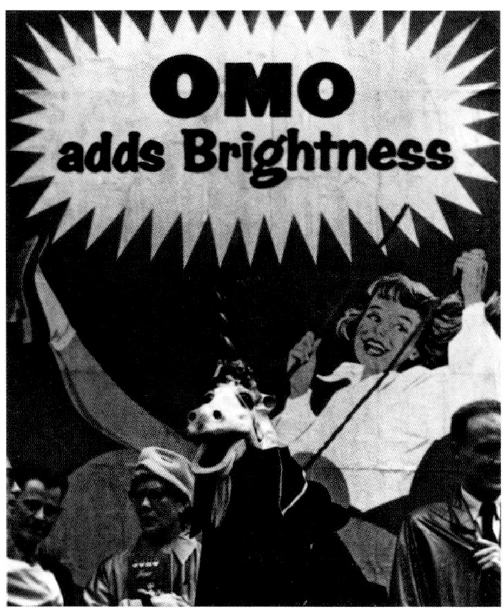

31 Soho, photographed by Ida Kar, *c.*1956

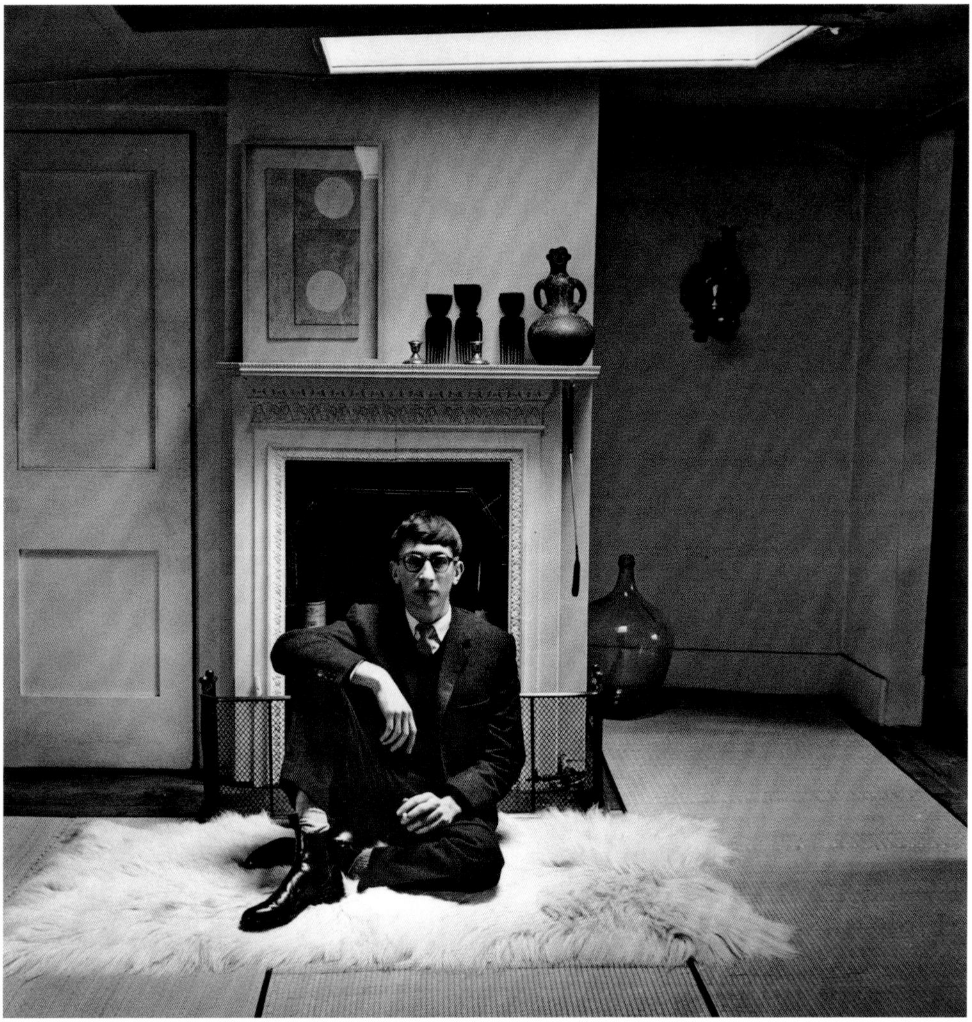

32 John Kasmin at home in Fouberts Place, photographed by Ida Kar, 1959
National Portrait Gallery, London

with Eliot in 1956 when it became clear that Kar did not know who he was. He also prodded her to take her photography in a different direction, to supplement her heavy view camera with a portable Rolleiflex and venture into the streets, pubs, and arcades around Soho to create saleable documentary picture stories. These stand up in comparison with the more celebrated contemporaneous work of Nigel Henderson and Roger Mayne, one print (fig. 31) thoroughly in the spirit of the moment featuring a strange pantomime unicorn flanked by passersby in a kind of frieze below a billboard advertisement emblazoned with a grinning girl on a swing and the slogan "OMO adds Brightness."

In 1959, some time after their liaison had ended, Kar photographed the now-married Kasmin (fig. 32) in outwardly

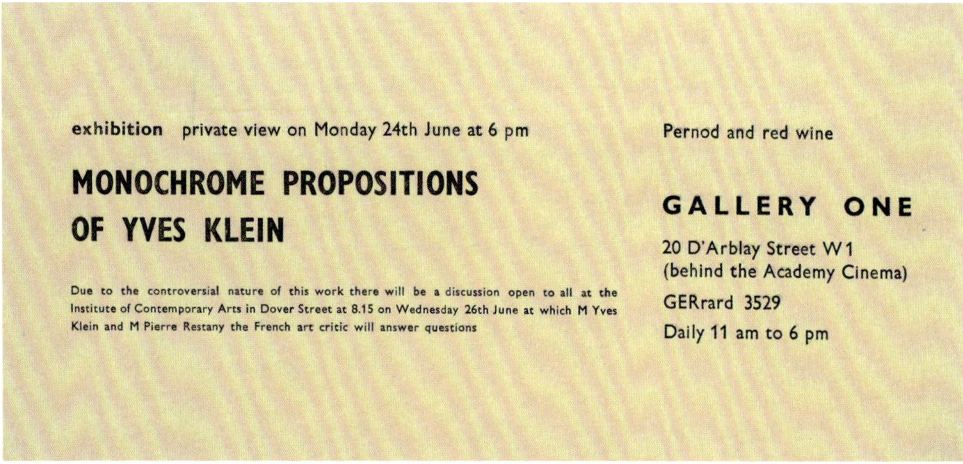
exhibition private view on Monday 24th June at 6 pm

MONOCHROME PROPOSITIONS
OF YVES KLEIN

Due to the controversial nature of this work there will be a discussion open to all at the Institute of Contemporary Arts in Dover Street at 8.15 on Wednesday 26th June at which M Yves Klein and M Pierre Restany the French art critic will answer questions

Pernod and red wine

GALLERY ONE

20 D'Arblay Street W1
(behind the Academy Cinema)

GERrard 3529

Daily 11 am to 6 pm

33 Invitation to *Monochrome Propositions of Yves Klein*, Gallery One and Institute of Contemporary Arts, 1957

respectable Mod turnout, betrayed only by a bohemian rumpled sock exposed by his cross-legged pose (above the mantle hangs a small abstract relief by Ben Nicholson, his wife Jane's uncle). Before leaving the year before, he had witnessed Gallery One attracting figures who have already played parts in the present narrative. In 1957, on the lookout for unheralded talent, Musgrave had spotted Robyn Denny at the Royal College of Art and offered him a show. Denny was then appearing in the pages of Coleman's *Ark* at work on the large abstract canvases that put him at odds with his tutors, but the small dimensions of Musgrave's premises may well have led to his exhibiting some uncharacteristic efforts in mosaic.[4] From further afield, Yves Klein mounted his "Monochrome Propositions" at Gallery One in June of the same year, their first exposure outside of France (fig. 33). The ICA deemed the occasion significant enough to stage a public discussion with the artist and the French critic Pierre Restany. Ralph Rumney, friendly with Klein, claimed a mediating role in arranging the affair, much as he had deployed his Parisian affiliations to broker, as discussed in the previous chapter, the notorious 1955 screening at the ICA of Debord's *Hurlements en faveur de Sade*. Kasmin, when bedding down on top of the single bathtub in D'Arblay Street, was aware that Musgrave rarely used it, preferring the Marshall Street baths. Vince, Bill Green's nearby boutique in Newburgh Street, drew a good part of its clientele for continental male fashion from that gathering place, though the gallerist always wore the same black corduroy suit on public occasions, his style adventures being channeled into outings dressed as a woman.[5]

No wonder that Kasmin could declare in looking back:

> *the whole of life at this time for me was so exciting I can't tell you, because everybody was such an exaggerated character you could hardly believe it possible that I knew so many people that were almost, were caricatures of their own ... they were people that were so full of being people you wondered how they had time to do anything, they were so intensely different from everybody else.*[6]

Another such person entered the Gallery One crucible in the youthful form of Terry Taylor. Accounts differ as to whether it was Kasmin or MacInnes who first met the precocious, London-born photographer, who made his living taking passport photographs in a Soho arcade, while circulating among the clubs at night shooting portraits of musicians and their fans. As the Flamingo, the principal jazz venue in Soho, was then next door to Gallery One (fig. 34), it would have been natural for Taylor to find his way over. But he recalls first meeting the author of *City of Spades* in a mostly African

34 Gallery One and the Flamingo club, D'Arblay Street, Soho, 1956. Still from *Sunshine in Soho* by Burt Hyams, 1956
British Film Institute Archive, London

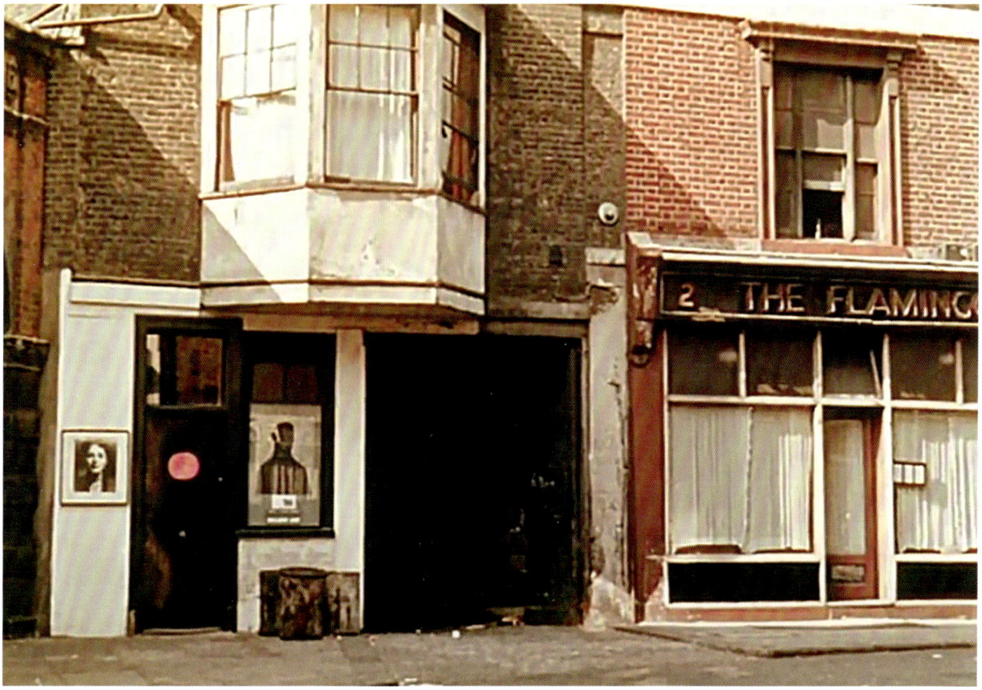

club, the Myrtle Bank in Soho's Berwick Street, which offered neither drink nor live music but where the jukebox, according to MacInnes, featured "highbrow jazz discs rather than the usual pops: currently, Dave Brubeck, Chico Hamilton, and old stalwarts like Fitzgerald, Armstrong, and Sarah Vaughan."[7] Kasmin, while he carried on managing Kar's business affairs, guided Taylor to taking his place as her romantic partner and assuming, owing to his vocation, the role of her able studio assistant.

Via this liaison, the new arrival became the template onto which the figure of the postwar teenager would be projected. In the invention of *Absolute Beginners,* MacInnes would distribute the salient aspects of Taylor's life over three of the novel's principal characters. Kasmin sketches some of that life:

> *a very good looking guy with lovely lips a bit like Mick Jagger's, you know, quite a lot of lip. He was a Londoner, he was maybe a year or two older than me ... He had a perfectly good way of earning money when he was functioning because his photography was mostly of musicians and in jazz clubs and night-time music and flash work and the night scene, and he worked for magazines and record covers and all that sort of thing. He certainly had a way of producing money. He did, I can't remember if he kept it secret at this time, but he did have a lady friend who was a prostitute called Gypsy, that was a very highly trained prostitute ... but I think he'd split from Gypsy, that was it, he had been living with Gypsy and he'd split from her. He was trying to turn over a new leaf and he moved in with Ida ...* [8]

For the purposes of his story, MacInnes assigned the life of peripatetic, freelance photography to his nameless narrator, as he did sympathetic affinity with black immigrants in districts like Notting Vale, where they resided, and leisure-time haunts like the Myrtle Bank, where they shared their music and style. To Wizard, the flawed, streetwise sidekick, went the intermittent habit of living off the prostitution of a female partner. The narrator's admired friend Dean, the "sharp modern jazz creation," acquired Taylor's refined musical connoisseurship, along with the drug use common among American jazz exemplars. In both cases, at least according to Kasmin, that habit extended to heroin: Taylor's "problem was that he was a heroin addict and every now and then he accidentally OD'd and he needed help and like most heroin addicts, every now and then he'd be trying to get off it. And Ida quite liked … the fact that he needed help … "[9]

As explored in the previous chapter, the 1959 *Place* exhibition at the ICA connected with emergent Mod culture across a web of allusion and indirection. The Gallery One hot-house, however, launched two strong attempts by older artists to capture the Mod as a type and a representative individual, both via the persona of Terry Taylor. MacInnes distributed him across the London terrain of *Absolute Beginners*, as just noted, while Kar posed him in photographic allegories of his febrile existence. She shot one series in 1957, in the aftermath of a portrait session (doubtless arranged by Kasmin) with a visiting American big-band singer named Judy Johnson, in a way that riffed on the idea of a smoky jazz boîte as den of vice (fig. 35). In several, as here, a standing Johnson remains in the darkly atmospheric frame, her back turned in a sleeveless sheath, dark hair spilling down her back. A soft-focus Taylor, illuminated in the foreground, is caught mid-inhale

35 Terry Taylor with Judy Johnson, photographed by Ida Kar, 1957
National Portrait Gallery, London

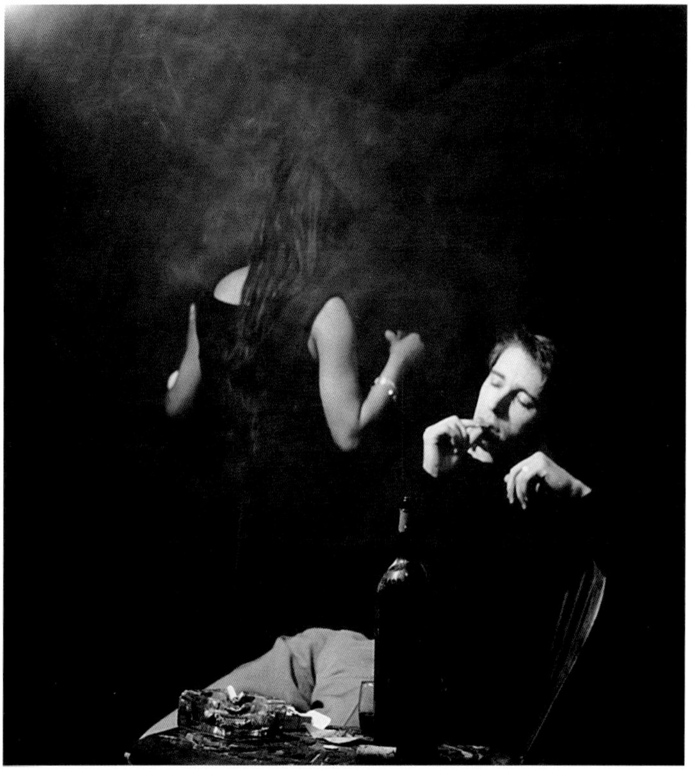

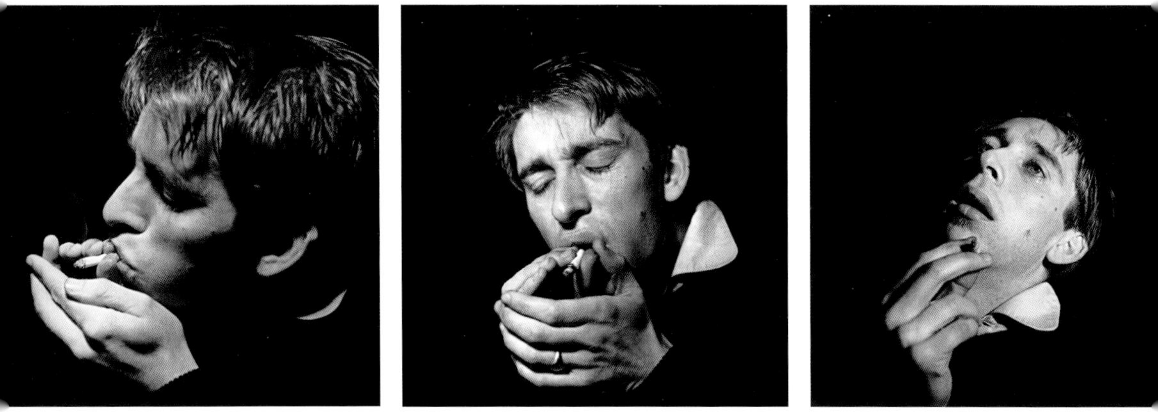

36a–c Terry Taylor, photographed by Ida Kar, 1957

National Portrait Gallery, London

on a marijuana joint ("charge" in his parlance), its discharge suffused in the air. The overflowing ashtray makes for a telling still-life vignette in the lower left corner.

Accompanying these two-figure compositions were close ups of Taylor in a series anatomizing the stages of getting high (fig. 36a–c). "That's the great thing about Mother Charge," he later wrote,

> *you never know which way she's going to take you. You think after a time you know all the different paths you can travel on, but you soon find out there are others. Monday, a laughing one. Tuesday, a serious one. Wednesday, a working one. Thursday, a lazy one. Oh man, isn't it exciting? A thousand paths to travel on and each one different ...*

The words belong to a drug-dealing character in Taylor's 1961 novel *Baron's Court, All Change*. MacInnes had repaid the young photographer's contribution to *Absolute Beginners* by encouraging him to write, and his protégé duly produced its effective sequel two years later. In addition to "charge," sharp dress and up-to-date jazz remain at the core of the protagonist's sense of self. When he first makes a profit from dealing, he immediately has clothes on his mind: "I felt like a millionaire. I wanted to go to Cecil Gee and buy half their stock up or something crazy like that. This was two months' wages ... " His reflections on jazz are rhapsodically detailed, as he skewers the false Mods, in his eyes, who had appeared in the interim and pretended to jazz connoisseurship as a pretext for vapid social display.[10]

Later, Kar followed him into less lurid moments in his daily round, one particularly telling shot finding him in contemplative reverie, prone on the floor next to his record player (fig. 37), a character vignette with resonant attributes akin to those in a Netherlandish portrait. The LP sleeves fanned out next to him tell the story of the sitter's advanced taste: *Ray Charles in Person*, issued in 1959, is a one-off live recording (captured by one microphone at the center of a Georgia baseball ground) that still stands as a high point in that performer's career: interspersed with scorching, gospel-inflected numbers are the big-band jazz instrumentals less remembered as staples of Charles's early repertoire. The

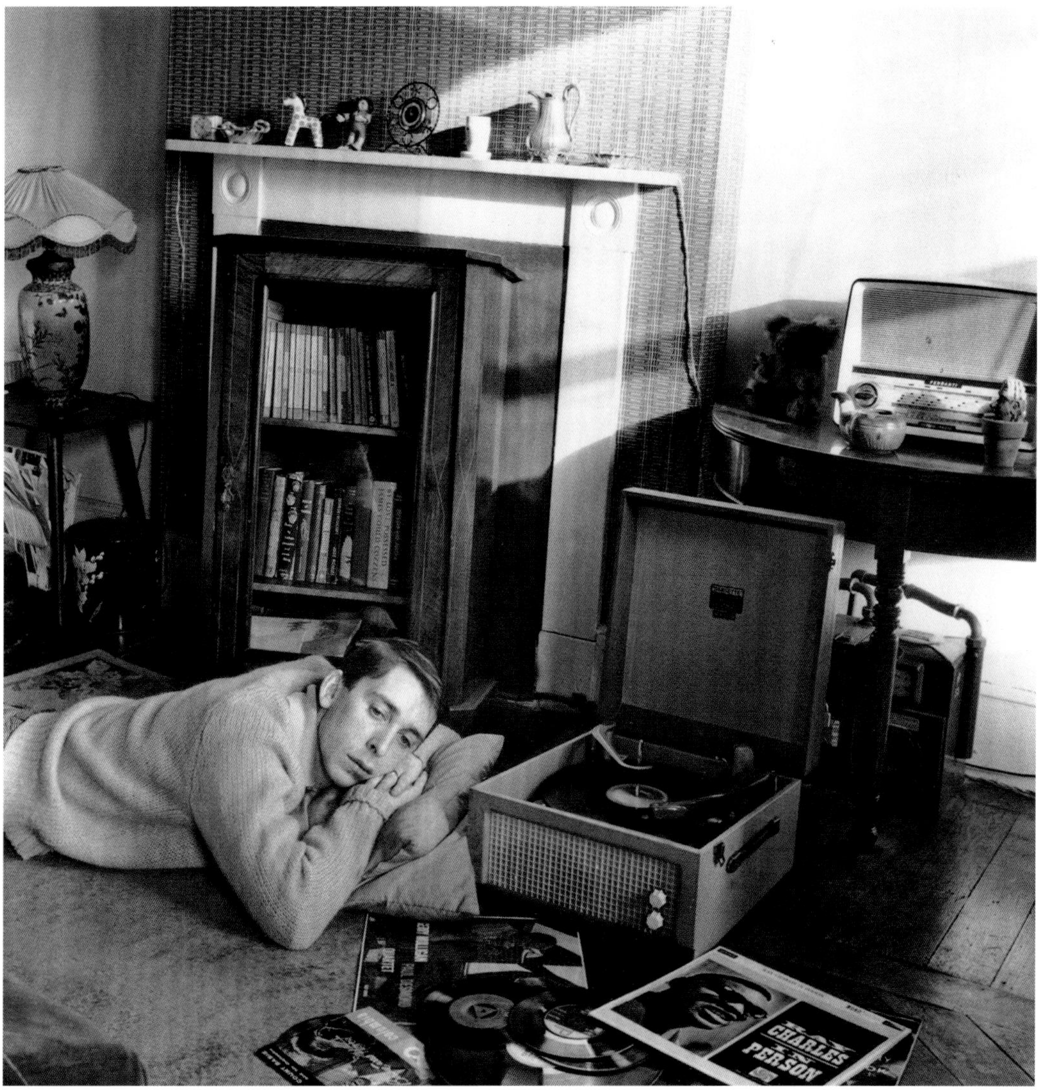

37 Terry Taylor, photographed by Ida Kar, *c.*1961
National Portrait Gallery, London

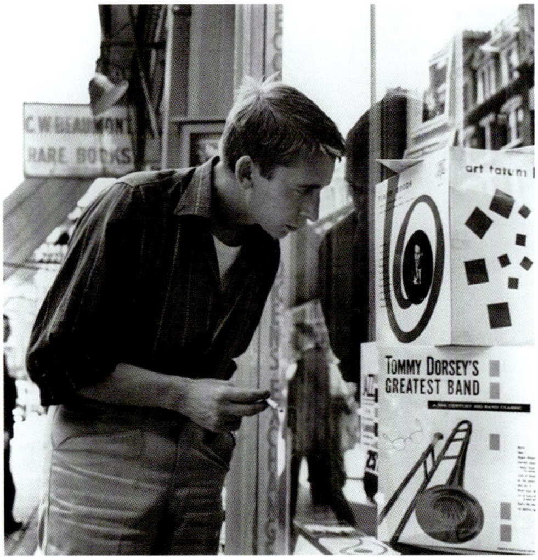

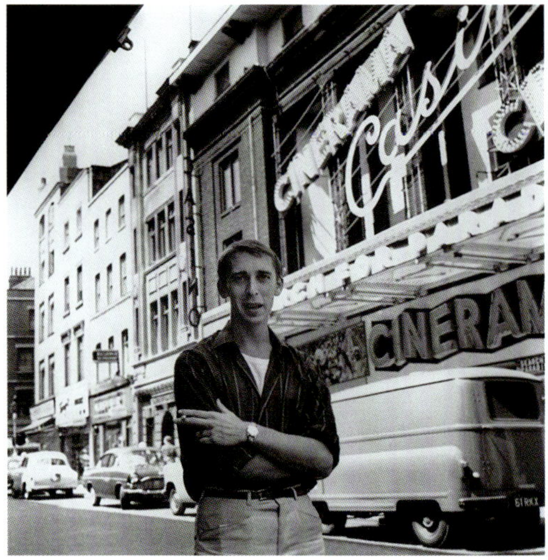

adjacent Count Basie record suggests that these tracks were to Taylor's liking, while the 1960 twelve-inch by white West Coast players Gerry Mulligan and Paul Desmond (baritone and alto saxophone respectively) announces affinity for the cooler American tendency.

Kar ventured out into Soho, Rollei in hand, to document Taylor in 1961, the year in which *Baron's Court, All Change* was published (fig. 38). College-boy coiffed, cigarette in hand, he peers at artfully arranged reissues devoted to past jazz masters, the pianist Art Tatum and the white swing bandleader Tommy Dorsey, in the display window of the Charing Cross Road bookshop (just along from Cecil Gee) maintained by the balletomane author and publisher C. W. Beaumont. In another pose (fig. 39), snapped by Kar in Old Compton Street (home to the 2I's coffee shop), Taylor stands in front of the Casino cinema, striking the very figure that Wollheim extolls for having "rejected the conception of the city as a solid three-dimensional environment that shapes and enfolds his life, and instead regards it as a kind of highly coloured backcloth against which he acts out, and upon which he projects his fantasies."[11]

38 Terry Taylor, photographed by Ida Kar, 1961

National Portrait Gallery, London

39 Terry Taylor, photographed by Ida Kar, 1961

National Portrait Gallery, London

The sequence from which these images are drawn represents an inspired, unexpected collaborative project that joined Kar's documentary art to Taylor's self-fashioning. Kasmin, having

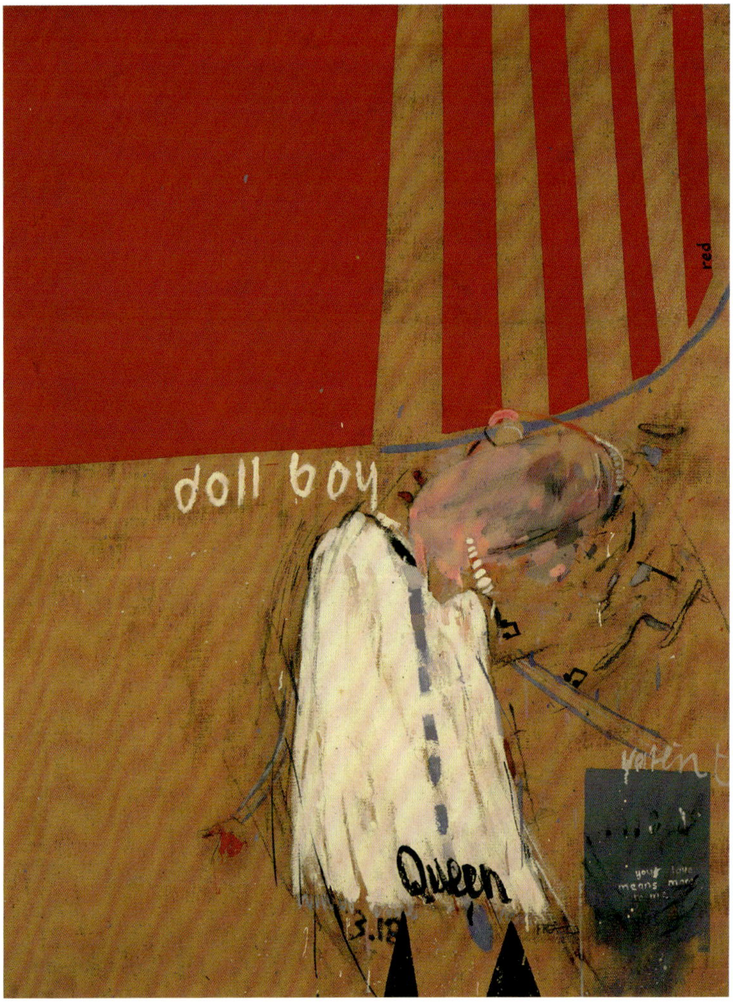

40 David Hockney, *Doll Boy*, 1960–1
Oil on canvas, 122 × 99 cm
Hamburger Kunsthalle

helped bring them together, had in the meantime parlayed his Gallery One experience into employment with a more upscale art dealer of established modern masters, better paid but lacking the excitement of the Musgrave milieu. Encouraged by the proprietors to scout for unknown artists, his quest led him, likewise in 1961, to a painting in the *Young Contemporaries* exhibition by David Hockney. Not knowing the artist, he bought *Doll Boy* (fig. 40) for forty pounds, intrigued, he says, by a work that seemed to partake equally of figuration and abstraction.[12] Both halves of this equation are distinctly Pop in character: the red and gold fairground bunting above presses on the drag "doll boy" below, advertising itself as the pop singer Cliff Richard, who had recently reached the charts with a song called "Living Doll." The musical notes issuing from the lips of the bent-down head might have given Kasmin a further clue, even without knowing that Hockney had festooned his studio space with Cliff pin-ups, that the young painter was unabashedly announcing homoeroticism as his artistic and personal signature – literally in the scrawled word "Queen" in black script at the hem of the crotch-length shift that drapes the figure. Reassuring for Kasmin might have been the treatment of the face in the borrowed manner of Francis Bacon's mottled grays and pinks, underscored by the carnivorous mouth (which does double duty as a cross-dresser's string of pearls): simultaneously homage to Bacon as *the* postwar prototype for gay eroticism in painting.

The confident, wholly unintimidated attitude conveyed by *Doll Boy* echoes the generally arrogant affect of the Soho Modernist, who refused all dowdy social shibboleths on principle. The charismatic gay character of the Fabulous Hoplite in MacInnes's *Absolute Beginners* speaks for this attitude, as does the existence of a significant contingent of

41 Barrie Bates with his submissions, *Young Contemporaries* exhibition, RBA galleries, London, 1961

42 Barrie Bates, poster for the Jazz Society, Royal College of Art, London, 1961

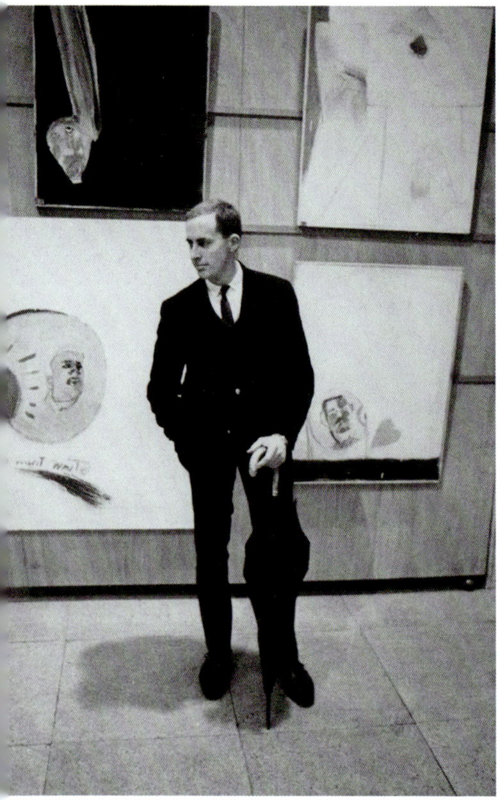

gay Mods frequenting Le Duce club in Soho or El Sombrero in Kensington.[13] Infatuation with a tepid Elvis imitator, in contrast, would have been entirely out of keeping with the sophistication of Mod musical preferences. At that point, too, the panache that comes across in the painting found little correspondence in his personal dress and demeanor. Kasmin, now a family man with a Fulham address, followed up his purchase by inviting Hockney round for tea: "He was very shy when I met him, still young and black-haired and nervous of women. I arrived home late from work, and there he was with his National Health specs and black crew cut sitting shyly with my wife. Neither of them was saying a word."[14]

That reticence was about to change in a hurry, abetted by a Royal College classmate who lived up to a number of Mod criteria, despite having recently arrived from the furthest reaches of the Commonwealth. The New-Zealand-born Barrie Bates (better known to posterity as Billy Apple, about which more shortly) adopted the Modernist's close-cropped hair and sharp, trim style in suiting, which he wore to the studio every day (fig. 41). In more casual moments, he stayed with an American collegiate uniform of turned-up Levis, white oxford shirt, and white Keds sneakers. Where jazz was concerned, he was as Modernist in taste as in dress. With a friend at the London School of Economics receiving rare up-to-date releases straight from New York by post, Bates soon set up weekly lunchtime listening sessions, for which he designed all the posters. His Modernist bearings are amply evident in the impeccable economy of his poster for Miles Davis's 1959 *Kind of Blue* (fig. 42), where the trumpeter extended the innovations of "Milestones" into an entire, haunting album from slowly evolving modal harmonies. The watershed character of that set – amply affirmed by its posterity – beggared the capacity of art to offer an equivalent beyond the evocatively muted abstraction of Bates's three-dimensional design. In March 1961, the prominent trade design magazine *Print Review* included some of Bates's poster designs in a feature titled "Top Drawer: Design by Music."[15] When Thelonious Monk received dispensation to play a concert at the Royal Festival Hall a month later, Bates was there.

As the leader of a jazz ensemble deploys the contributions of skilled specialists into a larger whole, Bates adapted a parallel approach to his art making. Admitted to the comparatively new school of graphic design, he made difficulties from the start but nonetheless impressed the head, Richard Guyatt, that he was the leading talent of his class. So much so that when he proposed transferring to the painting school, there to join his friends Hockney and Derek Boshier, Guyatt enticed him to stay by giving him license to use the resources of all the schools. Whatever the rough edges of his personality, Bates proved adept at enlisting photographers, ceramicists, metal casters, or printmakers to labor on projects that went out under his name. To his mind, he was more an art director than a studio hand with ink, glue pots, and T-squares (exhibiting a Mod's reluctance to engage in any activity that disheveled one's suit). He seems to have steered clear of actually working on *Ark*, perhaps the better to revive Coleman's late 1950s legacy of obviating the difference between fine art and design, now by working in both pursuits simultaneously.[16]

A winter holiday internship with an expatriate American advertising designer sharpened his desire to visit New York. Hockney shared the same determination for his own reasons, and both won monetary prizes in spring 1961 that provided the necessary funds – Hockney having discovered $99 fares on the charter carrier Flying Tiger. Various acquaintances gave them lodging during the two-month sojourn, and neither would return to London unaltered by the experience. For Hockney, arguably, the greatest attraction lay in the freer and more open gay scene. However beleaguered it might still have been in the pre-Stonewall decade, that life would have appeared light years ahead of London, where homosexual acts remained a crime. He was not disappointed, as attested by *I'm in the Mood for Love* (fig. 43), the travel-diary in paint he completed immediately on his return: his self-image as a horned and bespectacled devil, wedged between priapic skyscrapers, wears a heart on one sleeve and swings the other arm in the direction of "QUEENS UPTOWN."

For his part, Bates leapt immediately into the jazz paradise that was Manhattan clubland. On his first night in the city, his English host took him to the Village Vanguard to see the Miles Davis quintet, his *Kind of Blue* listening session back at the RCA come to glorious life. "Throughout July alone," writes Anthony Byrt of the artist's nightly rounds, "Bates would have had the opportunity to see Eric Dolphy, and then [Ornette]

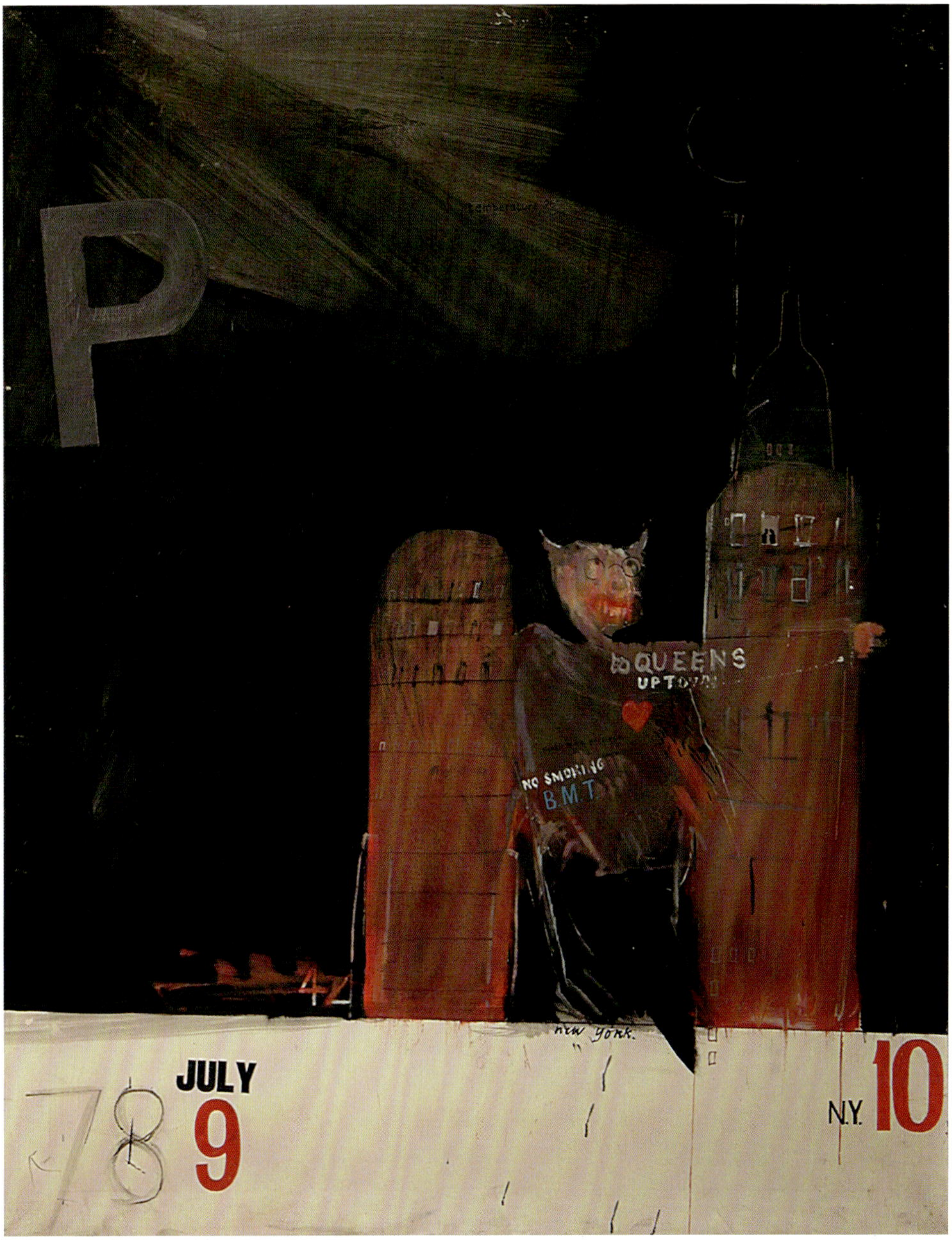

43 David Hockney,
I'm in the Mood for Love,
1961
Oil on canvas, 127 × 101.6 cm
Royal College of Art, London

Coleman at the Five Spot; Coltrane and Art Blakey at the Village Gate, Buddy Rich at Birdland, and Monk at the Jazz Gallery." Bates wrote to a friend back in New Zealand that he had "seen every one who's anyone."[17]

A memorable series of photographs (fig. 44a–d) document the two of them that summer on a lark at Coney Island. In

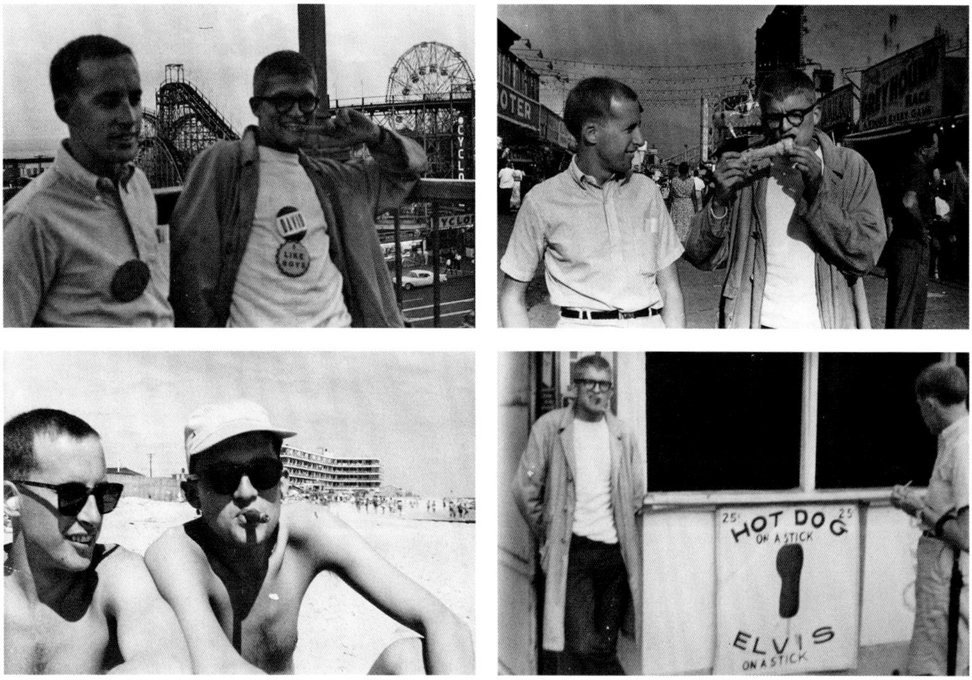

44a–d Barrie Bates and David Hockney, photographed by Mark Berger, Coney Island, New York, summer 1961
Billy Apple Archive

professional terms, however, the two young artists largely went their separate ways. Hockney carried a portfolio of etchings and an introduction from a London tutor to Alexander Liberman, the curator of prints at the Metropolitan Museum of Art. Liberman purchased one for the Met collection and offered his help both in finding buyers for the rest and locating a press in Manhattan where Hockney could make more. Bates carried his own letter of introduction to the leading typographic designer of the period, Herb Lubalin, and secured a month-long internship at the latter's Madison Avenue agency Sudler, Hennessey & Lubalin. After visiting their offices, Hockney drew a portrait of Bates titled *Madison Avenue. Lie$ Lie$ Lie$,* depicting his friend in a "drip-dry" suit with the hanger still in place. Bates had plainly needed to keep up appearances for the sake of his corporate-style workplace, with this particular summer-weight garment also carrying a certain symbolic significance in the period (fig. 45). Inexpensive enough for Bates to afford, the synthetic fabric signified up-to-date efficiency and careless elegance, rather than the cheap connotations that the word polyester has come to acquire.

Low-priced enhancements to one's appearance became a theme of their summer. While watching television with Hockney's new local companion Ferrill Ammacker, the three were regaled with the slogan for Lady Clairol hair dye: "Blondes Have More Fun." They made an immediate pact, went out to acquire the product and went blonde together that night, a state of peroxided splendor that the naturally dark-haired Hockney would maintain for decades.

After an interval long enough for his own darker hair to grow back out, Bates re-appropriated Hockney's summer portrait in the deadpan photographic piece *Portrait of the Artist in a Drip Dry Suit* (fig. 46), the image taken by his RCA colleague Robert Freeman, in which the telltale hanger protrudes from the collar. For his part, Hockney had acquired his own drip-dry suit before departing New York. In a studio portrait (fig. 47), datable to 1963 by the two paintings in progress (*The Hyptonist* and *Domestic Scene Notting Hill*), he probably donned the same costume for the photographer Tony Evans, high-water trouser length in evidence, along with the cognate Ivy-League accessories of penny loafers and narrow knit tie (a rare moment for him of impeccable Mod turnout).

Another young Yorkshireman, Terry Atkinson, recently arrived in London for his own postgraduate art degree at the Slade School, soon perceived the RCA outpacing the conservative Slade in conspicuous innovation. "Insofar as I could without being too intrusive," he recalls, "I nosed a lot around their various painting spaces at the RCA." He had known about Hockney, he says, "on the Yorkshire art school grapevine." But

45 Haspel seersuckers advertisement

46 Barrie Bates/Billy Apple, *Portrait of the Artist in a Drip Dry Suit*, 1962
Offset lithograph on canvas, photograph by Robert Freeman

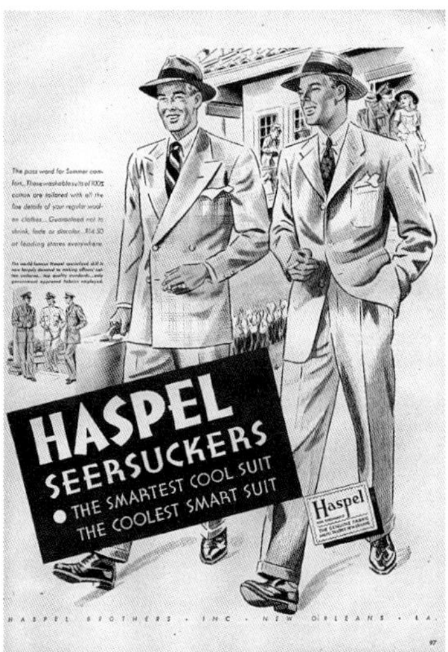

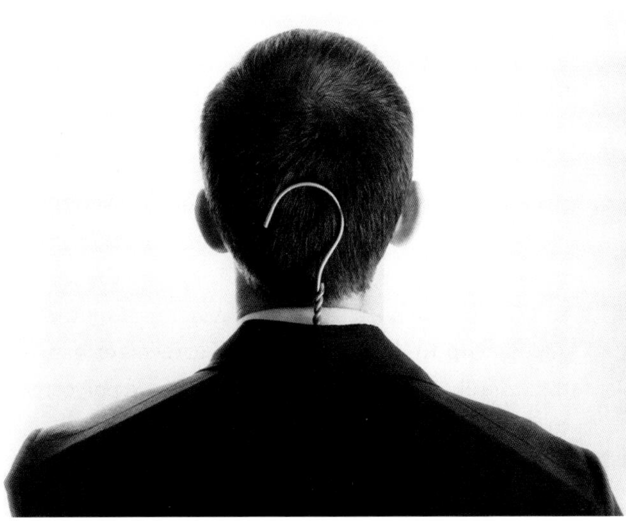

that had hardly prepared him for the dazzlingly transformed Hockney he encountered in London: "his presentation of his own body," as Atkinson puts it, "dyed hair, gold suit, etc., presented another kind of relief ... as inspiring, I do not use the word glibly, as Chuck Berry et al." For Atkinson, to equate Hockney with the first wave of American rock and roll represented his highest possible form of praise, recognition of the advantage held by the Royal College in the role of what he called "receiver and transmitter of Pop art iconography and ideology coming then from the United States."[18]

The gold lamé jacket had become so indelibly a part of Hockney's public image that Atkinson's memory backdates it; it was in fact the occasion of Hockney winning the gold medal for painting at his graduation that marked its public debut. Not everyday wear – and the opposite of Mod discretion – the jacket called to mind the gold suit Elvis Presley famously wore for the cover of his 1959 LP, *50,000 Elvis Fans Can't be Wrong*. The fact that Lord Snowdon, the husband of Princess Margaret, photographed Hockney wearing it in 1962 (fig. 48) proved beyond a doubt the publicity value of the self-fashioning he had begun in New York the year before. No longer the poorly dressed, diffident figure Kasmin had initially encountered, his emerging identity as a public figure began almost at once to attract an inestimable surplus of recognition for his art. While never alluding to his friend by name, Bates had reached a point where he could no longer proceed as an artist still pretending that the machinery of publicity was somehow an extraneous supplement to one's practice. The next chapter tracks the diverging paths followed by the two artists. Bates would soon adopt an invented new name and a public persona as cognizant as possible of the inherent contrivance of any marketable artistic identity. That sustained undertaking presages what came to be called Postmodernism, thus diverting his story to one side of what remained of modernism as unfinished business. His old mate Hockney, by contrast, found himself still with more than one modernism to work his way through.

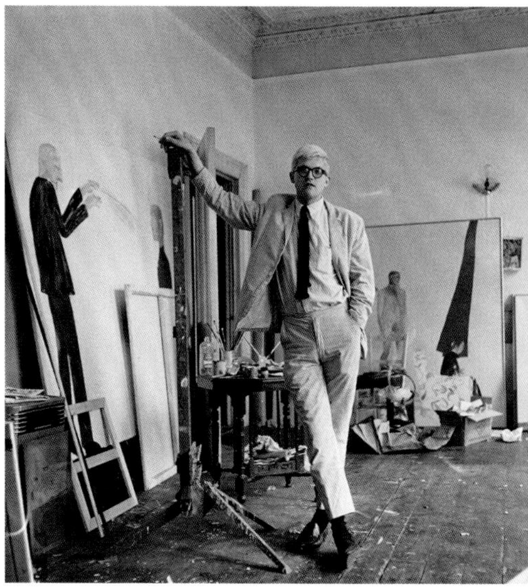

47 David Hockney, photographed by Tony Evans, 1963

48 David Hockney wearing his gold lamé jacket, photographed by Lord Snowdon, 1962

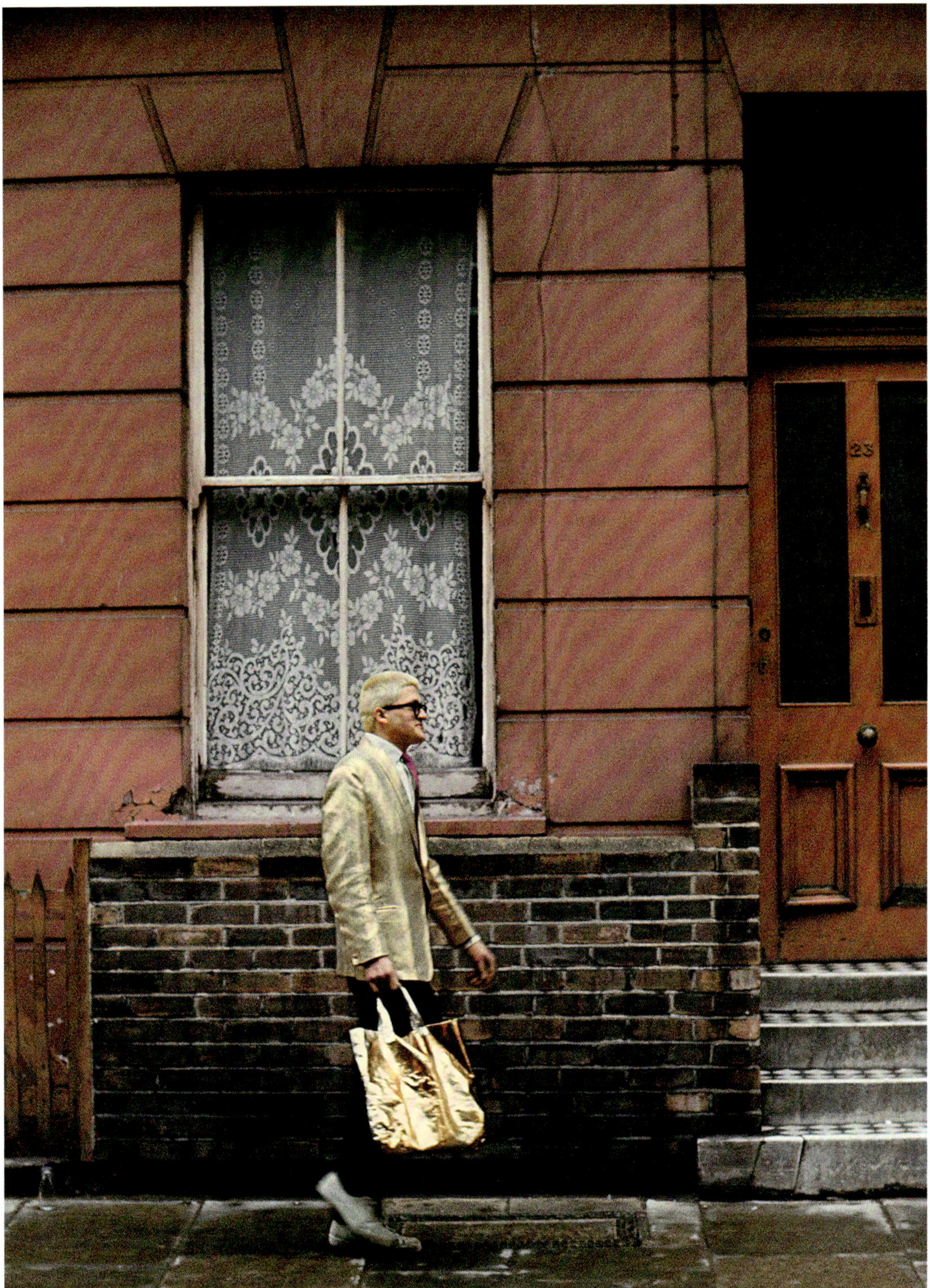
23

CHAPTER THREE
APPLE ARRIVES AS HOCKNEY TAKES OFF

IN NOVEMBER 1962, IN A KIND OF PRIVATE CEREMONY held at the studio of Richard Smith, Barrie Bates underwent the ceremonial erasure of his birth-identity to emerge as a new personage named Billy Apple. The baptismal font was once again a container of Lady Clairol blonde hair dye, the moment captured in a slide (fig. 49) taken by Smith (and later designated an inaugural Apple work). Trademark registration affixed, Billy Apple became the only appellation to which he would henceforth respond, the idea being that the identity of the artist as an artifact of publicity and market promotion would no longer remain an unruly add-on to an "authentic" body of work. Instead, the artist would necessarily become one more signifying component to be subsumed

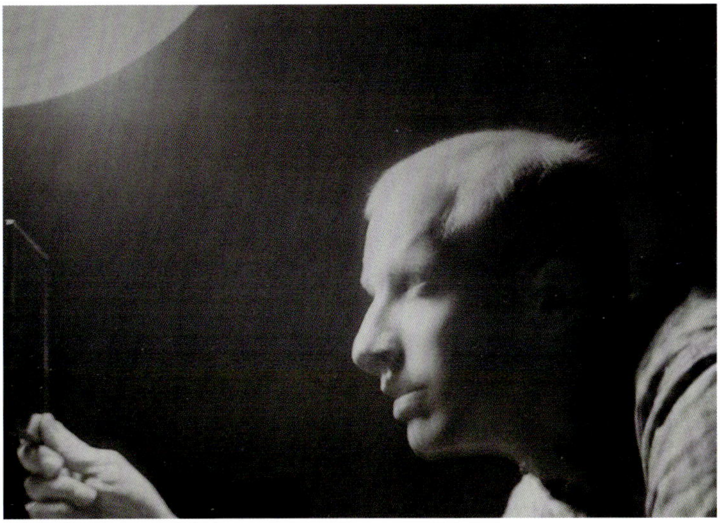

49 Billy Apple, *Billy Apple Bleaching with Lady Clairol Instant Crème Whip*, November 1962
Photograph by Richard Smith

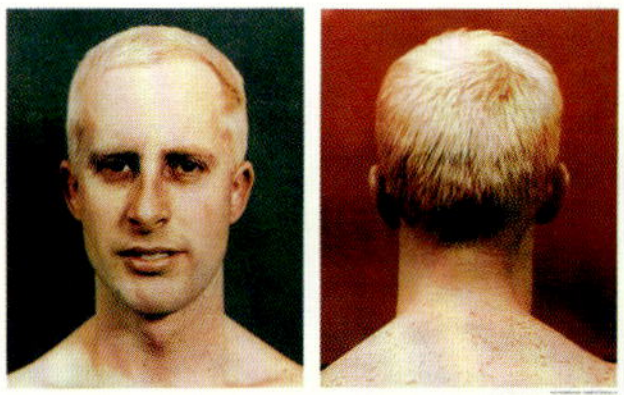

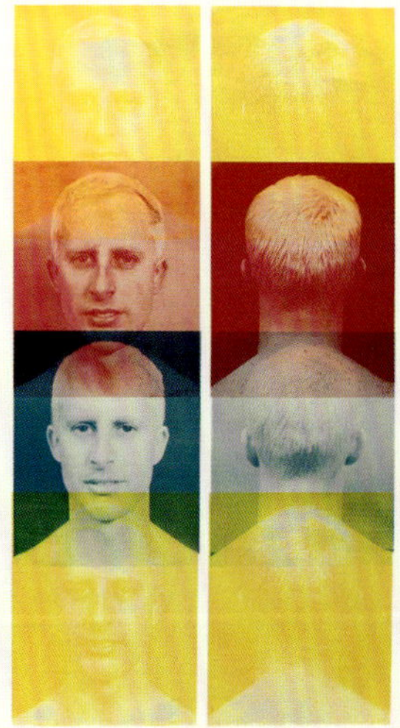

within that body of work, therefore just as susceptible to aesthetic and cognitive control as any other artistic product.

He unfurled the manifesto of his new condition in April 1963 at the latest incarnation of Victor Musgrave's Gallery One, now relocated to North Audley Street off Grosvenor Square, the site of the American Embassy. For *Apple Sees Red: Live Stills*, he took over the entire space, painting the walls black in order to control the entire environment. Along one wall were twelve identical portraits, analogous to the *Portrait of the Artist in a Drip Dry Suit*, but pointedly stripped of any telltale accessories, indeed any clothing at all. Likewise photographed front and back by Robert Freeman and printed as offset lithographs by Roy Crosset (fig. 50), the bare-shouldered Billy Apple reveals himself clothed in effect by nothing but the bleaching of his hair and eyebrows. One variation surrounded the frontal portrait with the framing of a signed identity card, while a third set (fig. 51) broke the double portrait down into the color separations used in the printing process, coherence of the self disintegrating into the mechanics of reproductive technology. On sculptural plinths, with a nod to Jasper Johns, were trios of cast apples (fig. 52)

50 Billy Apple,
Self-Portrait (Apple Sees Red on Green), 1962–3
Offset lithograph
Photograph by Robert Freeman

51 Billy Apple,
Vertical Progression, 1963
Offset lithograph
Photograph by Robert Freeman

going from whole to half-eaten to core, their skins red, green, or gold, their pulp black (he titled them *2 Minutes 33 Seconds* for the time it took him to consume the apple). On a tray, with a nod to Marcel Duchamp, there was also a bronze cast of the (prominent) Adam's apple of Billy Apple.

Press reactions caught the mortuary chill of the exercise, "live stills" for still life, with or without awareness of the death rites of Barrie Bates hanging over the advent of this new hybrid being. Gallery One maintained its trajectory of provocative statement begun with its installation of Yves Klein's *Monochrome Propositions* in 1957 (someone went to the trouble of shooting a bullet through the display window during the Billy Apple show). Kasmin even played a certain part; owing to his New Zealand connections, two Kiwi assistants had come to work at the gallery, which eased the way for Billy Apple. But the early part of 1963 was also the moment of Kasmin's unveiling his own aesthetic epiphany on the stage of the London art world. "The trigger," he relates, had been "a [1960] show of Morris Louis's paintings at the ICA. I was swept off my feet ... Here were these vast paintings that were exciting beyond belief. I thought, 'That's what people should be looking at in painting, instead of pottering about with John Minton and Julian Trevelyan and Lucian Freud's dreadful little drawings.'"[1] By 1963, in the service of that enthusiasm, Kasmin succeeded in opening his own Mayfair gallery in New Bond Street, keyed to the effective display of work like Louis's, which by itself changed the way that alert Londoners looked at art.[2]

52 Billy Apple,
2 Minutes 33 Seconds, 1963
Painted cast bronze
Edition of 3
Private collection

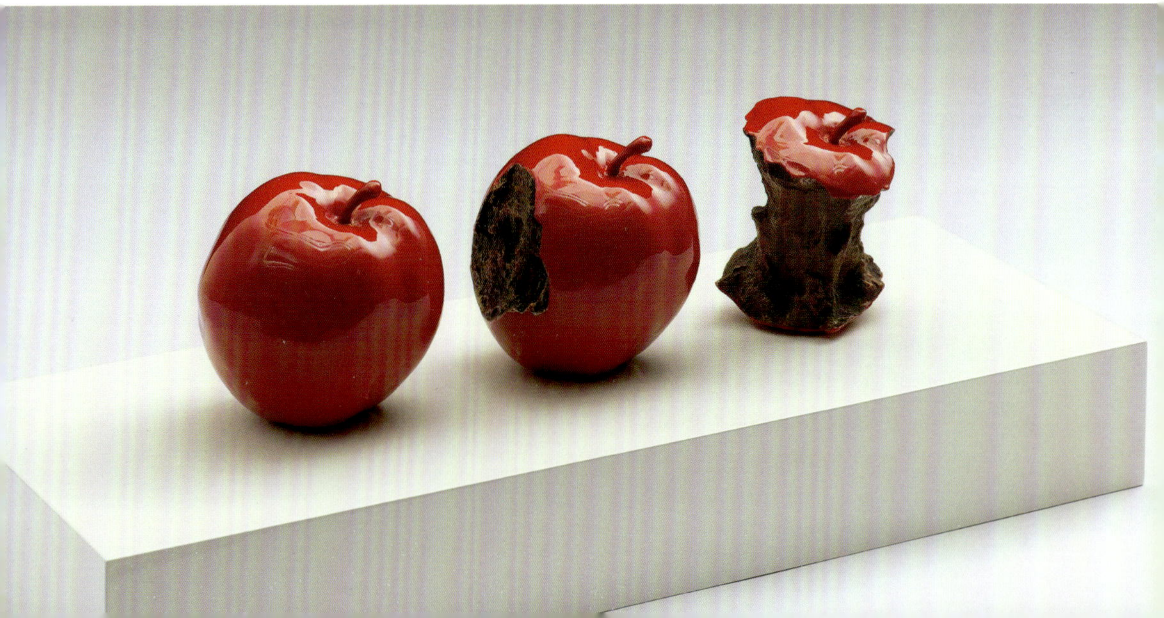

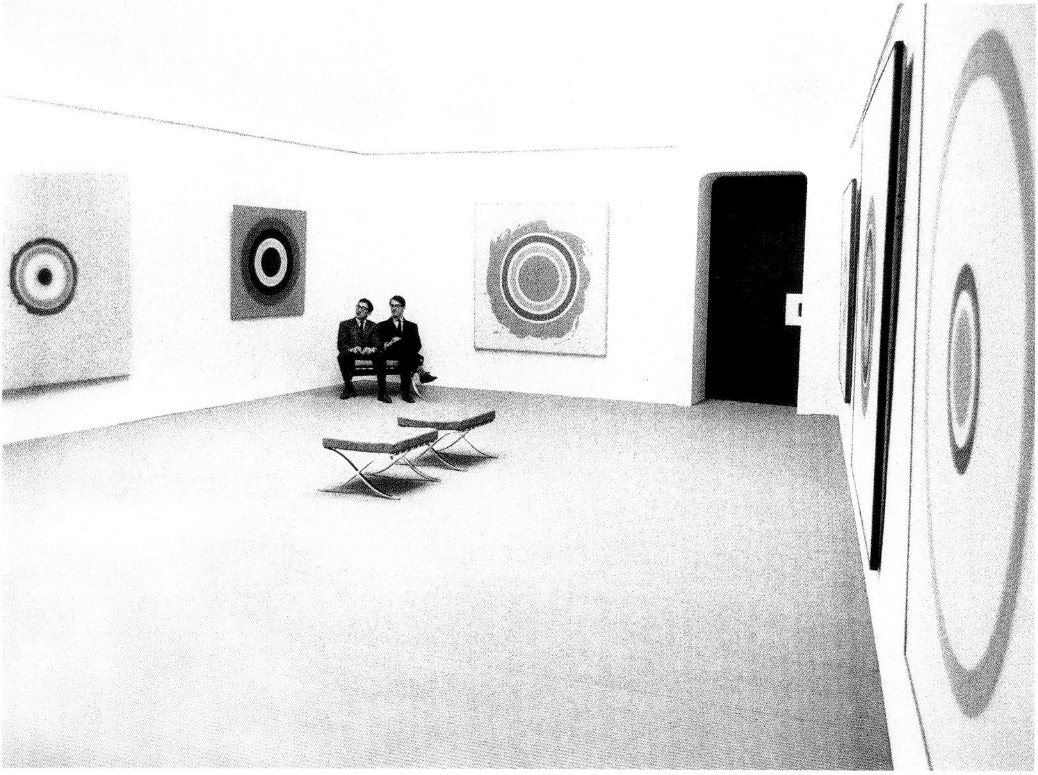

53 John Kasmin and Sheridan Blackwood in the Kasmin Gallery with paintings by Kenneth Noland, photographed by Lord Snowdon, April 1963

Through a classical portal squeezed between two shopfronts, one entered a plain, narrow corridor, which rounded a corner at the end to reveal a space then unlike any other in London. The clarity and spaciousness of its top-lit spaces, the industrial chic of its Pirelli rubber floor, all designed by the architect Richard Burton, proved a revelation in itself. A suite of photographs (fig. 53) by Snowdon – whose participation speaks volumes for the gallery's instant cachet – capture Kasmin with his financial partner Sheridan Blackwood, Marquess of Dufferin, contemplating the first exhibition in the new gallery: the concentric circle canvases of the American Kenneth Noland, a close friend of Morris Louis and exactly the kind of artist for which this environment had been engineered. In this endeavor Kasmin gained the immediate support of the power dealer Lawrence Rubin, who had recently established his own beachhead for these New York painters in Paris; Rubin wrote to him in June 1962: "Should you get a place with good space you can count on my help with all the American artists I handle: Louis, Noland, Frankenthaler etc., in the younger generations and

Motherwell and Gottlieb in the older generation. I have lots of ideas on the subject."[3] Kasmin subsequently wrote to Noland after a visit to Rubin in Paris: "Larry and I made a list of paintings he proposes sending me for the show, 8 in all, mainly big ones, so that even if you do not bring some newer ones with you we shall have a knock-out show anyway."[4] This phalanx was truly as imported a Modernism as post-bop jazz had been, as much a new style of critical judgment as it was a statement of thoroughgoing abstraction in art.

The London sculptor Anthony Caro had grown close to Noland on his American visits and was in turn being celebrated in cognate terms by the American Modernist critics Clement Greenberg and Michael Fried. At about the time of Kasmin's opening show, the St. Martin's School sculptors around Caro actually pitched in to cover Greenberg's airfare so they could receive critiques from the American arbiter of quality, the added attraction being Kasmin's affirmation of his taste on foreign soil. As that taste went under the name of high Modernism on its home ground, there were now two ways to think like a Modernist in central London, this new variety having nothing to do with the jazz scene or men's boutiques of Soho, but arguably partaking of a cognate formal rigor. And it was in this context that Hockney's first solo exhibition opened at Kasmin's in December (fig. 54), some six months after Billy Apple's rebirth as a brand.

Hockney may have twitted (the former) Barrie Bates's advertising life during their New York summer of 1961, drawing his likeness under the title *Madison Avenue. Lie$ Lie$ Lie$*, but his exhibition with Kasmin shared nothing of his friend's ambivalence and irony about the commerce in fine art. Fifteen substantial paintings, including the two glimpsed in the artist's "drip-dry" portrait, were

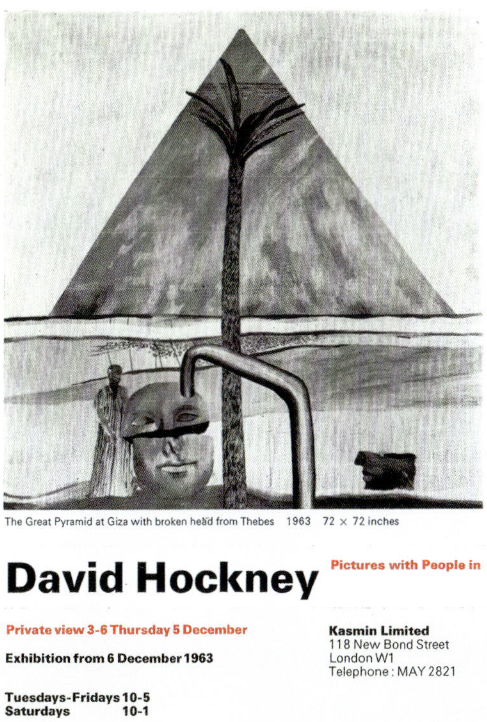

54 Announcement for *David Hockney* private view, designed by Gordon House, Kasmin Gallery, London, December 1963

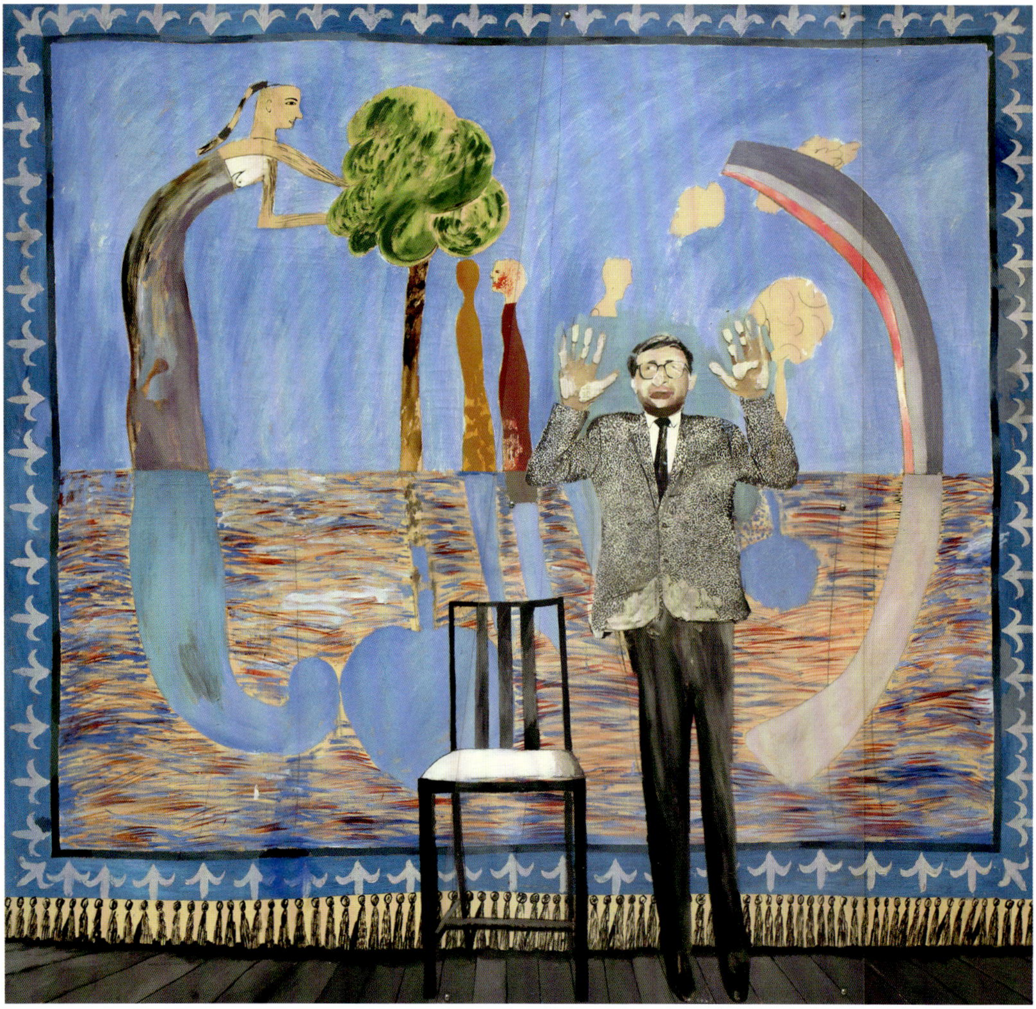

mostly priced at £350 or £400 – commensurable to the prices Noland had been commanding.[5] The latter figure would represent some £7000 in today's currency, which Kasmin regarded as less than the market would maximally bear but conducive to the works going to deserving collectors. The surviving gallery checklist shows only two canvases unsold or unreserved.

Conscious of his odd-man-out position vis-à-vis the abstract painters in the Kasmin stable, Hockney gave his show the slightly apologetic title "Pictures with People In." But he grappled with the problem in a more consequential, even aggressive manner via one painting in the show, *Play within a Play* (fig. 55), onto which he bolted a top-to-bottom trapezoid

55 David Hockney, *Play within a Play*, 1963
Oil on canvas and plexiglass, 182.8 × 198.1 cm
Private collection

of clear Perspex. A standing figure beneath it – dressed in proper Modernist attire – seems trapped and desperate to escape. The illusionistic perspective of the floorboards and chair work against the actual adherence of the transparent plastic to the painted surface, suggesting a narrow shelf of space that does not actually exist. The panicked figure squeezed into the impossible space is Kasmin.

Francis Bacon's characteristically distressed figures always appeared behind glazing, and Hockney could be alluding to that prototype for theatricalized agony. But there was a more proximate correlate for so emphasizing the plane of the canvas surface, Greenberg's core precept being that painting had come to define itself by attributes it shared with no other art form, these being "flatness and the delimitation of flatness."[6] The so-called color-field approach shared by Louis and Noland, with their thinned-down pigments stained into raw cotton duck, ratified these propositions by making the actual matter of the painting and its abstract imagery physically coincident from one another. A highly curated selection of the reviews and essays in which Greenberg had developed this grand thesis over two decades had been published in 1961 under the title *Art and Culture*, thereafter circulating widely within the art world in readily digestible form.[7] Even if Hockney had not read any of it, as is likely, the dicta and formulae that defined this imported fine-art Modernism would have been abundantly available as second-hand chatter. The Perspex sheet makes literal and threatening the flatness of the fetishized picture plane, as it descended squarely on top of the Londoner's Modernist style code, a quality that Kasmin exemplified in his careful attention to grooming and dress. In this forced confrontation, *Play within a Play* may be a rare or even unique instance of the two Modernisms, London style and New York fine art, coexisting in equal measure within a single work of art.

The playful put-down in *Play within a Play* at the same time suggests a certain envy of American abstract Modernism as it had captivated his dealer and friend. How, Hockney might have been asking, even in the wake of the exhibition's success, could he become not quite so much the odd man out? "I have never thought my painting advanced," he later recalled, "but in 1964 I still consciously wanted to be involved, if only peripherally, with modernism."[8] His immediate concerns, however, lay in realizing his ambition to live and work in Los Angeles. The proceeds from the Kasmin sales gave him the means, augmented by the success of his ambitious portfolio of large etchings (fig. 56), published in 1963, a take-off on the *Rake's Progress* of Hogarth devoted to his (Bates-free) adventures over the New York summer of 1961. Plate 3, "The Start of the Spending Spree and the Door Opening for a Blonde," probably betrays an anachronism, as the door in question opens to reveal a setting sun on a beach with waving palm.

These two commercial triumphs not only gave Hockney funds for the trip, but might well have confirmed him in exactly what he had been doing to date, as exemplified by *Domestic Scene: Los Angeles* (fig. 57), which he painted in London shortly before his departure. He found his photographic source in *Physique Pictorial*, a low-rent magazine of euphemistic beefcake produced in Los Angeles by one Bob Mizer, supplied by a visiting American colleague at the RCA.[9] The apron and athletic socks worn by the central figure send up the artfully placed accessories that allowed nude photography to be sent through the U.S. mail. Luxuriant lilies and an exuberantly floral slipcover channel the subtropical California vegetation that the artist at that point only

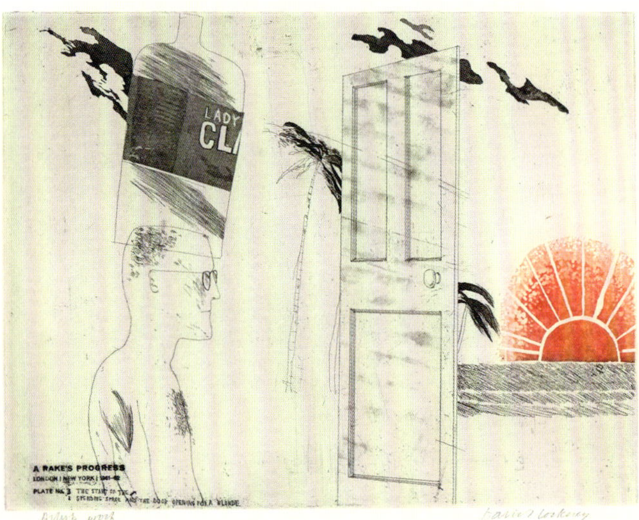

56 David Hockney, "The Start of the Spending Spree and the Door Opening for a Blonde," from *A Rake's Progress*, plate 3, 1961–3
Etching and aquatint on paper, red and black ink, 30.3 × 40.5 cm
Yale Center for British Art, Paul Mellon Fund

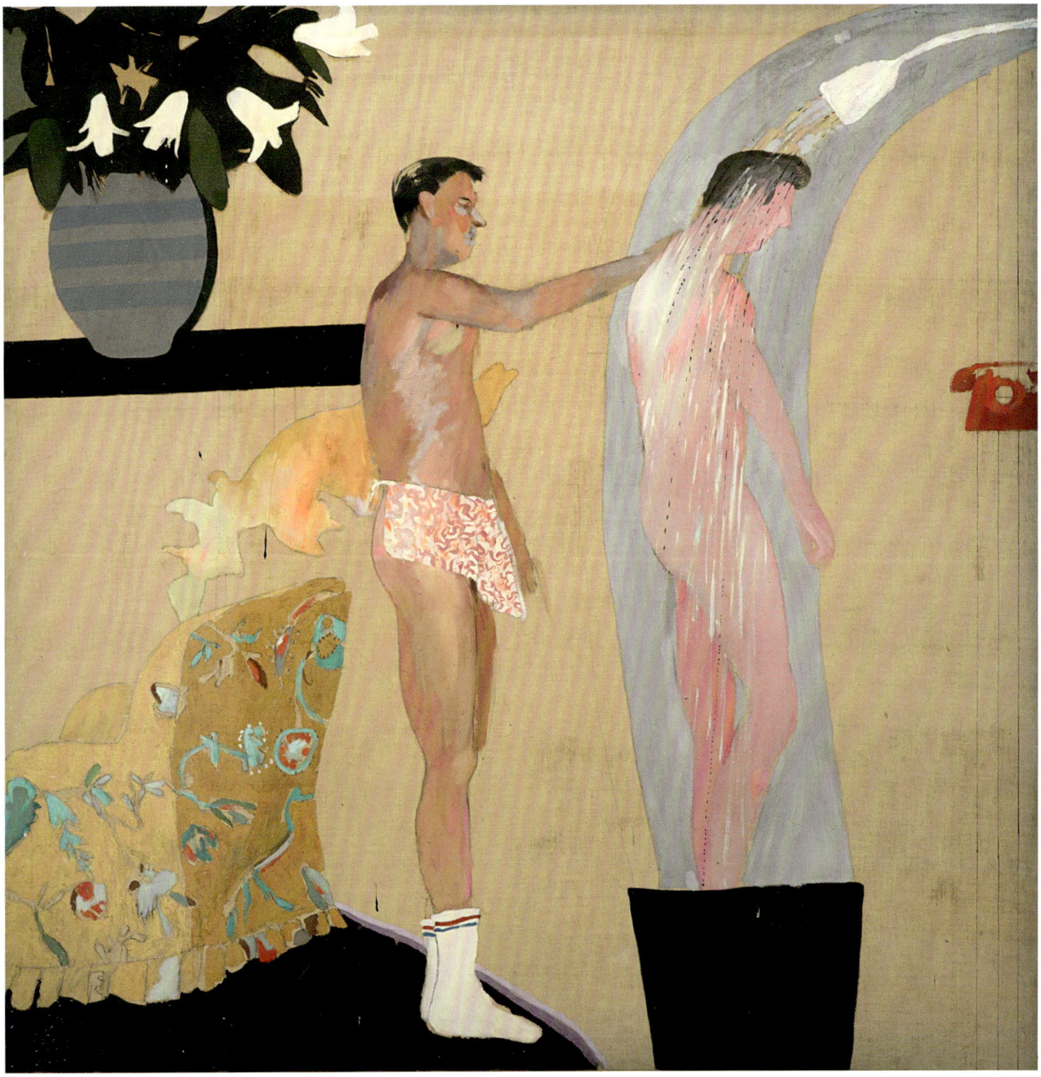

57 David Hockney,
Domestic Scene,
Los Angeles, 1963
Oil on canvas, 152.4 × 152.4 cm
Private collection

imagined with the aid of such scenarios, the absurdities of which he both indulges and mildly ridicules. The arc of pale blue pigment against the exposed canvas arguably carries an echo of Noland's stained stripes and circles, but any reconciliation between Hockney's observational comedy and the strict imperatives of color-field abstraction appears less than robust.

One fundamental difficulty lay in the wan imitation of an effect achieved by the American painters with the new, water-soluble acrylic paints. In California, Hockney discovered these and began to use them, but not at first to any great distinction from his pre-California output, even though he was now painting such scenes on the spot. One example is the 1964 *California Art Collector* (fig. 58). On the right side, Hockney takes note, not for the last time, of the odd popularity in California of the London sculptor William Turnbull's stacks of roughly shaped stones. That weighty attribute of the portrait subject nonetheless shares the insubstantial quality of all the other accessories, including the swimming pool in the distance. Although painted in California, the spindly overhang and floral upholstered armchair differ little in approach from the schematic staging of his imagined Los Angeles from the year before.

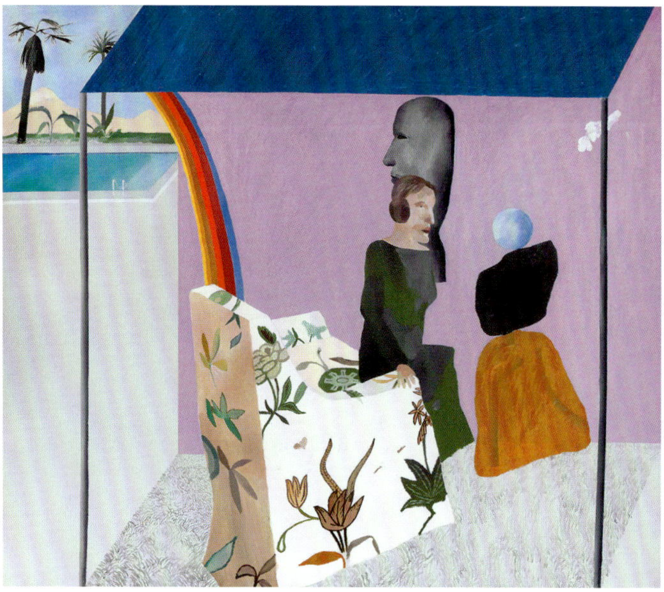

58 David Hockney, *California Art Collector*, 1964
Acrylic on canvas, 152.4 × 182.8 cm
Private collection

It was not until his second sojourn in Southern California, which began in mid-1966, that the key came to him, which made itself evident as he returned to the theme of collector's portraits. His subject, Betty Freeman, stood out for her artistic sophistication; she had been sufficiently prescient to have bought a drawing from Hockney in 1961. In the intervening years, Freeman had also come forward as an unparalleled private patron of modern music (a mission that began when she bailed out LaMonte Young on a Connecticut marijuana possession charge) and a significant photographer of musicians in her own right.[10] When Hockney renewed contact in 1966, as Freeman recounts, "David asked if he could come paint my pool. He came over and took little Polaroids. Sometime later,

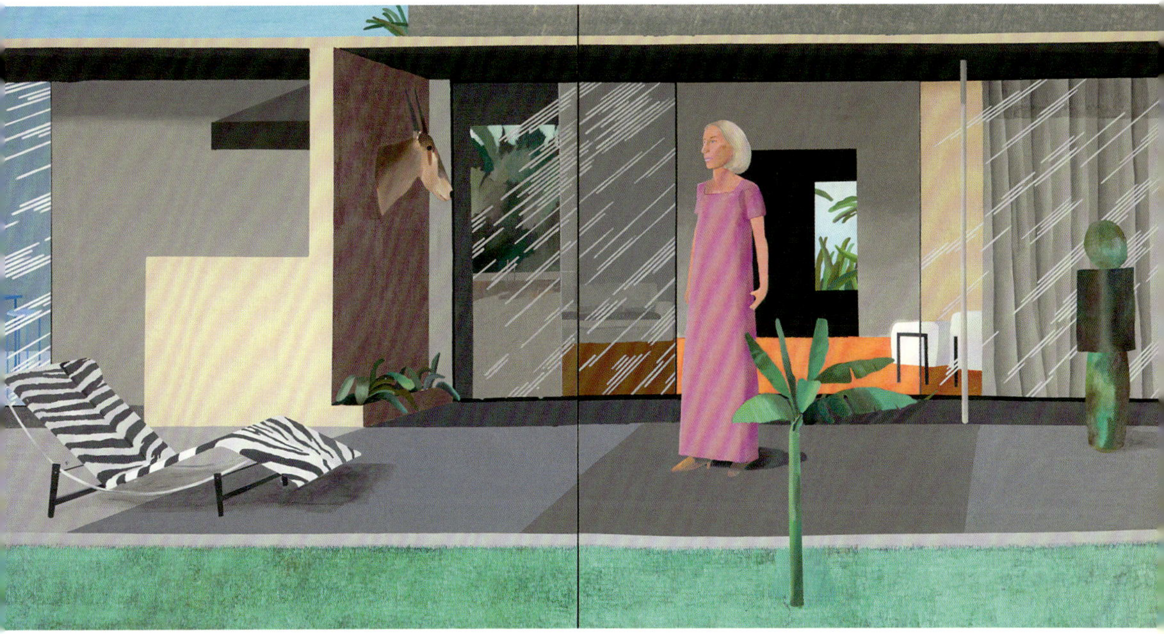

59 David Hockney, *Beverly Hills Housewife*, 1966–7
Acrylic on two canvases, 152.4 × 365.7 cm
Private collection

[the dealer] Felix Landau called and asked if I wanted to see the finished painting" (fig. 59).[11]

It comes as no surprise that she initially turned down the entirely unexpected and gargantuan outcome of his visit (two panels each six feet square), though she relented afterwards and sportingly purchased the work (posing with the artist for Kasmin's camera *in situ*; fig. 60). No pool is in sight, but her effigy-like figure in a floor-length housecoat of eye-riveting pink stands on the garden terrace of her house.

60 David Hockney and Betty Freeman with *Beverly Hills Housewife*, photographed by John Kasmin, 1966

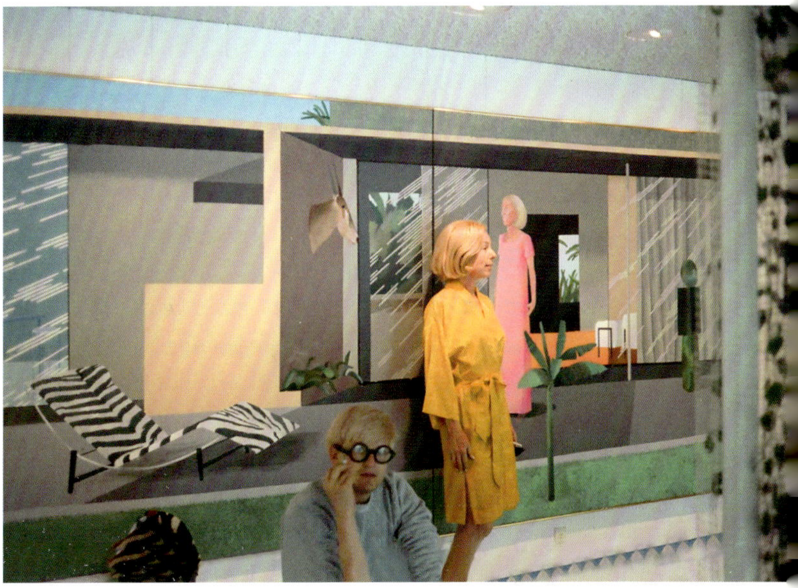

Against a rectangle of bright orange carpeting visible through the sliding glass doors, Freeman stands vacantly eye-to-eye with the head of an African antelope, a genuine trophy bagged by her husband. The crisp lines of the one-story, flat-roofed structure nonetheless acknowledge Freeman's formidable modernist cultivation, which Hockney borrows for himself via the geometric abstraction of the wall surfaces and glass reflections.

The architectural edifice and the composition of the painting as a whole are impossible to prise apart from one another, the robust pictorial structure a world away from the loose arrangement of *California Art Collector* from two years before, despite their ostensibly cognate themes. What had made the difference? One part of an answer would follow from Hockney seeding the picture with a Le Corbusier armchair (plus a zebra-covered knockoff) as tokens of the International Style in architecture and design, thus pointing to an additional, third distinct Modernism encountered over the course of this chapter. There are overlaps here with the graphic economy of the *Ark* designers in the later 1950s and with the Greenbergian rationale of truth to materials and optical self-evidence, but these three versions of Modernism belong to substantially different complexes of ideas and practices. And Hockney, over these few years, set about rehearsing all three of them.

Early in the following year of 1967, Hockney sought out and enjoyed the company of the American Modernist artists on a sojourn to New England and New York. He wrote to Kasmin: "Just driven back from Boston (I still don't have a license yet, but am driving illegally). Met Kenneth Noland, Jules Olitski and Tony Caro at Bennington ... " Having returned to New York where he had a substantial exhibition with Charles Alan on Madison Avenue, he excitedly reports, "I just got some water tension breaker from [paint innovator] Lenny Bocour ... so now I can *stain* the canvas." Before coming back to California, basking in the sales at the Alan gallery ("six paintings and all the drawings at $300 each"), he spent another weekend at Noland's, proudly having broken even playing poker with the "ruthless" Noland and Olitski (the color-field airbrush master).[12] Back on the West Coast, deprived of the stimulation provided by the Bennington Modernists, Hockney dropped for the moment the thought of staining his canvases in a color-field mode.[13] But he hardly lacked for contact with another, arguably stronger genealogy of historical Modernism in architecture – one that appears to have been on his mind for a considerable period of time.

In a 2009 statement, he reflected on the two main enticements that occupied his mind in anticipation of migrating to Los Angeles for the first time.[14] The second of these, as embodied in *Domestic Scene Los Angeles,* was the all-male idyll conjured by the issues he had seen of Mizer's *Physique Pictorial*; but "the first," he recalled with fascinating specificity, carried a contrastingly upscale cachet: "a photo by Julius Shulman of Case Study House #21" (fig. 61). As initiated by the editor of *Art and Architecture,* John Entenza, the purpose of the Case Study project was to foster and publicize Modernist truth to industrial materials in prototype

61 Pierre Koenig, Case Study House 21, 1960
Getty Research Institute, Los Angeles, Julius Schulman Photography Archive

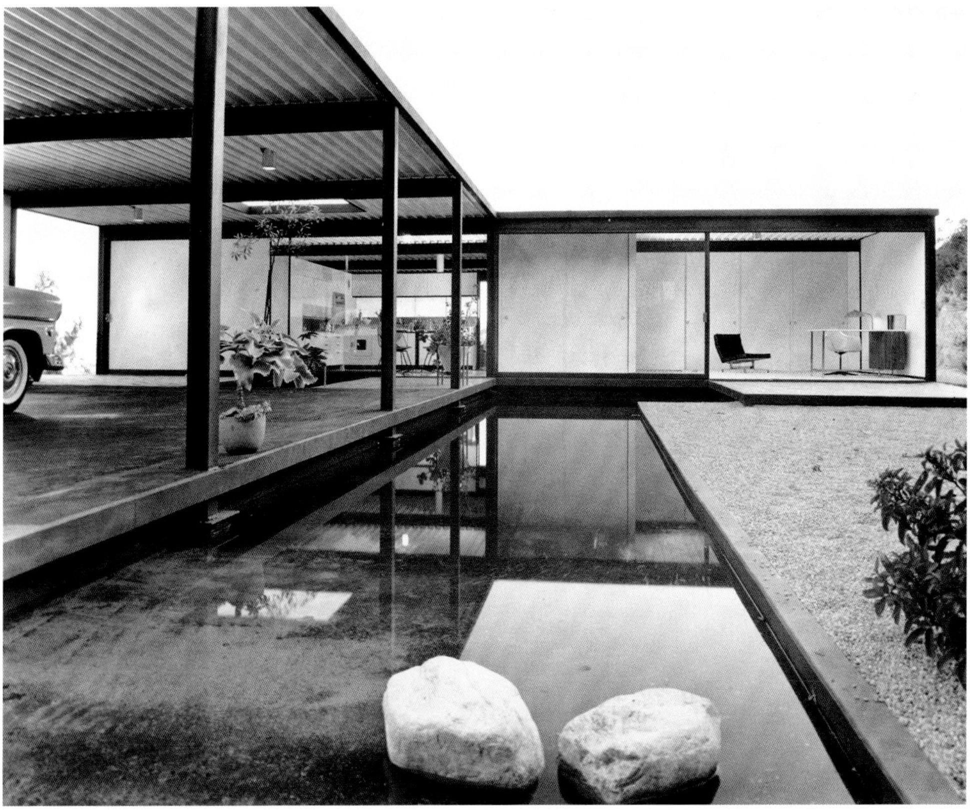

dwellings suitable for the city's rapidly growing middle-class population. Pierre Koening, a young, experimentally minded local architect, had designed the structure in question, called the Bailey House after its first owners. The tensile strength of welded steel and freedom from heavy foundations made possible the siting of such structures in dramatic sites along the Hollywood Hills and Santa Monica Mountains, drama made all the more memorable by the inspired photography of Julius Schulman – the Bailey House having been the first of his Case Study subjects.

Schulman had made his career as an architectural photographer in tandem with the burgeoning practice of the expatriate Austrian Richard Neutra. Drawn from Vienna in the 1920s to work with Frank Lloyd Wright during the latter's period of practice in Los Angeles, Neutra had stayed on to become the architectural doyen of Modernism adapted to private residential use, attracting adventurous, usually affluent clients – among them the department store magnate Edgar Kaufmann, patron of Wright's Falling Water in Pennsylvania. Both as a structure and occasion for Schulman's twilit magic, Neutra's 1946 Kaufmann House in Palm Springs (fig. 62) exemplifies the sensibility that Koenig's American-born generation would inherit and modify according to a less exclusive outlook, seeking to expand the reach of rarefied Modernist aesthetics to wider efficiencies of production from standardized components. It is an irony that Schulman's rendering of Koenig's Case Study #22 (fig. 63), the small and spare Stahl House of 1960, came paradoxically to belie these ambitions at the level of imagery. The internally illuminated nocturnal view of the women in party gowns suspended at a vertiginous height above the lighted street grid soon became and remains an ideal vision of Los Angeles glamor and opulence. Hockney's preference for #21, set in an enclosed canyon precinct, speaks to another aspect of Koenig's and Schulman's sensibilities, one more inner-directed and subtle in its screen-like interplay between opaque and transparent surfaces, its ensemble of rectilinear uprights, pond, pavement, and spare garden calling forth contemplative associations with Japanese temples and teahouses.

The night in 1963 when Hockney first arrived in Los Angeles, he found a room in a small motel called the Tumble

62 Richard Neutra, Kaufmann House, Palm Springs, 1946

Getty Research Institute, Los Angeles, Julius Schulman Photography Archive

63 Pierre Koenig, Case Study House 22, 1960

Getty Research Institute, Los Angeles, Julius Schulman Photography Archive

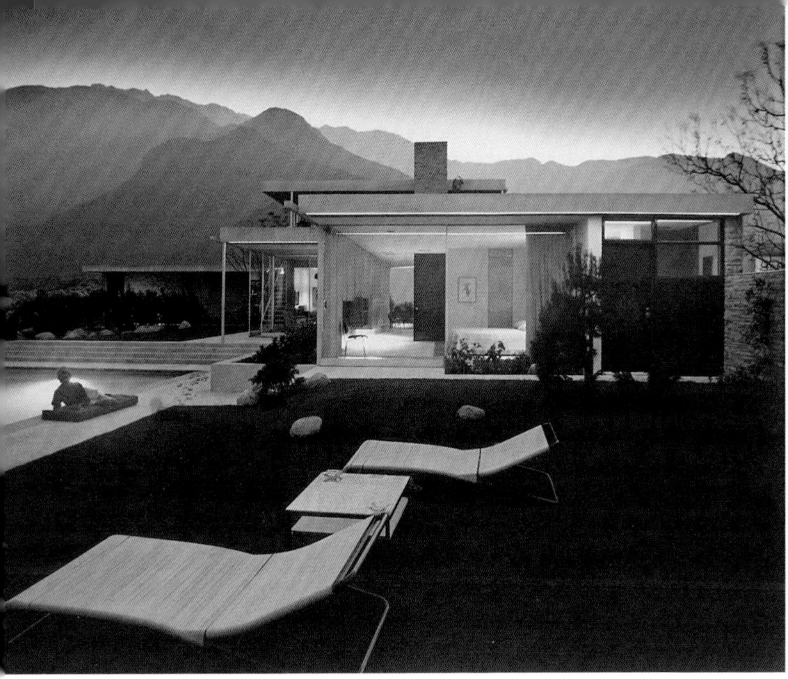

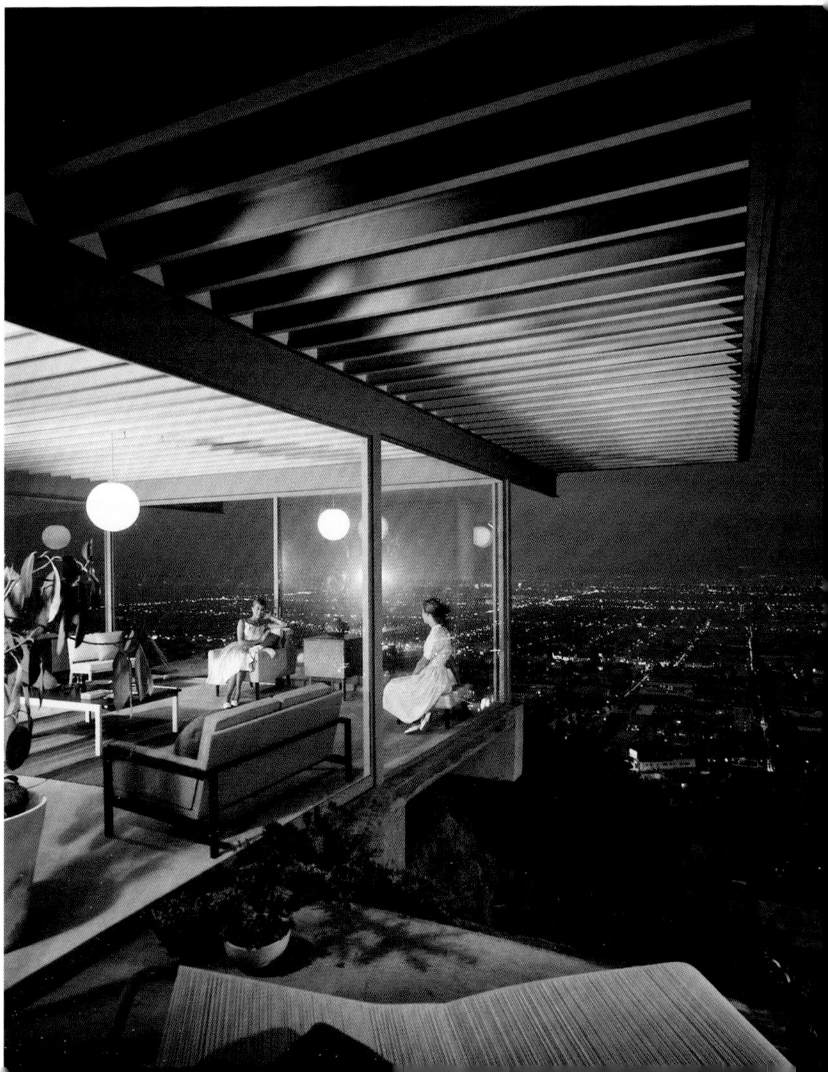

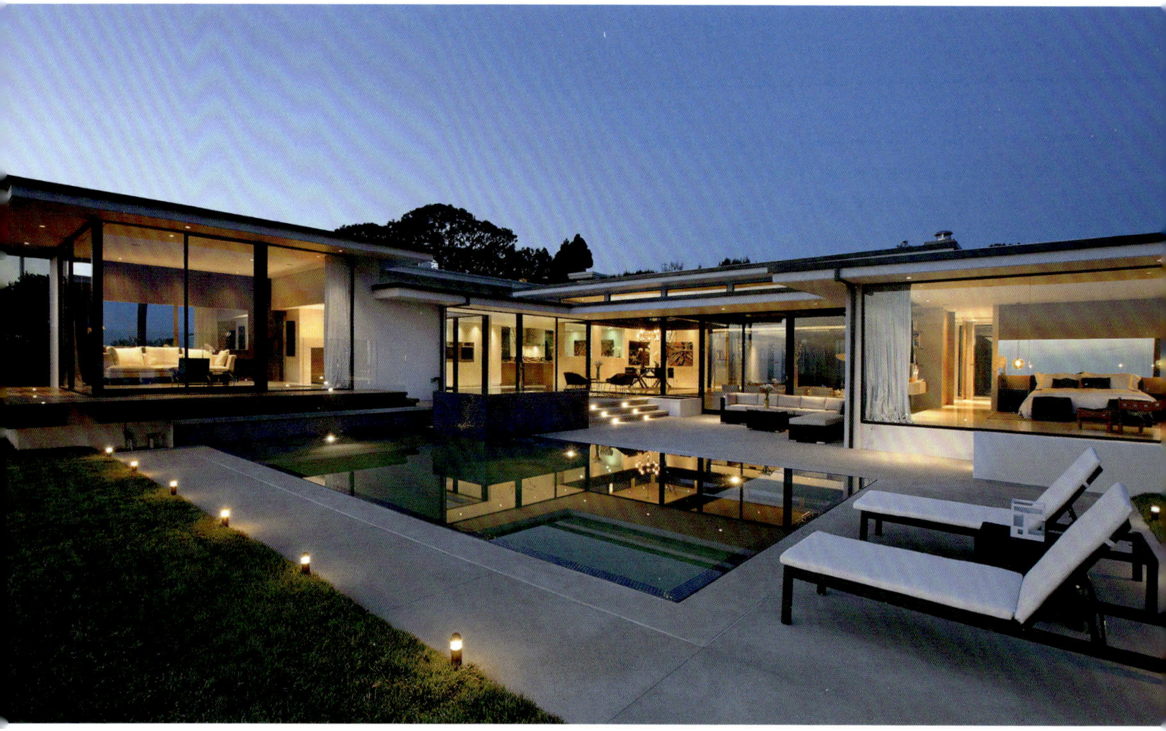

Inn at the mouth of Santa Monica Canyon, where Channel Road meets the Pacific Coast Highway. Did he know then that he was staying not a hundred yards from another of the storied Case Study dwellings, the one belonging to the renowned designers Charles and Ray Eames, likewise proponents of the democratizing benefits of good design in everyday life? By 1967, however, his intervening years among the Los Angeles collecting class had considerably leavened the idealism implicit in his faraway fascination with Koenig's refined experimentation. Alongside these celebrated examples, there existed less rigorous and more numerous interpretations of the Modernist ethos that tempered industrial rigor and transparency with brick facing, rendered walls and softening decorative touches. During the 1950s, an entire residential development called Trousdale Estates climbed the hillside along the eastern boundary of Beverly Hills, exemplifying this locally adjusted Modernism (fig. 64). Betty Freeman, the "Beverly Hills Housewife," did not live in Trousdale; her house on North Hillcrest, categorized in property records as Spanish style, had two stories and pitched roofs. But

64 House in Trousdale Estates, Beverly Hills, California, photographed by Jim Bartsch, 1964

one would never know that on the evidence of Hockney's painting. He carefully framed the glass-fronted, one-story extension giving on to the unseen pool so that her house is in effect transferred to Trousdale and she herself into the involuntary personification of this domesticated Los Angeles Modernism.

His satire of Freeman is gentle, and she played along. For another collector portrait, however, he found less reason to refrain from overt comedy: as he wrote to Kasmin at the beginning of 1968, "I have started a portrait of Fred and Marcia Wiseman [*sic*] – I can't help calling them Fred and Marcia Flintstone, but as you never watch television the joke will be lost on you. They really are a mad couple." Their interaction over lunch, he relates at length, "was just like a scene from a situation comedy, but substitute the morning newspapers for 'Art in America' and Sotheby's catalogues."[15] The Weismans (fig. 65) were collectors of great local prominence – she being the sister of Norton Simon, corporate buccaneer and mega-collector, and he being Simon's business partner. Hockney undertook the work on commission: "she

65 David Hockney, *American Collectors (Fred and Marcia Weisman)*, 1968
Acrylic on canvas, 213.4 × 304.8 cm
Art Institute of Chicago

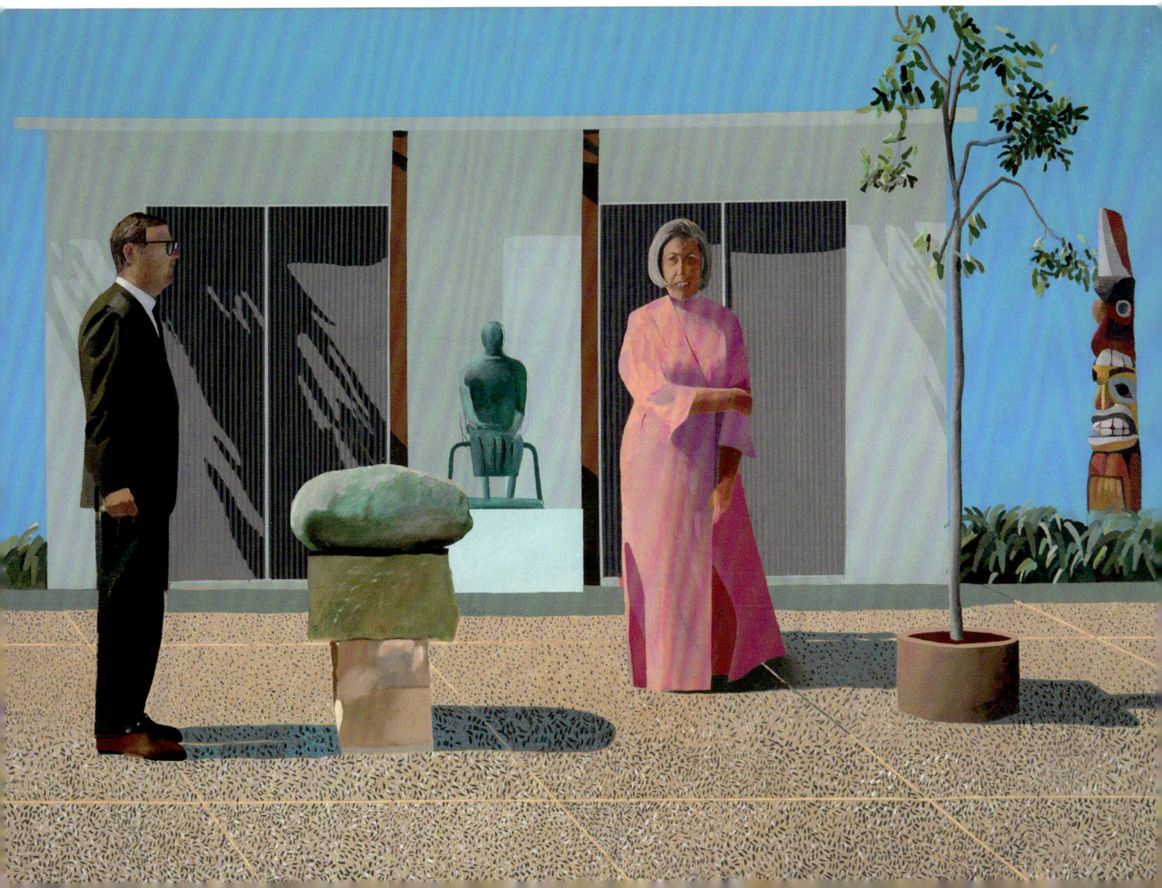

talked me into starting their portrait," the artist told Kasmin. Their self-regard and his ambition yielded a gargantuan, ten-by-seven-foot canvas, to which he attached the generic title *American Collectors*.

As Hockney had played up the safari theme in his portrait of Freeman, he emphasized the taste for a fashionable primitivism in his treatment of the Weismans. Yet another stack of irregularly hewn stones by Turnbull stands like a monstrous pet between the couple, overlapping with a hieratic female figure by Henry Moore housed in an apparent niche at the center of small modernist pavilion. The totem pole, as Hockney emphasizes, aligns an actual native-American carving of great refinement with these British strivings toward the authenticity of rough simplification, which find an echo in the planes of her voluminous robe (even though she stands a long pace behind her husband, their heads align horizontally, and she somehow seems the larger of the two). The ruthless logic of these arrangements becomes clearer when comparing the painting to a surviving collection of snapshots, held by the Hockney Foundation but sadly barred from reproduction, taken by Hockney as a guide to its composition. Two head shots point up the unkindness in his treatment of the Weismans' features, her teeth especially enlarged in an obvious analogue to the maw of the Northwest-Coast spirit to her left. Moore's sculpture actually stood on a shelf that projected outward from the pool house, but Hockney introduced a geometric play of light and shade in a way that suggests an altar-like niche. An opaque rectangle of bright turquoise serves as sole vestige of the otherwise suppressed swimming pool; the rather untended, overgrown foliage of its site survives in no more than a spindly potted tree and low subtropical hedge.

The Weismans, like Freeman, only kept their portraits for a short period before selling them on, the overt satire serving Hockney's self-regard far more than that of his sitters. By their sheer size, both paintings amplify their humor to the point of bombast; at the same time, however, he exploits their quasi-architectural scale to another, more cognitive end. Abetted by the even coverage and intensity available in acrylic paint, the symmetrical pavilion behind the Weismans – rendered more as a diagram rather than a plausible structure – makes architectural Modernism over into a discrete motif, its configuration governing the entire arrangement of the picture. With all the fascination that Hockney's Californian subject matter has exerted on his admirers, it is striking that the angular austerity of his depicted buildings, by comparison to the vivid attributes he places around them, has received little attention. When he opined in 1964, "I still consciously wanted to be involved, if only peripherally, with modernism," he may or may not have seen this solution; but this third Modernist input, doubly imported from Vienna via Los Angeles, provided that involvement and a distinct mode of art – harder, more spare, more decisive – directly traceable to his experience there. That experience comprised the surface aspects of sunshine, water in the desert, and tanned bodies, but dug down, without his habitual irony, to this legacy of technical and aesthetic Modernism.

If that is true, however, then why all the eye-catching details? There is something of the misdirecting stage magician in Hockey, that is, giving the viewer something so tempting to look at that you miss the logic of the trick. *A Bigger Splash* (fig. 66), his 1967 painting of a similar poolside patio, serves as the quintessential, most reproduced summation of his LA manner. But just how much of the picture surface does the titular spray of white paint actually take up? Is it the main event, or is it a calculated distraction, a symptom of Hockney's aversion to over-seriousness? And just how original is it anyway? Alongside the standard comparisons to the liberated gestures of De Kooning-style Abstract Expressionism, Francis Bacon had already made such jets of white an unsurprising device. But Hockney's version holds a sly surprise in that he painstakingly rendered every splatter and rivulet with small and delicate brushes, making its pretend spontaneity of a piece with the meticulous precision of every other part of the canvas.

Much more to the point of Hockney's Modernist progress is the raw canvas on which it is painted, visible in the quasi-Polaroid border around the image, harking back to the Noland works on display at the launch of the Kasmin Gallery four years before. His transmutation of the received Modernist aesthetic lies in the rigidly anti-naturalistic pattern of intensely hued, evenly spread plastic pigment, adhering to the canvas support like a viscous membrane. The stretched

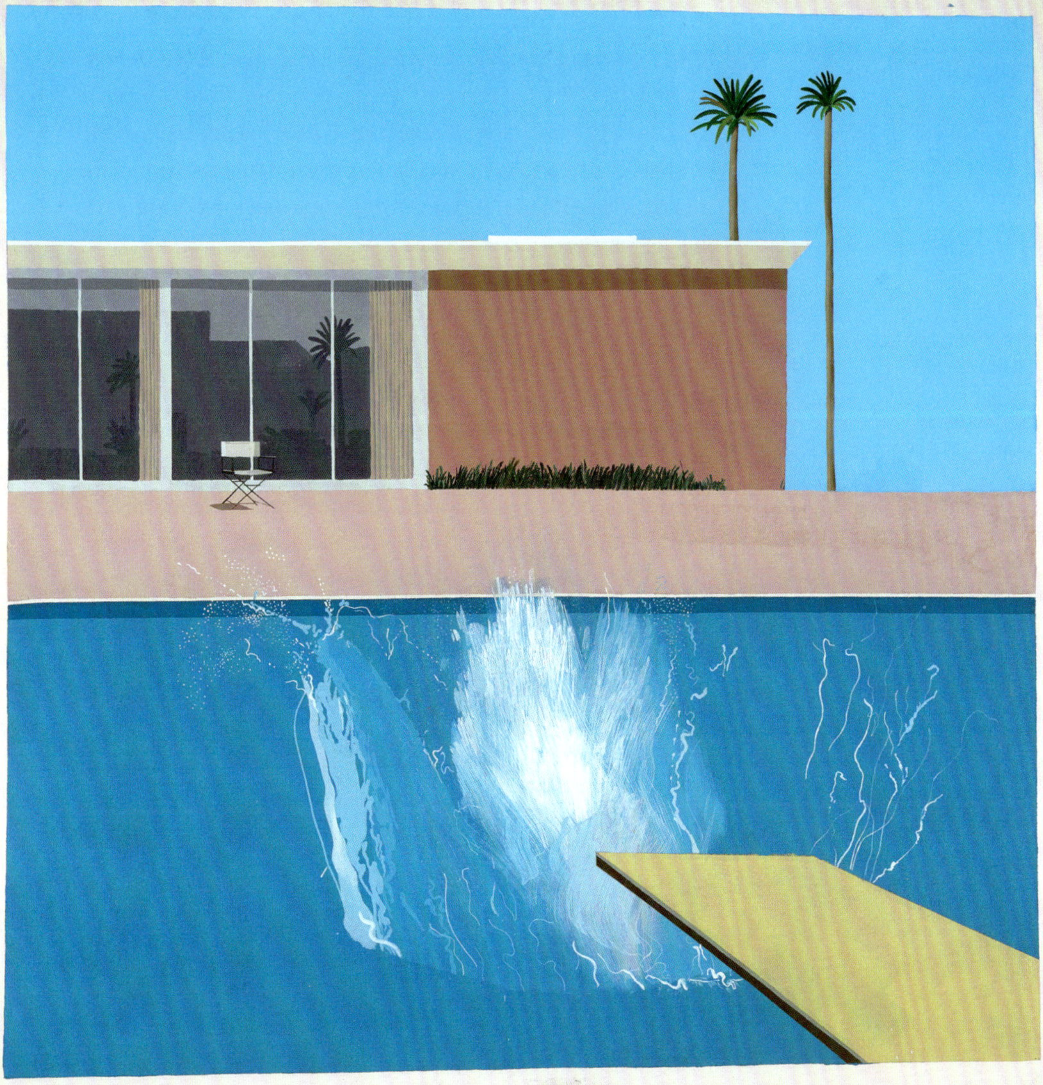

66 David Hockney,
A Bigger Splash, 1967

Acrylic on canvas,
242.5 × 243.9 cm
Tate

spatial depth of the painting paradoxically reinforces its two-dimensional pattern. Just un-focus a little bit, let that pattern emerge, and it is as if the Constructivist and De Stijl manner of painting, which had fed the vocabulary of architectural Modernism, had latterly re-emerged in a new subtropical palette.

That act of re-invention brings to a provisional end one long arc of development around the term Modernist that has extended over these first three chapters. It has extended the thread far from the London nexus from which it began. The artists most closely aligned with the sensibility of the Soho Modernist, Terry Taylor and Barrie Bates, had by the later 1960s both drifted off: Taylor migrated to the nascent counterculture and the sacrament of LSD, spending increasing amounts of time in North Africa; Bates, now as Billy Apple, decamped for New York in 1964, just as his friend Hockney made his choice for Los Angeles. There, over a decade or more, he embarked on a series of under-sung experiments in framing art as process and product dictated by its contextual circumstances.[16] Maturity and growing commitments take their toll, as Kasmin could attest. The next phase in this account requires a return to London and to the early years of the 1960s. Having traversed boundaries of race, nationality and sexual orientation, it is time to proceed from the signal contributions of Ida Kar to the emergence in that moment of two more key women artists, part of a formidable female cohort across the other arts.

CHAPTER FOUR
PAINTING SENSATIONS: PAULINE BOTY AND BRIDGET RILEY

IF DAVID HOCKNEY HAD A PEER IN COMMANDING THE London spotlight in 1962, it would have been the young painter Pauline Boty. She was one of four young artists – and naturally the only woman – showcased in Ken Russell's BBC film *Pop Goes the Easel*, made for the *Monitor* television program in that year (fig. 67). In a disco party scene, filmed in the studio of Richard Smith, she conveys confidence and composure at odds with Hockney, in an uncredited cameo, flailing about in the background.

Recognition as the leading, perhaps only female member of the Pop cohort at the Royal College had been, as might be imagined, more uncertain and circuitous a process than her male counterparts had enjoyed.[1] Over the objections of her rigidly philistine father, Boty had studied at the art

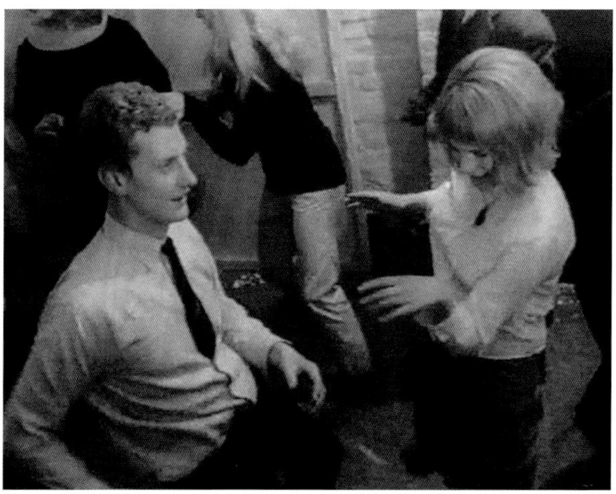

67 Derek Boshier and Pauline Boty in *Pop Goes the Easel*, for *Monitor*, BBC TV (dir. Ken Russell) 1962

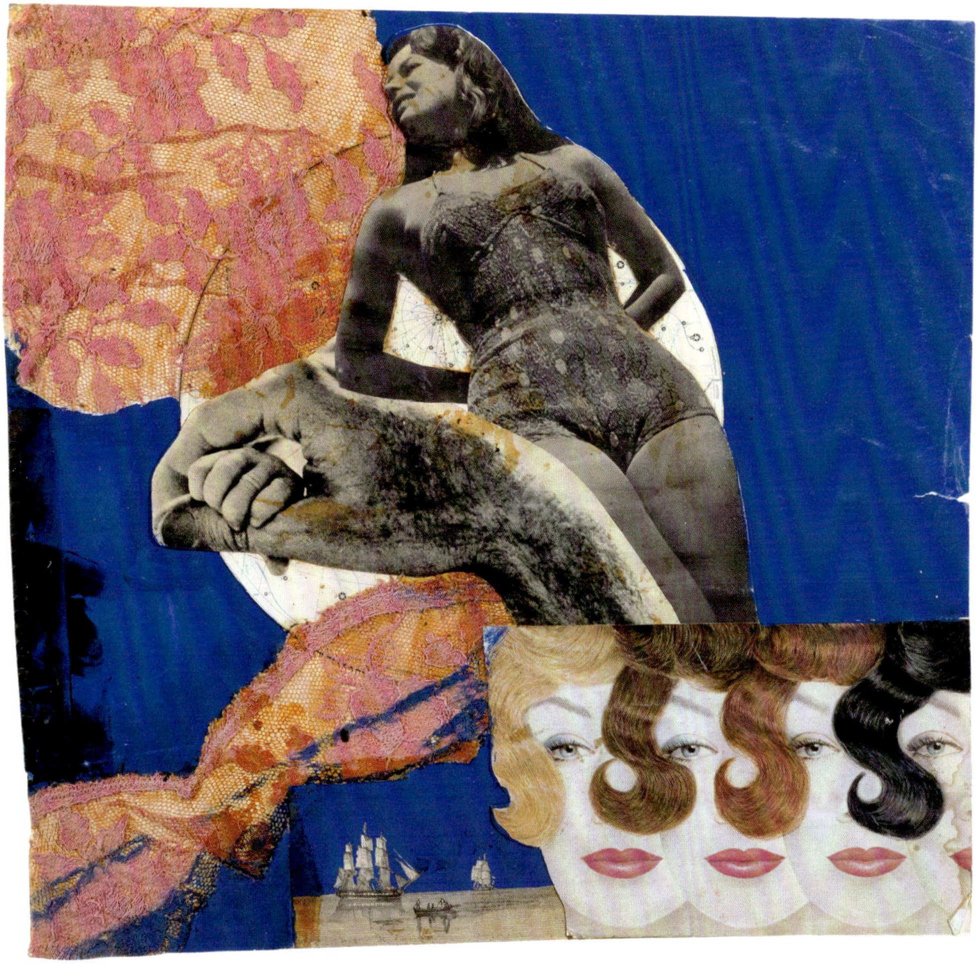

college in her home London suburb of Wimbledon, where she performed with enough distinction to gain entrance to the Royal College as part of the class of 1958. But she found herself, contrary to her preference for painting, channeled to the school of stained glass, its emphases on handicraft and a certain piety deemed more suitable for a female applicant. Her considerable attraction to the profane nonetheless found an outlet in an extra-curricular practice of collage, not then as common a medium as it has since become. Her efforts hover between the Dada antecedents of Hannah Höch and Max Ernst, on the one hand, and something incipient that flowered in the youth culture of the coming decade, mindscapes where atavistic Victorian survivals melded freely with the flotsam of contemporary vernaculars.

68 Pauline Boty, *Untitled (with paint, lace and hair colour advert)*, 1960–1.
Collage and paint on paper, 37.2 × 39.7 cm
Women's Art Library Collection, Goldsmiths, University of London

In her 2016 novel *Autumn*, Ali Smith weaves Boty through the present-day narrative, at one point having a fictional character, an aging pop songwriter who knew her in their shared youth, close his eyes and describe from memory all the details of one actual collage (fig. 68). "A friend of mine did it, an artist," he tells his young female neighbor, whose powers of fantasy he is hoping to encourage, asking, "How did it strike your imagination?" She answers, "Like it would be if I was taking drugs," though quickly reassuring him that she had never ever taken any. "But if I did," she goes on, "and everything was in my head all at once, all sort of crowding in, it would be a bit like it."[2] Smith recognizes that the incongruities of the untitled 1961 collage in question surpass any bookish affinity to Dada or Surrealism, that its suspensions of logic served a wider social purpose at this historical crossroads, as it was becoming possible for young people to test different ways of thinking and feeling beyond the inherited norms that their parents had by and large internalized without serious question. Mind-altering drugs functioned on a continuum with the imaginative potential of art. Psychic adventurers like Terry Taylor were still relatively few, but the need for mind expansion, in the service of figuring out new ways to be in the world, new ways of fashioning an inner life, could manifest itself without – or at least in advance of – pharmacological assistance.[3]

This cerebral dimension has its carnal counterpart in the expansions of sexual freedom, as the old proprieties and means of control steadily weakened. That change found an incipient reckoning in Anne Jellicoe's 1962 play *The Knack*, a frenetic farce in which a lothario and his mates suffer a rude comeuppance at the hands of a seemingly vulnerable waif (originally played by Rita Tushingham); yet unsanctioned love conquers all as she selects the least assertive of the men to set up house without benefit of marriage. And Boty figured in the landmark success of her friend's play, designing the poster for its Cambridge tryout (fig. 69), which became the cover of the program at the Royal Court in

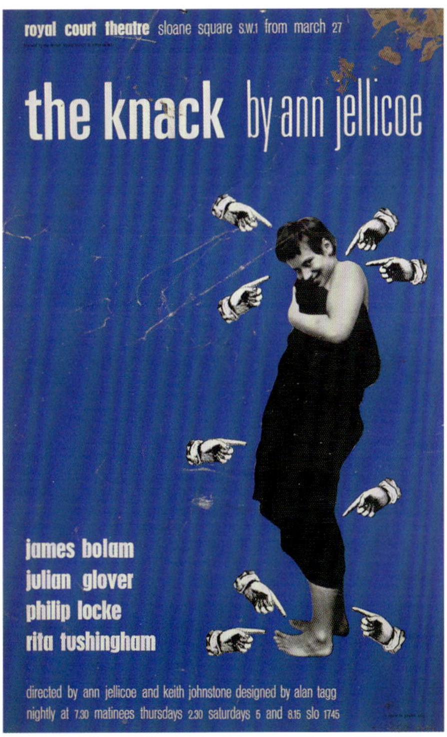

69 Pauline Boty, poster for the production of *The Knack*, Royal Court Theatre, London, 1962
Victoria and Albert Museum, London

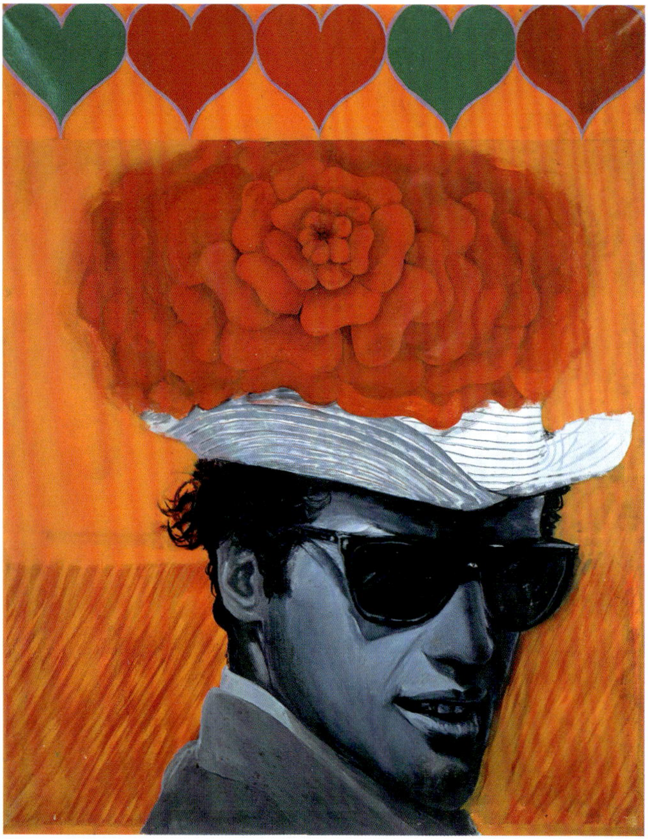

70 Pauline Boty,
With Love to Jean-Paul Belmondo, 1962

Oil on canvas, 150 × 122 cm
Private collection

London.[4] She drew on the lessons of collage with more stringent economy and a sure hand with condensed, sans-serif type, multiplying the old printer's device of the pointing hand around a grinning Tushingham's naked yet covered silhouette, the fingers signaling both a chorus of accusation and the menace of unwanted contact impinging from all sides.

From 1961, the year of her graduation from the RCA, Boty had also begun to carry her assemblage procedures of collage into a manner of painting unlike anything she had ventured before, one built from flat, eccentrically shaped components distinctly set apart from one another in bright, saturated colors. For a time these remained largely abstract, though with manifold figurative intimations from fairground banners to military insignia to postcard landscapes. But 1962 witnessed her throwing aside any protocol that serious painting must be allusively indirect and abstract. Henceforth, she would assemble her compositions from fully realized components in incongruous but telling juxtapositions, much as she had done in collage. But these works would be on a wall-filling scale, and she would render the juxtaposed elements in her own rough-and-ready manner of handling oil paint.

By 1962, London Mod enthusiasm for continental style had been broadened by the arrival of French New Wave film, announced by Jean-Luc Godard's *À bout de souffle* (*Breathless*) in 1960, with its startling debut of the former stage actor Jean-Paul Belmondo as its magnetic star. In making her transition to collage-in-paint, Boty's *With Love to Jean-Paul Belmondo* (fig. 70) seized on this vogue in a manifesto of assertive identity as a painter along with unabashed sexual connection to her subject. The large centered rose and line of hearts follow from the decorative Victoriana that she had pursued in her college days, but intensified in eye-searing hues, while her rendering of Belmondo's face (in the black and white of *Breathless*) resembles the workmanlike, photo-based modeling of fan tributes more than the technique of a practiced painter. In this quality lies both self-exposure as an earnest amateur in the medium and a capture of that general impulse of fan culture for a self-conscious and successful work of art. As she wrote the following year:

> *There's another kind of hero now. And I think the nearest thing to a contemporary romantic image is Jean-Paul Belmondo ... He lives carelessly, like young people of today, and according to his own morality. He's lawless. He creates about himself a feeling of anarchy. You feel he is completely free. He has no guilt, and I think this in particular is a contemporary feeling. His freedom makes him full of a marvellous kind of wild energy, and he belongs to the here and now. James Dean was the rebel image for rebel teenagers some years ago, and Jean-Paul Belmondo is an idol of the freedom of youth today.*[5]

It would be difficult to surpass this text as a credo of the narcissistic male Mod as an ideal type; but the ascription of his affect to "young people of today" entails a claim from the female side. This passage comes from her script for the BBC radio program *The Public Ear*, for which she had been enlisted as a representative voice of her generation. At this juncture, the Modernist sensibility, so predominantly male in its prior development, belatedly begins a shift toward encompassing a female outlook. Boty's 1962 portrait of her friend Celia Birtwell (fig. 71), the soon to be renowned fabric designer, bookends the Belmondo and makes the terms of this claim explicit. Its full title is *Celia Birtwell Surrounded by Her Heroes*, who include Elvis Presley in his gold lamé suit next to her right hip, their friend in common, David Hockney, as photographed by Lord Snowdon in red cardigan and accessorized by cigar, and the Everly Brothers (in exceptionally stylish suits). But that starry male iconography attends a member in good standing of a new female Mod elite, among whom Boty could count herself. Birtwell's state of *déshabillée* attests to that: insouciant provocation unconcerned with conventional propriety.

The Only Blonde in the World (fig. 72), painted in the following year, has justifiably become Boty's best-known painting. Absent is the here-and-there compositional pattern

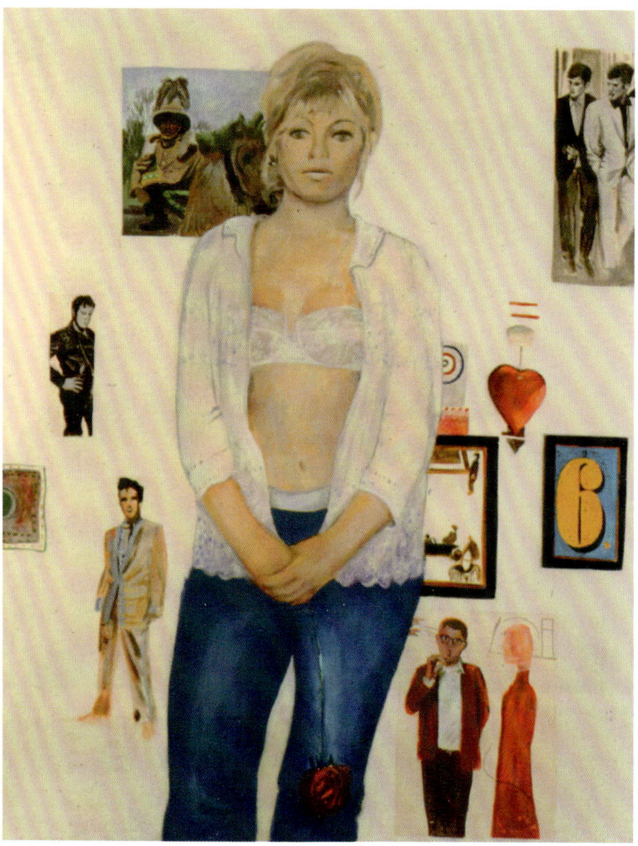

71 Pauline Boty, *Celia Birtwell Surrounded by Her Heroes*, 1963

Oil on canvas, 152.5 × 122.5 cm
Museu Coleção Berardo, Lisbon

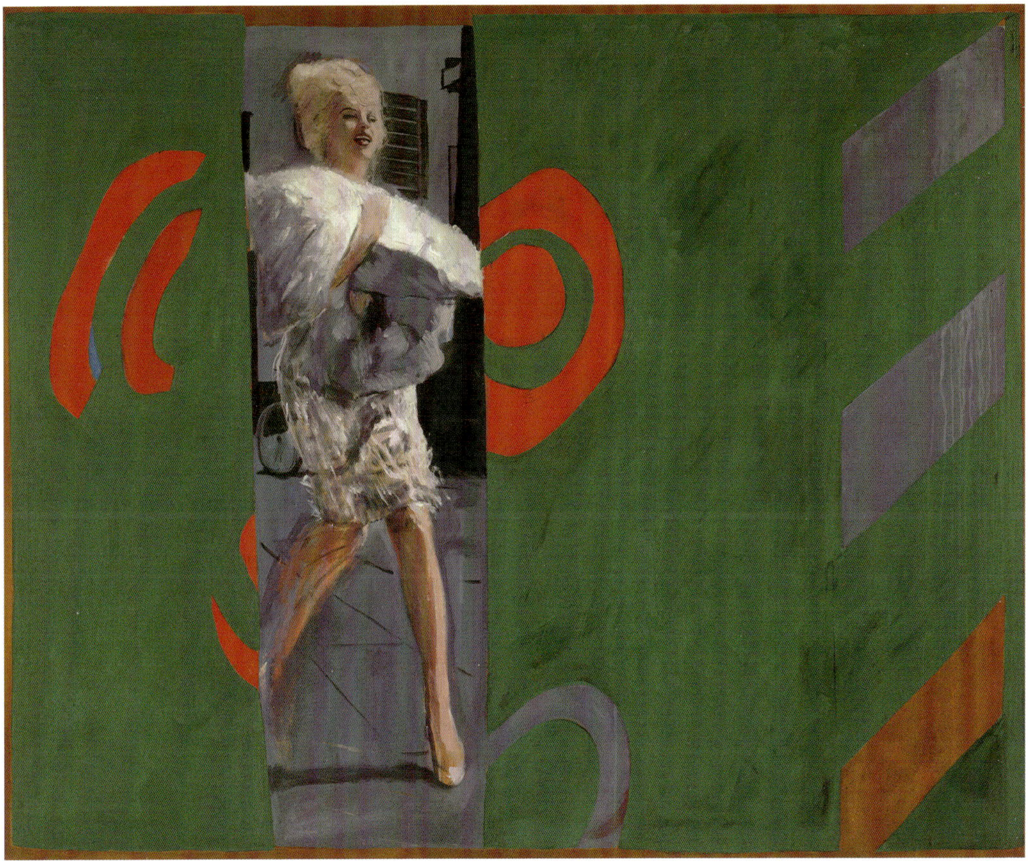

72 Pauline Boty, *The Only Blonde in the World*, 1963
Oil on canvas, 122.4 × 153 cm
Tate

borrowed from collage; the painting instead organizes itself into five roughly equal vertical bands. Of the two narrowest, one contains all of the work's mimetic function, staging a confrontation between the figurative Pop of the Royal College class of '59 and the abstraction pursued by their immediate predecessors like Robyn Denny and Richard Smith, as urged on by Roger Coleman and Lawrence Alloway. The painstaking awkwardness of the fan-rendering style is likewise absent; Boty conveys her Monroe figure, though derived from a magazine photograph, with confident imprecision. Although her skill with the brush had not reached Hockney's level, she was finding comparable acumen and judgment in knowing when to leave off. In Sue Tate's words, "The loose brushwork gives a tactile immediacy, evoking the shake of the hips and the flounce of the tassels."[6] Fairground lettering and Victorian filigree, which she had incorporated into *With Love to Jean-Paul Belmondo*, reduce themselves to an array of abstract signs set within a freely brushed matrix of green paint,

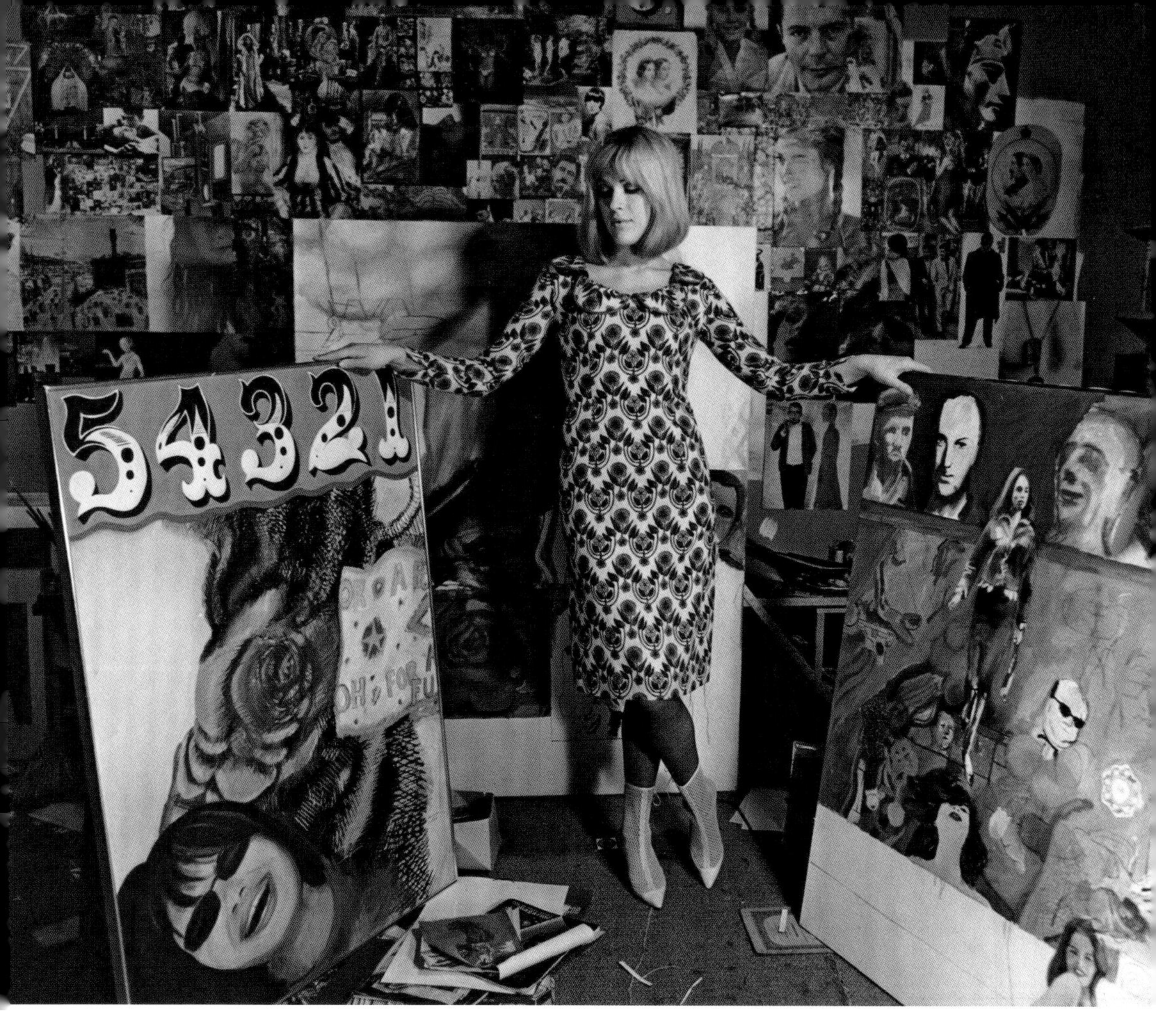

their syncopated irregularity the only memory of the ornate emblems condensed into them. The vividness of those abandoned, archaizing motifs transposes itself into intensified contrasts of hue, notably between the complementary colors of red and green. Tate also draws attention to the internal frame in gold, which appears to be in front of the green field at the bottom and behind it at the top, thereby slightly tilting and detaching the virtual plane of the painting from the literal surface of the canvas.

Like Andy Warhol's renowned series of Monroe portraits, Boty's *Only Blonde* is a memorial painting, the actress having died in August 1962. The delicate blur of her portrait signifies absence, even disappearance. When Boty turned to female glamor in the here and now, by contrast, her style assumed a blunt, even raucous edge. In a 1963 photograph by Lewis Morley (fig. 73), Boty stands against the collage mural on

73 Pauline Boty, photographed by Lewis Morley, 1963

Bromide print, 29.3 × 35.6 cm
National Portrait Gallery, London

her studio wall. With her left hand, she props up a work in progress devoted to the 1962 Profumo affair, the sex-and-espionage scandal named for the compromised Conservative minister whose indiscretion had nearly brought down the government. A sexual triangle involving the sometime actress, sometime escort Christine Keeler lay at the heart of it, and she became its public face, in part because of the notorious photograph taken by Morley (before the scandal broke) of Keeler naked sitting astride a black modernist chair. As Boty developed her now lost painting on the subject, she later substituted that pose at its center, but began, as seen here, with another full-length walking pose, which she surrounds with grotesque portraits of the rogues' gallery connected with the case.

With her right hand, Boty supports a painting (fig. 74) that includes another brunette glamor figure of the moment, but one of benign rather than sinister reputation. Pressed to one side beneath a furiously cross-hatched English rose is a portrait of Cathy McGowan, presenter of the new Independent Television weekly program *Ready Steady Go!* Entirely in keeping with its subject, she returns to the unassuming, fan-portrait technique. The much-loved McGowan (fig. 75) had

74 Pauline Boty, *5-4-3-2-1*, 1963
Oil on canvas, 125 × 100 cm
Wolverhampton Art Gallery

75 Cathy McGowan, photographed by Tony Galey, 1963

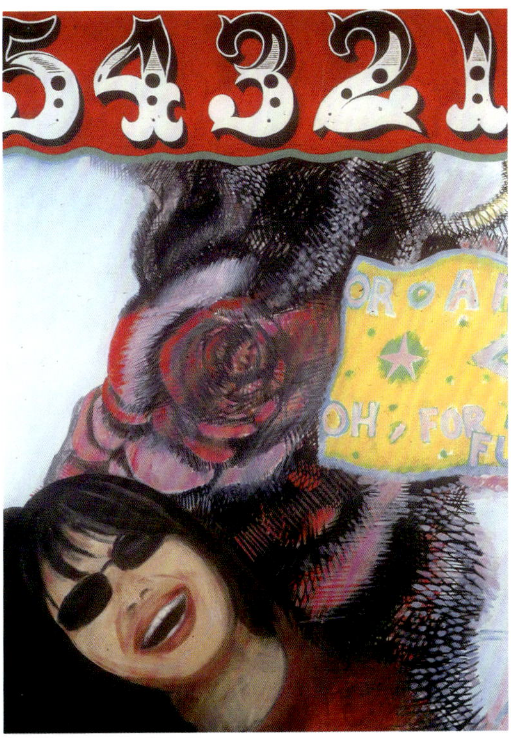

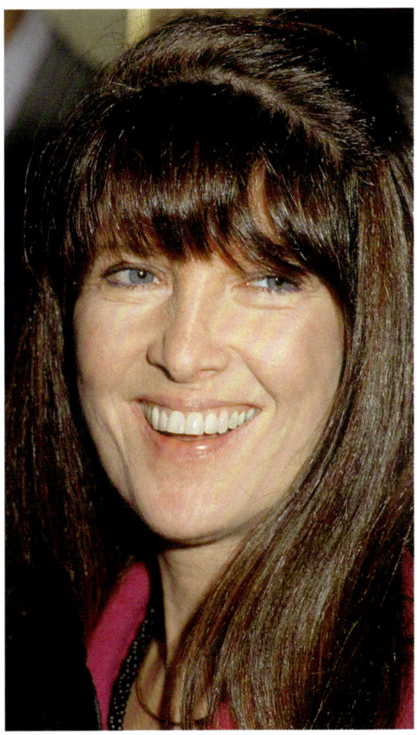

famously been recruited from an office job at the magazine *Woman's Own* and almost never made it through a weekly program without flubbing her lines. But her cheerful amateurism, along with the sterling quality of music, helped save the program from being dismissed as a slick show-business sell-out. In the words of Vicki Wickham, then a producer on the show: "She was the *perfect* Mod."[7]

Boty does not, however, allow that perfection to remain a family-friendly proposition, as she unfurls a yellow banner at the right of her painting emblazoned: "OH, FOR A FU..," that sentiment presumably a bond between artist and subject – one that voiced the kind of excitement promised by the music behind the euphemisms of television propriety. *Ready Steady Go!* had made its debut in 1963 and instantly established itself as the prime pop-music showcase in the UK.[8] The titular countdown formula, *5-4-3-2-1*, that surmounts her composition is the title of the show's theme song, a hit for the blues-oriented band Manfred Mann (Boty's reaching back to old-style fairground lettering stands out in its crisp delineation from the loose paint handling below, emblematizing her own oxymoronic coinage, "nostalgia for now"). The invited

76 The Supremes performing on Independent Television's *Ready Steady Go!*, photographed by David Redfern, 1965

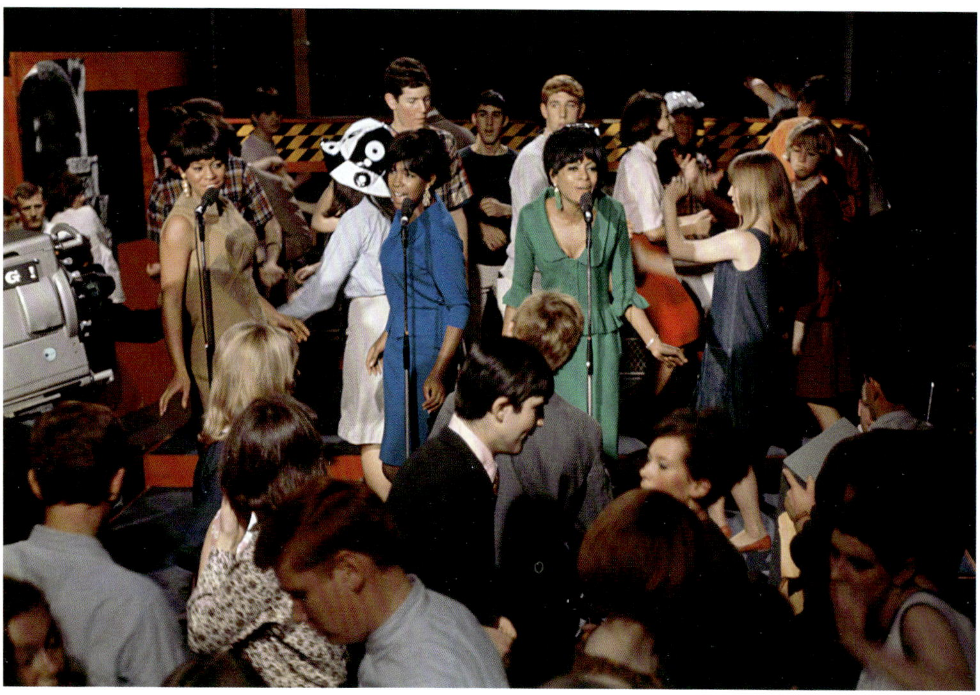

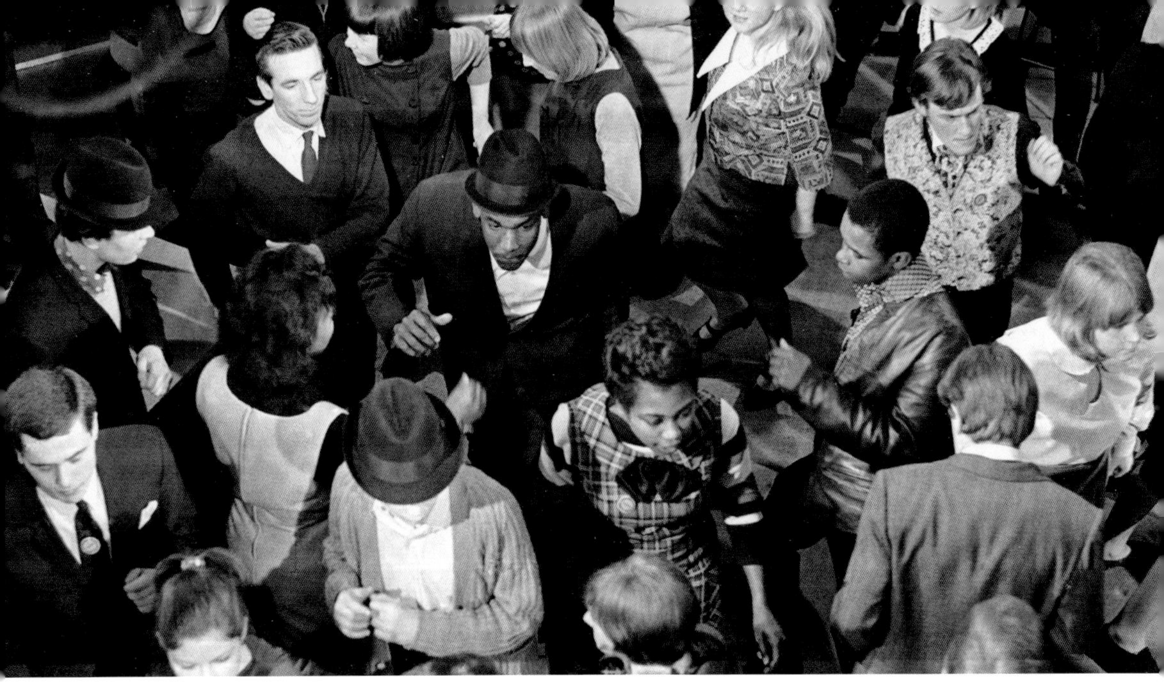

77 Dancers on Independent Television's *Ready Steady Go!*, photographed by Tony Gale, February 1964

performers, in something of a miracle for television, were mostly respectable from the perspective of discriminating Mod taste, especially with the growing admixture of black rhythm and blues artists from America – performers from the southern Stax studios like Otis Redding, Carla Thomas, and Wilson Pickett or the northern, urban Motown like the Miracles, Supremes (fig. 76), Temptations, and Martha and the Vandellas – all lending the aura of their talent and professionalism to the British performers who appeared alongside them. A formidable local peer like Dusty Springfield would be there to cheer them on and join in. In the Morley photograph, Boty appears styled in dress and attitude to make an appearance as a dancer on the show, which she in fact did on the debut broadcast and regularly thereafter. The classic pattern of a Modernist's non-stop weekend now assumed staying in long enough on Friday evening to watch *Ready Steady Go!*

Beyond its entertainment value, there was valid, even essential information on dancing and clothes to be gleaned from it (fig. 77). Some original Modernists decried this massification of their ethos (the formative jazz identification migrating decisively to the more danceable rhythm and blues), but one capital thing that it accomplished, by breaking up their old exclusivity, was to open space for women to carve out leading roles in what had been exceedingly male-dominated territory. One bemused observer, looking back from

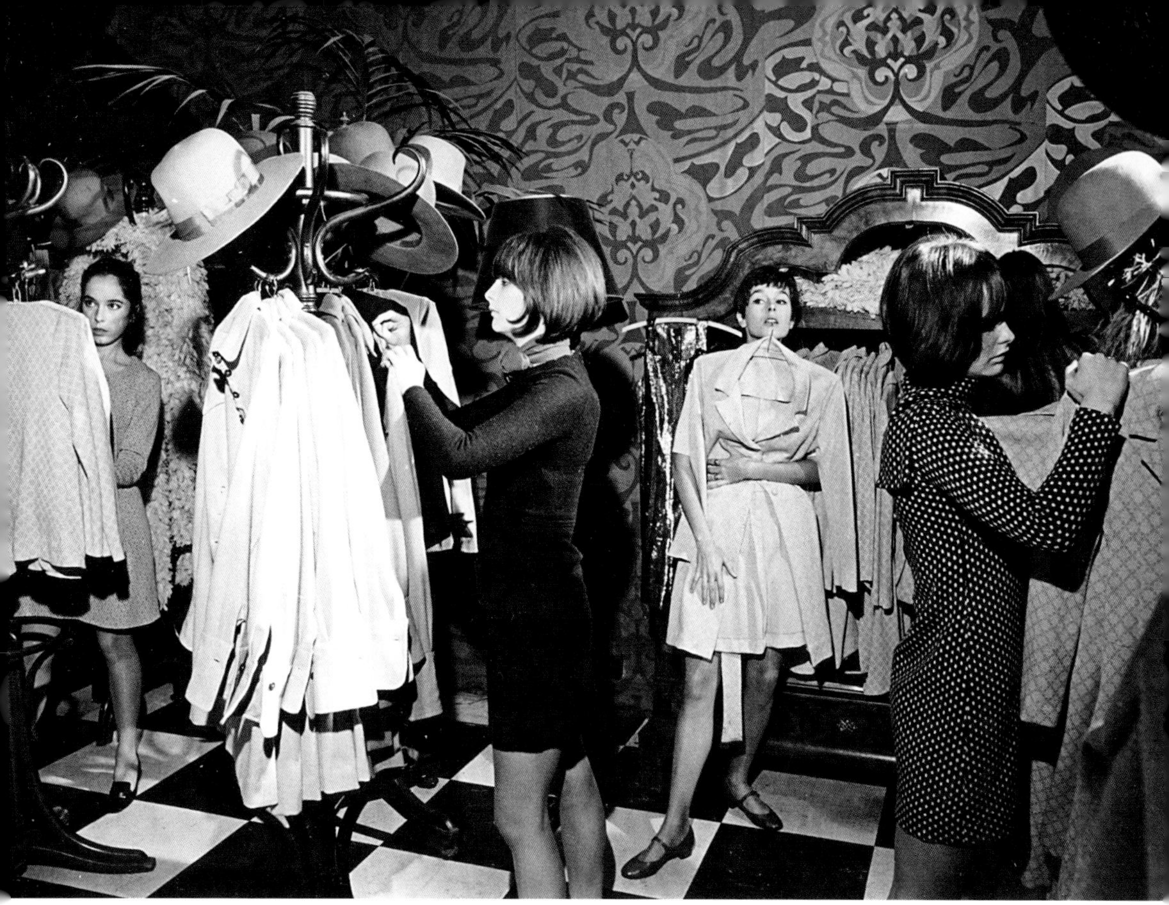

78 Biba fashion boutique, Kensington Church Street, 1965

the close of the 1960s, observed that the new dance styles showcased on *Ready Steady Go!* had upended the old gender hierarchy, under which "there was always a strong emphasis on the masculinity and aggressiveness of the male who was expected to lead the woman, and the coyness and delicacy of the woman who followed. Now the female dances in exactly the same fashion as her male partner and in many instances appears to be even more aggressive."[9]

It was also with the McGowan phenomenon that a strong female counterpart to the male Mod style could be said to have surfaced – with a markedly different mode of transmission. The original Soho Modernists had picked and chosen from clothing items not designed with them in mind or had their suits custom tailored to their own specifications. No prominent fashion designer ever emerged from their ranks (the core Modernists never identifying with the peacock aesthetic promoted by John Stephen, the entrepreneurial "King of Carnaby Street," nor with the Carnaby scene in general). McGowan, in contrast, had in her corner the visionary designer Barbara

Hulanicki, then twenty-seven, who had founded her first, mail-order business on the premise that young women of ordinary means ought to be able to afford innovative design. "With Cathy McGowan endorsing our clothes by wearing them nearly every week on TV," Hulanicki recalled, "there was a sort of underground grapevine which was growing everyday ... throughout the clubs and the offices ... "[10] From the day she opened her first Biba boutique in September 1964, she found the premises packed every Saturday morning in the wake of the *Ready Steady Go!* broadcast the previous evening (fig. 78).

That phenomenon might attest to no more than the promotional power of television had not Hulanicki been offering styles that took the circumstances and outlook of her youthful clientele fully into account. She had the theory that rationing and austerity had ushered a whole new body type into the relative affluence of the 1960s: "the postwar babies who had been deprived of nourishing protein in childhood and grew up into beautiful skinny people. A designer's dream. It didn't take much for them to look outstanding. The simpler the better, the shorter the better." The linear profile of these outfits combined with the severity of Sassoon-style haircuts made for a sudden spectacle of the feminine unprecedented in its vividness and threatening in its seeming androgyny – abundant provocation for the misogyny still dominant across the media landscape.[11]

Hulanicki describes in her memoir one night at Biba just before closing:

> *a tiny blonde girl came in and began taking the clothes off the hatstands. Instead of trying them on behind the dangerously wobbly screens, she stripped off in the shop and proceeded to try on smocks and trouser suits ... She was magnetic – her skin was like marble and her features larger than life. It was Julie Christie getting her wardrobe together for the film Darling.*[12]

Christie's acting out in the Biba boutique crystalized the release of unsupervised behavior customary in the shop, which served as a music-filled domain for young women largely free of male scrutiny. But the film role for which she was preparing would transmit a different message altogether.

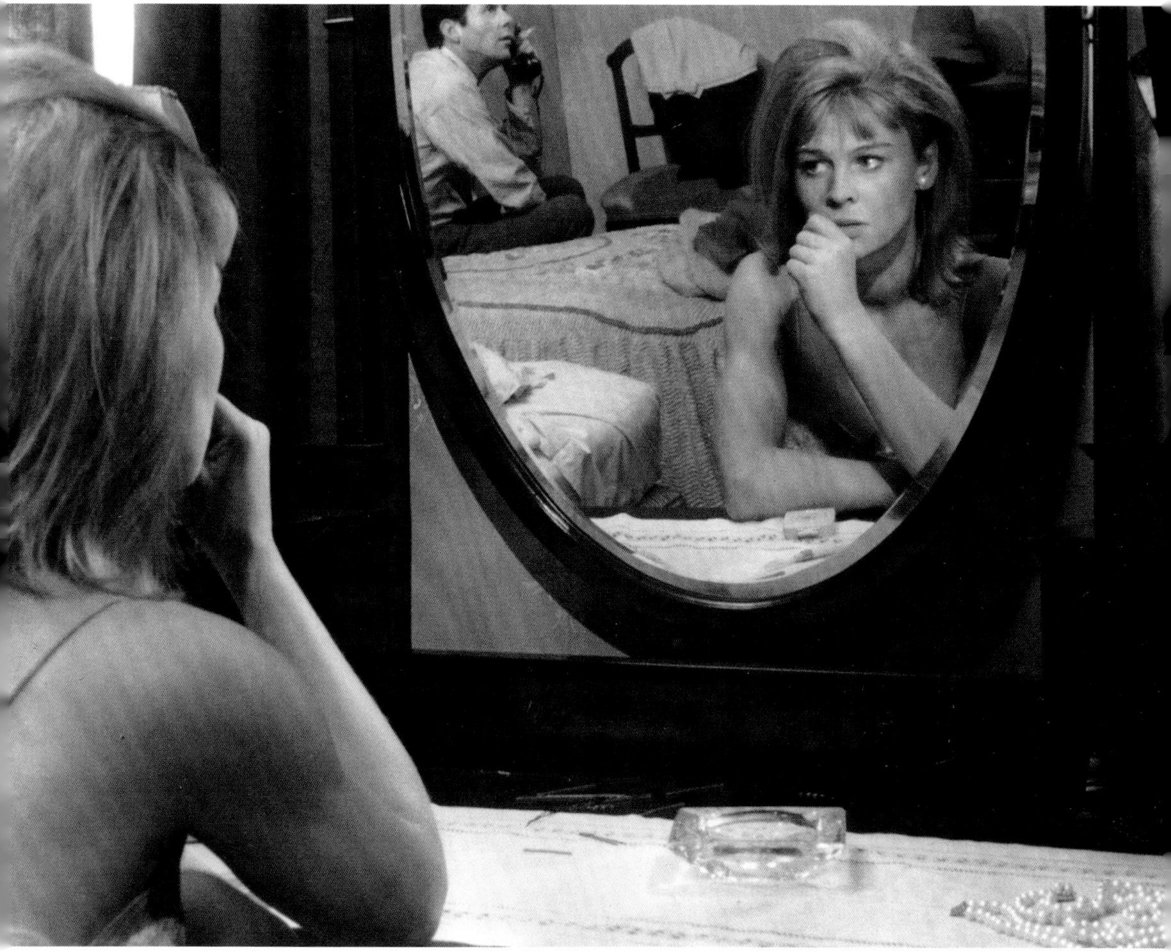

John Schlesinger's film *Darling*, its script by Frederic Raphael and title role of Diana Scott played by Christie (fig. 79), premiered in August of 1965. Although rarely discussed or even much remembered now, its story of a London model – ruthlessly out for herself and undone by her ambitions – proved a notable international success at the time, exceptionally so for a British film: it gained Academy Awards for Raphael and for Christie in just her third film; Schlesinger was nominated for best director and the film for best picture. There are many ways it can be taken as a mordant look back along the lines of "What have we wrought?" in allowing a youthful, pop aristocracy to upend the hierarchical order that the Oxbridge-educated Raphael and Schlesinger still took for granted, however with-it they might have tried to appear.

79 Julie Christie and Dirk Bogarde in a publicity still for *Darling* (dir. John Schlesinger), 1965

To this end, the film's authors took full advantage of Pauline Boty's persona and career.

Boty had mixed with Schlesinger before, having been considered for a role in the director's previous film, *Billy Liar*, in 1963. She would have played a generously free-spirited young woman who shakes herself loose from the drab industrial north for the bright lights of London (but failing to entice the reclusive title character to join her on the adventure). Her chances had been rated highly enough that she rehearsed with both Albert Finney, who had starred in the original play by Keith Waterhouse, and Tom Courtenay, who would do so in the film. But Schlesinger in the end cast Christie, fresh out of the Central School of Speech and Drama, in her first significant film role – to which the director added both tribute and insult to Boty's rejection by translating the artist's personal style into Christie's look and performance.[13]

For his purposes in *Darling*, Schlesinger helped himself less to Boty's personal manner than to significant portions of her biography. The most consequential of these provided the central plot element, an affair between Scott and a married television producer played by Dirk Bogarde. Boty had likewise been involved in an affair with a married television producer, Philip Saville, but, by 1963, had left Saville for Clive Goodwin, the literary agent, writer, and actor, whom she married shortly after their first meeting. With Goodwin, a thoroughgoing man of the Left, she enjoyed what seemed to those around them a fulfilling and egalitarian bond, none of which suited the requirements of Raphael and Schlesinger. Their Diana Scott ends her story in a loveless marriage to an indifferent Italian aristocrat: smiling on the outside, crying on the inside, as in countless such moralizing fables. Given Boty's subsequent, self-sacrificing death from cancer in 1966 (she refused chemotherapy because she was pregnant), the insult came to grate even more.

Where *roman à clef* correspondence left off, however, the film puts forward a venomous account of the Pop painting with which Boty was identified, thus going from revenge on the person to revenge on her vocation. In one key sequence, Schlesinger's social-climbing heroine meets her lover at a posh Mayfair gallery opening. The artist is a recently released convict, portrayed as a caricatured primitive, who produces brash, simplified icons of criminality (fig. 80), plainly intended by the film's designers to read as contemporary Pop. Preening art critics from the BBC and the quality papers ponder their profundity and vie for interviews. The crudely simplified icons of criminality designed for the film send up the vogue for Pop Art as vacuous pretension exploitable by a con artist in both senses of the term. But that strained comedy comes bound together with the film's pervasive theme of duplicity and deception, as Diana Scott's older married lover seizes the occasion to confront her with the evidence of her betrayal with Laurence Harvey's rakish interloper. As they descend, in medium shot, what one takes as the long escalator in the Bond Street underground station, Christie's character retaliates with high-volume abuse in the abrasive cockney accent of both the convict painter and her own version of the common whore he has just accused her of being. Pop painting thus figures in *Darling* marked by the superficiality and bad faith of the film's lead character and by extension the new media landscape where she and her lovers make their way.

Boty had been called on occasion the Wimbledon Bardot, an ascription she sought to turn against the male objectifiers by embracing the role on her own terms. But others facing the same condescension would have no reason or inclination to

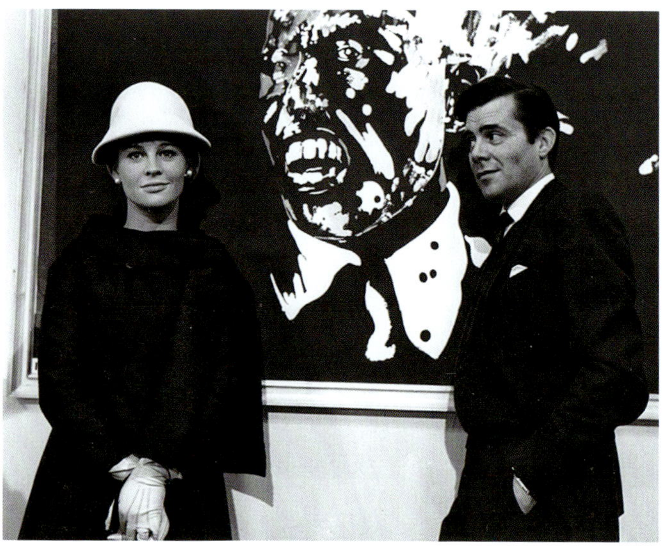

80 Julie Christie and Dirk Bogarde in *Darling* (dir. John Schlesinger), 1965

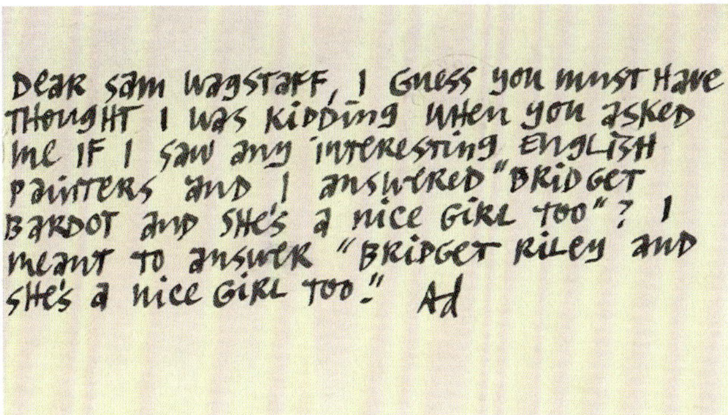
Dear Sam Wagstaff, I guess you must have thought I was kidding when you asked me if I saw any interesting English painters and I answered "Bridget Bardot and she's a nice girl too"? I meant to answer "Bridget Riley and she's a nice girl too." Ad

81 Ad Reinhardt, postcard to Samuel J. Wagstaff, 23 July 1964

Archives of American Art, Smithsonian Institution, Washington, DC, Samuel J. Wagstaff papers, 1932–85

do likewise. In August 1965, the American painter Ad Reinhardt wrote a note of apology to the curator Samuel Wagstaff in his typically elegant calligraphy (fig. 81): Reinhardt, known to admire Bridget Riley's work, could not recall her first name without the intrusion of an erotic association, along with the demeaning use of "girl." That same year *The Guardian* likewise referred to her as a "slight, dark-haired girl, unassuming and unspoilt," though she was then thirty-four and already an international art star in full command of her career.[14] It was true, nonetheless, that her success still seemed fresh. Her period of study at the Royal College in the mid-1950s had drawn none of the precocious attention that Hockney, Boty, and others of their cohort had enjoyed – in fact she barely attended her classes and left without a qualification, afterwards suffering a nervous breakdown. On her recovery, Riley was able to secure an income working in the art department of the J. Walter Thompson advertising agency, supplemented by some part-time art teaching on the side. Obscure and fiercely proud, all she would have to answer the misogyny of the period would be her art.

The break that made her answer possible and decisively changed the global landscape of 1960s art came about in a scene that might have come from a movie scenario. One evening in 1961, leaving the Mayfair premises of J. Walter Thompson in the direction of Grosvenor Square, she was caught in a downpour and ducked into the nearest storefront. It took her a moment to realize that she was sheltering in the entryway of an art gallery, namely Gallery One at its new location in North Audley Street. Victor Musgrave invited her in. Noticing that she carried a portfolio, he induced her to show him the contents, which led to him visiting her studio and after some months arranging for an exhibition at the gallery, which came in April 1962.[15] The chief reason for the delay had been her then lacking an adequate amount of finished work; but the work she did have to show Musgrave, once he

82 Bridget Riley, *Kiss*, 1961
Acrylic on linen, 122 × 122 cm
Private collection

had fully absorbed its significance, represented such a clear advance and fresh departure from the prevailing norms in British abstract painting that an exhibition must have seemed imperative.

In the way that Riley ducking out of a downpour and finding herself in Gallery One can seem almost too neat a narrative, her achieving the breakthrough painting that Musgrave saw in her studio seems a moment of epiphany torn from the pages of a romantic artist's biography. Alone in her studio in 1961, hopes for a painting career slipping away, a routine existence in teaching and advertising illustration looming in its place, she sought to make the most basic artistic statement she could conceive. Placing a panel, four-foot square, directly on the floor, she undertook to divide it using the most basic contrast of black and white pigment, in this case a water-soluble casein that yields a smooth, matte finish – so no calligraphic flourishes, just unrelieved dark and light. Seeking a way to trace rational curves, she pounded a nail in the floor at a distance from the panel, which served as the pivot of a string compass. Shifting the panel allowed her to vary the arc until she had achieved the nearly asymptotic approach of the upper black mass to the rectangle below. That tenuous interval gave the panel its title, *Kiss* (fig. 82).[16]

The year before, Lawrence Alloway had coined the enduring term "Hard-Edge" to characterize work by an all-male group of southern Californian painters, all of whose compositions arose from carefully executed planar geometries. Working with Stefan Munsing at the United States Information Agency, he mounted a show of their work under this rubric at the ICA (fig. 83), believing that these modestly scaled exercises offered a corrective to the slacker arrangements of London abstractionists. The quality that Alloway prized in this art was not balanced order; it was instead "incertitude economically presented ... which hits the spectator's eye in ways that encourage a kind of 'illusion'." Their consequent "optical flash" connoted for him the urban and contemporary – very much in the manner of a Soho Modernist's ideal state of continuous alertness and acuity.[17] But no abstract painting in London, the home of this sensibility, had yet matched the fortuitously sharp tests for the eye emanating from the bedroom suburbs of Los Angeles. With *Kiss*, Riley had found her way at least to the brink of releasing a similar energy, as she herself was the first to recognize. For all of its coherence and authority, however, it remains an exceptional experiment within her body of work, a way station perhaps too close to the crisply poised compositions of Ellsworth Kelly (fig. 84) – well received in London when likewise shown by Munsing – who tended to place a similar pressure on small intervals against large areas of black or uninflected color.

83 Exhibition catalog cover for Lawrence Alloway's *West Coast Hard-Edge*, Institute of Contemporary Art, London, 1960

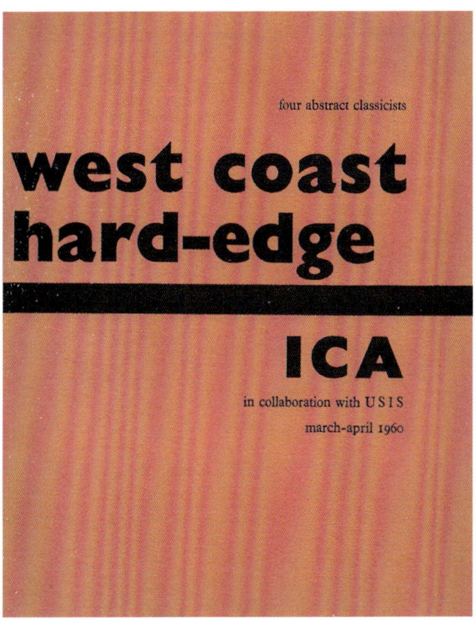

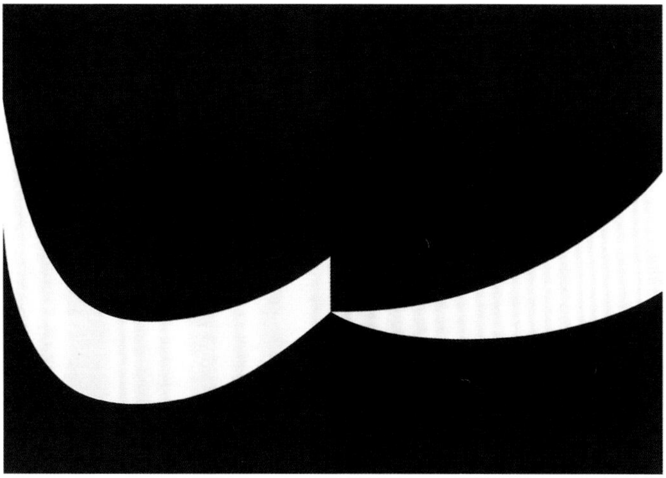

84 Ellsworth Kelly, *Atlantic*, 1956
Oil on canvas, 203.5 × 292.9 cm
Whitney Museum of American Art, New York

Proceeding from the large, simplified elements of *Kiss*, it struck Riley that a straightforward next step would be to reduce the elements in size but multiply them in number. In the likewise four-by-four-foot *Movement in Squares* (fig. 85), she took each row of what would otherwise be a checkerboard grid and systematically reduced and then expanded the width of its elements (a process that appears to have paused in the

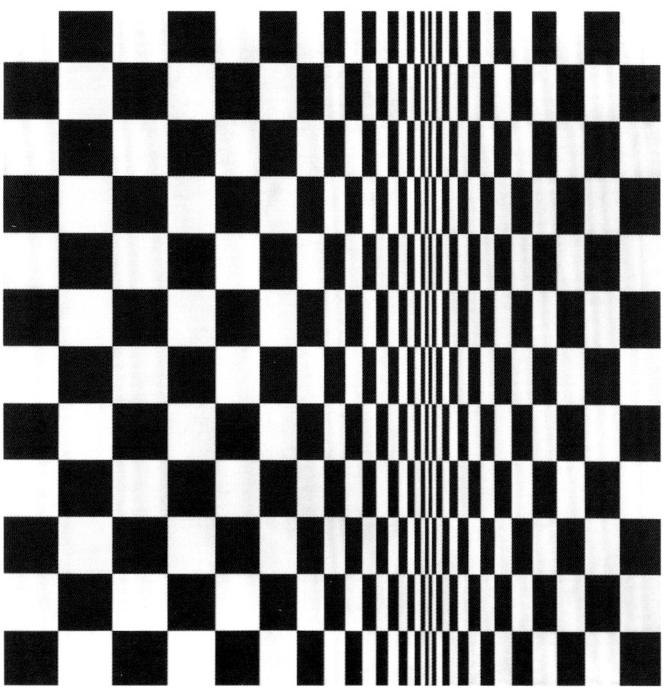

85 Bridget Riley, *Movement in Squares*, 1961
Tempera on board, 123.2 × 121.3 cm
Arts Council Collection

column at the far left). A simple algorithm could fully describe the operation, and there is nothing about the formula that departs from an easily graspable pattern on a flat surface. Yet the effect proves to be qualitatively different from what such a systematic description implies, in that the sum of her calculated variations in shape and tone is to induce an overriding optical effect that seizes the perceptual faculties of the viewer. Simon Rycroft aptly observes that Riley's painting, in decisively turning away from the mimetic representation of nature, instead "enacts nature and its properties" in ways "not corporeally limited to the eye and mind of the viewer, but thoroughly embodied; internalized as a changing set of physical responses and realizations."[18]

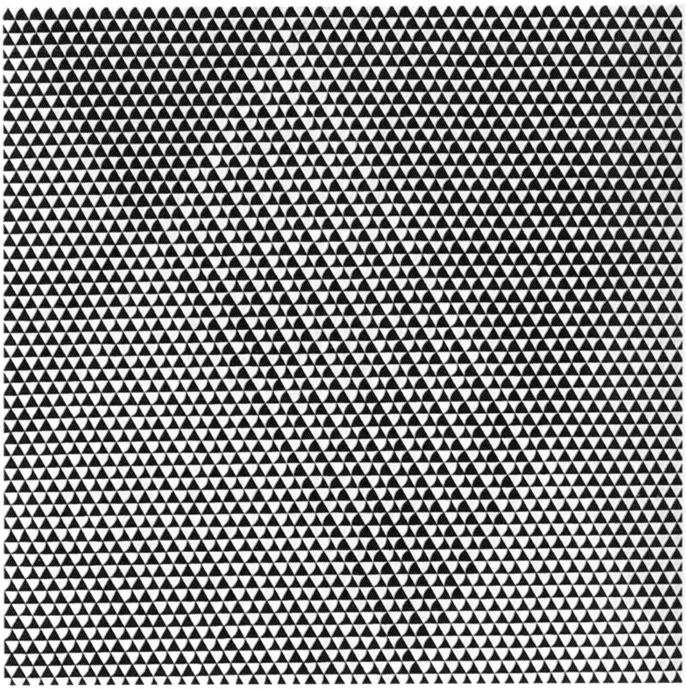

86 Bridget Riley, *Tremor*, 1962
Emulsion on board, 122 × 122 cm
Kunstmuseum Den Hague

Such were the two completed panels that Musgrave saw on his first visit to Riley's studio, along with a number of drawings that mapped further permutational exercises, from which she was able to generate eight further finished panels in time for her first solo exhibition at Gallery One. To look closely at a more intricate painting like *Tremor* of 1962 (fig. 86) is to grasp the compositional process for what it is: a set of variations on small equilateral triangles set in rows, whereby one or another of the sides is bowed in a convex or concave curve. Riley's principle of repeating small units of one geometrical type establishes what one intellectually comprehends as a stabilizing grid subjected to easily comprehensible variations. Viewed close up, the sober logic of shape-transformation that governs each row dominates. But pull back to take in the whole composition and the

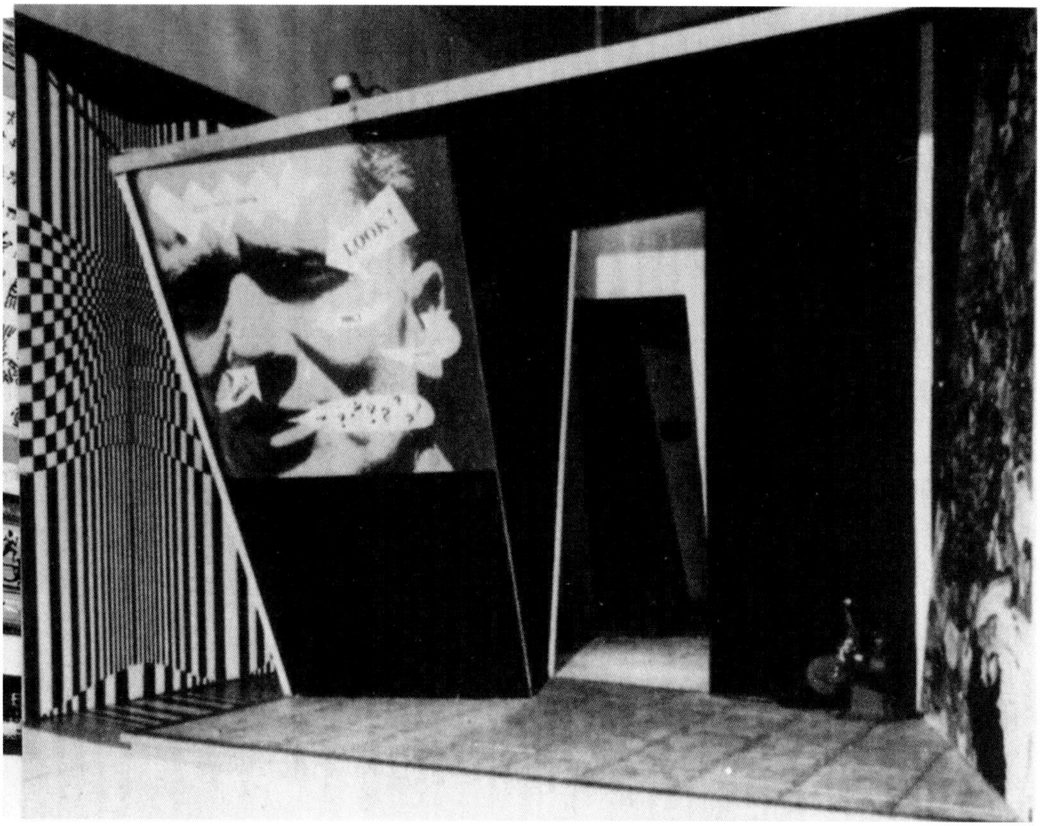

involuntary apperception of waves and undulations decisively takes over, amply affirming the pertinence of its title.

That her paintings reward in equal measure both levels of attention departs from the investigations into perceptual ambiguities by members of the Independent Group, as famously displayed in the optical corridor built into the "stand" constructed by Richard Hamilton and his group for the Whitechapel exhibition *This Is Tomorrow* of 1956 (fig. 87). Hamilton and John McHale mined the psychology textbooks with the idea that postwar technology and consumer abundance were transforming the human sensory capacities. Riley, by contrast, started from logic supplied by abstract fine art, seeking to re-animate the expressive possibilities of painting within the terms established by advanced painting in London around 1960. In the process, she more than confirmed Alloway's take on the possibilities of Hard-Edge abstraction to signify heightened alertness on the part of the spectator and at the same time to induce it on the spot, whether the spectator desires it or not.

87 Richard Hamilton, John McHale and John Voelcker, Group 2 installation, *This Is Tomorrow* exhibition, Whitechapel Gallery, London 1956

Alloway permanently departed London for New York in 1962, but his coinage lived on. David Sylvester, emerging as the prime arbiter in the London art world, briefly reviewed Riley's Gallery One outing towards the end of a round-up covering four other exhibitions. But the unqualified praise made up for its brevity: "Bridget Riley is a hard-edge abstractionist," he informed his *New Statesman* readership, "painting in black and white, mostly using squares, circles and parallel lines as units in such a way that they can seem to be jumping, flashing, bending." Having effectively acknowledged Alloway's "optical flash," Sylvester then shifts his attention to the calculated logic of shape transformation. Plainly speaking of *Movement in Squares* without naming it, he praises the "contrast, at once unnerving and reassuring, between all the frenetic activity that occurs where the squares are compressed and the serene stability of those which have retained their 'proper' proportions."[19] He was so taken by the painting that he purchased it as a representative of the Arts Council for the permanent collection of that body. He went further, seeking to buy another major panel, *Horizontal Vibration*, for himself (fig. 88).

In so doing, Sylvester hastened if not induced a key technical feature of Riley's practice. When he discovered that his chosen painting had already been sold, he seems to have made something of a fuss, proposing that an exact replica could be made for the other buyer. One was duly made, not by Riley herself, but by a professional letterer from J. Walter Thompson, and it was Sylvester who eventually received the copy.[20] And that, in the long run, made no difference, because execution of her compositions by skilled assistants became her normal procedure. Such abstention from the finishing

88 Bridget Riley, *Horizontal Vibration*, 1961
Emulsion on board, 44.5 × 141 cm
Private collection

process might suggest indifference to the object status of the work, but the opposite is the case. So crucial is the concrete execution to the success of each work that no preventable lapse of skill could be permitted. While Riley was issuing screen prints after her designs from the moment of her first exhibition, the double character of her paintings, Sylvester's paradox of the frenetic coexisting with the serene, can be fully apprehended only in front of the actual painted object. One has to see directly their precision of application in the texture and slightly raised boundaries of actual pigment, whereby the combined registers of intellectual and physical labour manifest themselves. Extended contemplation, of the kind Riley intended, allows a viewer momentarily to attend to the pattern of construction before being seized by the involuntary psychological response, that is, to negotiate and comprehend the electric jump that occurs between her discreet pictorial means and her spectacular, involuntary effects on the optical nervous system.

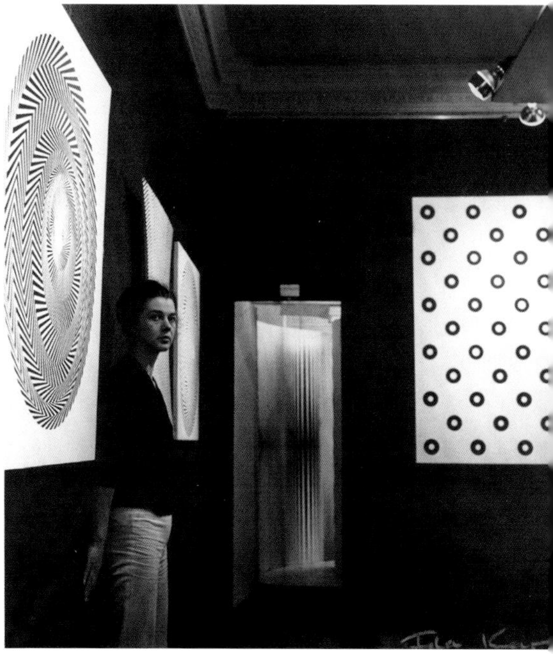

89 Bridget Riley in her exhibition at Gallery One, London, photographed by Ida Kar, 1963

National Portrait Gallery, London

But the normative term "original" does not precisely apply. As was the case with *Horizontal Vibration*, another could always be made, so that the prime physical encounter with her work is always shadowed by the mechanics of reproduction. Nor did Riley, with Musgrave's assistance, shrink from enhancing the intensity of her paintings by creating a dramatically immersive environment for them. In her second exhibition at Gallery One, mounted in September 1963, her paintings were set against black walls, possibly unchanged since Billy Apple's coming-out exhibition (as discussed in the previous chapter) mounted in the same space the previous April. But Riley plainly found such a backdrop conducive to unifying her black-and-white paintings, while at the same time isolating the individuated plunge into the unique perceptual world engendered by each panel.

The historical record for this dramatic approach to installation lies in images of Riley taken *in situ* by Musgrave's wife, the photographer Ida Kar, just as she had documented artists like Yves Klein shown at the old Soho premises of Gallery One, as well as the Mod-style excursions of her protégé Terry Taylor, also traced in Chapter Two. It had seemed natural that Pauline Boty would pose for the likes of Lewis Morley and David Bailey, given the emphasis she placed on her public persona as a means to direct attention towards her art. In obvious contrast to the fashionable Quant–Courrèges look cultivated by Boty, the more mature Riley adopted a sort of uniform of her own devising, black pullover with light-colored trousers, flat shoes, makeup minimal, her dark hair pulled away from her face (fig. 89). Unassuming but put-together fashion resonated with the pure tonal palette of her work, relative lack of adornment likewise signaling a studied professionalism and efficiency of execution as a counter to prevailing stereotypes of the feminine. Her presence in Kar's installation photographs further imparts a useful sense of scale, nowhere more than in the shots taken inside the pièce-de-résistance

90 Bridget Riley inside *Continuum*, photographed by Ida Kar, 1963
National Portrait Gallery, London

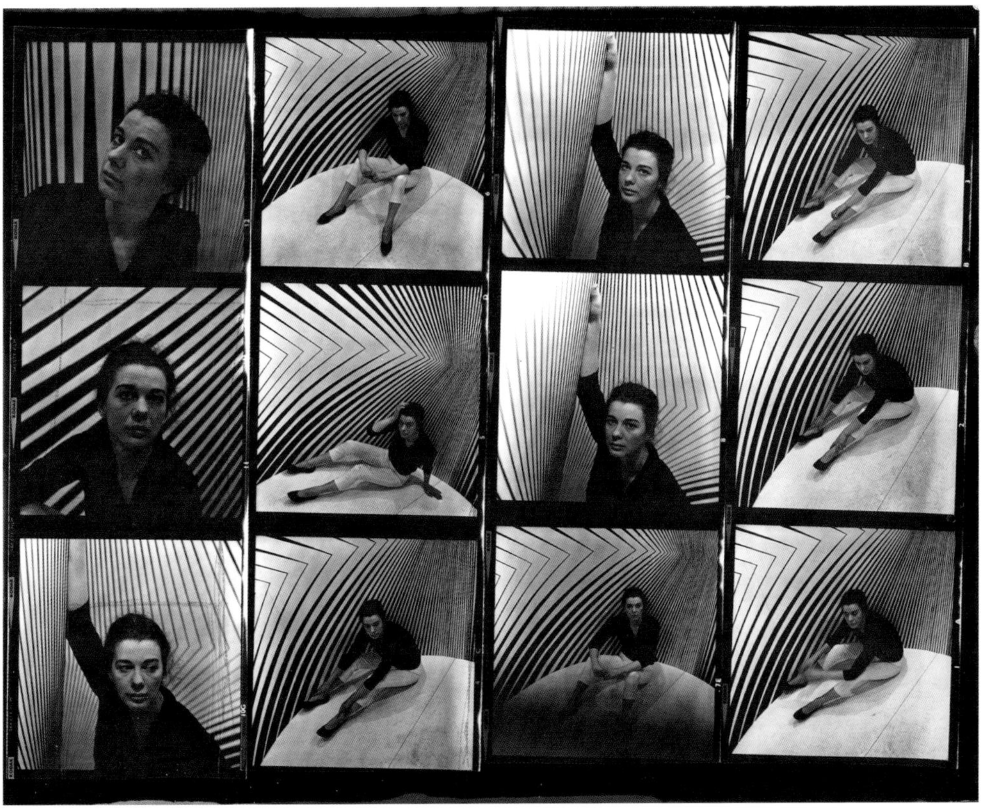

of the show, which she called *Continuum*, a feat of undulating construction whereby the spectator on entering lost contact with the external perceptual world (fig. 90). In the words of *The Times* reviewer: "a geometrically precise black and white pattern of compressed and expanded vertical stripes, six feet high and 28 ft. long, coiled in a circle so that you can stand in the centre of an endless surface." Instead of her patented disorientation taking place inside one's head, the effect inside *Continuum* was bodily: "The optical effect of the pattern," reported the same reviewer, "is such that only by keeping one's eye fixed on a set point can one confirm that the surface is actually within hand's reach."[21] Kar devoted her longest sequence of photographs to Riley inside of her creation.

Between spring and autumn 1963, many London art followers would first have taken in the light-washed white space of John Kasmin's new gallery, Kenneth Noland's splashes of chromatic pigment spaced artfully along walls at uniform eye level. By September, Riley's equivalently abstract panels offered themselves to visitors in an environment that disabled detached, self-possessed contemplation in favour of more heightened yet equally rigorous experience. In that same season, Boty had her most significant solo show at the off-beat but important Grabowsky Gallery in Chelsea. Norbert Lynton, writing for the *New Statesman*, reviewed both Riley and Boty in a single column. He pulled out the stops for the former: "Britain's most purposeful exploiter of the physiological limitations of human vision," he called her, extolling the show as a "highly dramatic flux of form and virtual space ... a splendid physical experience at once frightening and exhilarating." But the typically astute Lynton could not see Boty as any more than an acolyte of Peter Blake nor help himself from referring to her as "Princess Pauline of Pop and television."[22]

That year, 1963, is yet a long way from the onset of anything one can call a counterculture, yet the stark perceived contrast between these two emergent female artists will soften as that horizon approaches. Boty's fairground lettering and English roses anticipate the strong hippie tendency to ransack the past for its more florid relics. Beyond its counterparts elsewhere, British Pop had been more heavily invested in the atavisms and discards of the Victorian and Edwardian eras, densely accumulated in the everyday life of a country under an enduring monarchy just coming to the end of its Empire. From this followed a propensity for old-fashioned music-hall and end-of-the-pier amusements alongside the more up to date variety. The attraction of stepping outside of normal time in design and dress had its counterpart in stepping outside of normal space via altered perceptual states and mind-expanding practices. In this respect, the "particular alchemy" that Riley ascribed to her paintings anticipated the cult of direct experience and expanded perception that would be central to the hippie ethos.[23] Rycroft speaks of the encounter with Riley's paintings as inducing, "in the patient viewer, a state of heightened awareness and wakefulness to the previously invisible."[24] The artist's own lexicon also aligned the sensations she was aiming for with the pastoral yearnings ascendant in the counterculture: the viewer's involuntary cognitive responses, she later told Sylvester, should recall sensations of "running ... early morning ... cold water ... fresh things, slightly astringent."[25]

Each of these artists thus anticipated a key component of the altered sensibility that lay just over the horizon. Boty's death in 1966 makes it impossible to say how she would have navigated that landscape – though in all likelihood as adeptly as she had the Mod. In the absence of her charismatic presence, however, her painting fell into an invisibility that persisted for nearly three decades. By contrast, Riley gained via mass knock-off pastiches on posters and fabrics a visibility that worked to the detriment of her art. In the face of a newly enlightened mass media absorbing and superseding some of its most vital discoveries, where would fine art find an alternative path? The response on the part of some practitioners consisted in fashioning a counterculture of their own, but one that in visual aspect appeared at an opposite pole to the flamboyant, festive, and fantastic. In the process, sculpture overtook painting as the medium of choice, the play of visual illusion giving way to the earthy authenticity conveyed by plain matter, though in no way forestalling high imaginative flights of its own.

CHAPTER FIVE
HIPPY HIPPY SHAKE: SCULPTURE THROUGH THE COUNTERCULTURE

A 1967 MAGAZINE POLL NAMED BRIDGET RILEY ONE of the three most famous women in Britain after the Queen.[1] But the fact that the other two were Mary Quant and Twiggy (fig. 91) suggest that the character of her fame had likewise shifted, at least for that moment, into a frame further from Bond Street galleries and the ICA and closer to the King's Road boutiques, which had figured prominently in the emergence of the female Mod. But Chelsea and the King's Road had

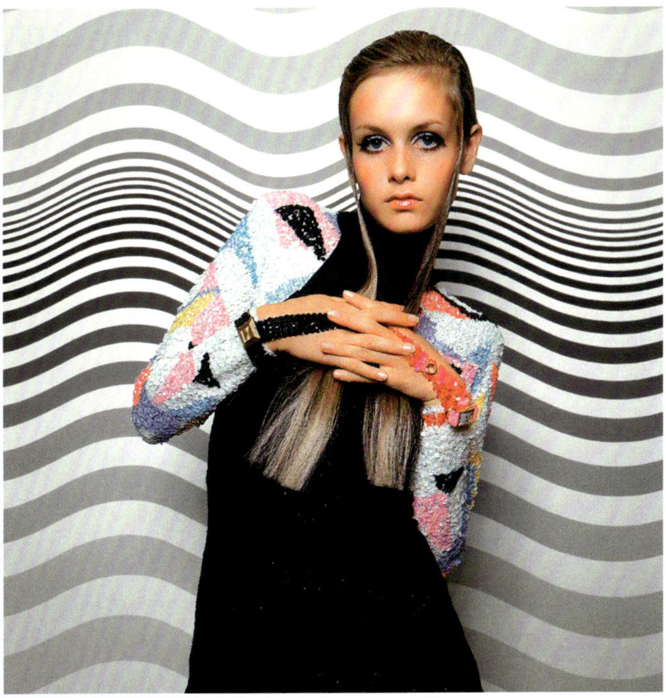

91 Twiggy in a sequined jumpsuit by Gene Shelley, photographed by Bert Stern, *Vogue*, 1967

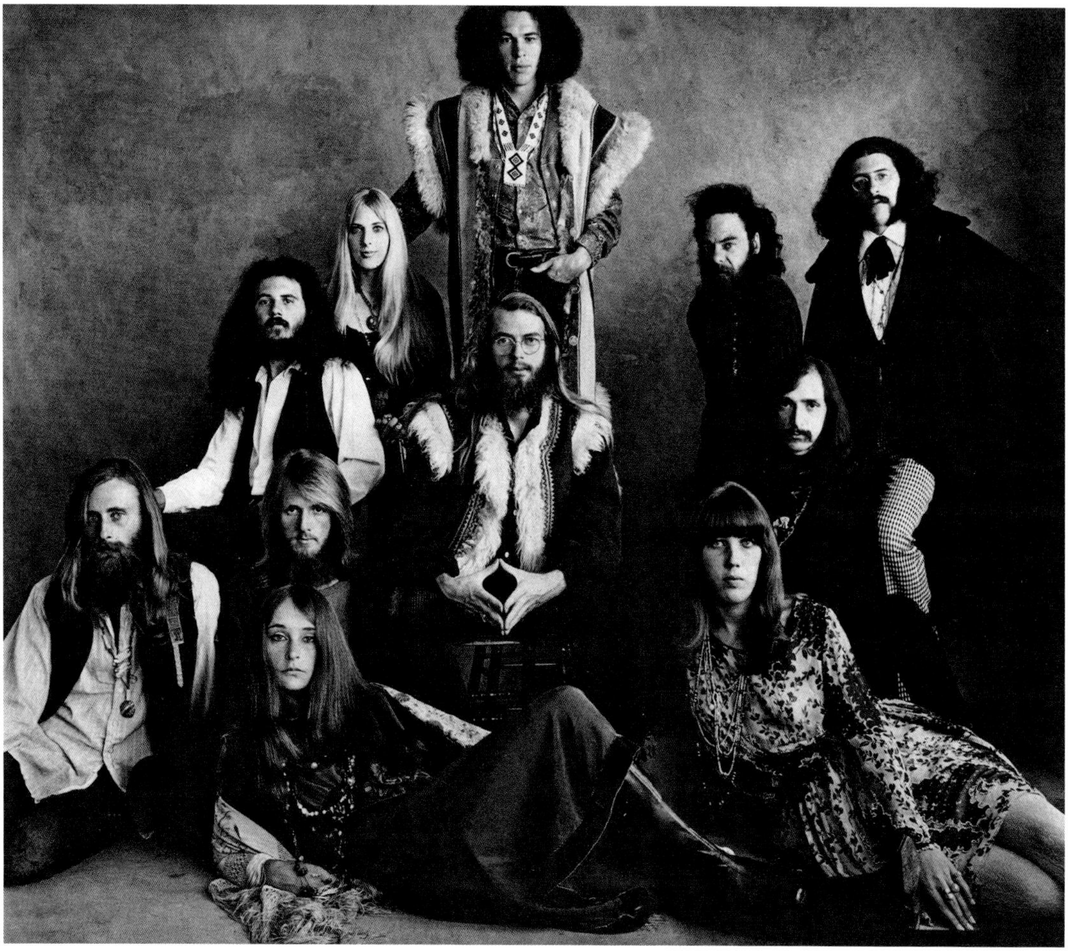

already undergone a considerable further evolution toward exotic pastoralism with Victorian and Edwardian revivals, as the locale came to anchor the international counterculture in its London incarnation.

92 Chet Helms and the Family Dog Concert Collective, photographed by Irving Penn, San Francisco, 1967

Counterculture comes as a loaded term, to say the least, with an unruly number of not always compatible tributaries.[2] It can be said at least that it was largely a movement of the young, though often encouraged by middle-aged figureheads like Allen Ginsberg or Timothy Leary. Inwardly, its adherents sought to reach enhanced or expanded mental states induced by imported techniques of meditation (Ginsberg) or psychedelic drugs (Leary and Ginsberg again). Outwardly, such aspirations manifested themselves in eclectically exotic appearance and conspicuous refusal of conventional jobs, careers, and political beliefs, though its relationship to the emergent New Left and anti-war movement was fraught from the beginning and only partially overlapping.[3] By 1966, all these tendencies had found a physical nexus in the Victoria-era wooden houses of the Haight-Ashbury district of San Francisco. Alongside cooperatively communal living, hippie commerce made its appearance, providing suitable drug paraphernalia, extravagant costume, trippy ballroom concerts, underground news sources (Jann Wenner's early *Rolling Stone* among many others) and splashy poster graphics for residents and tourists alike (fig. 92).

Although all these manifestations crossed over from California to London, the commercial dimension became a particularly conspicuous import. In the course of that shift, the new entrepreneurs were as often as not aristocrats, the old stigma of the bourgeois shopkeeper having somehow ceased to apply under the countercultural spell. Michael Rainey's Hung on You (fig. 93) started the trend in 1964.[4] The son of one

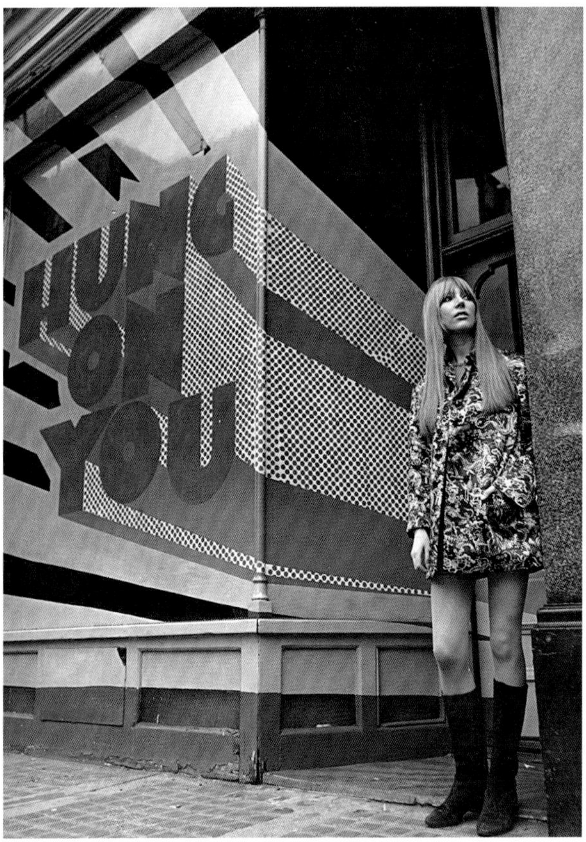

93 Model in front of Hung on You, 23 Cale Street, London, photographed by George Freston, 1965

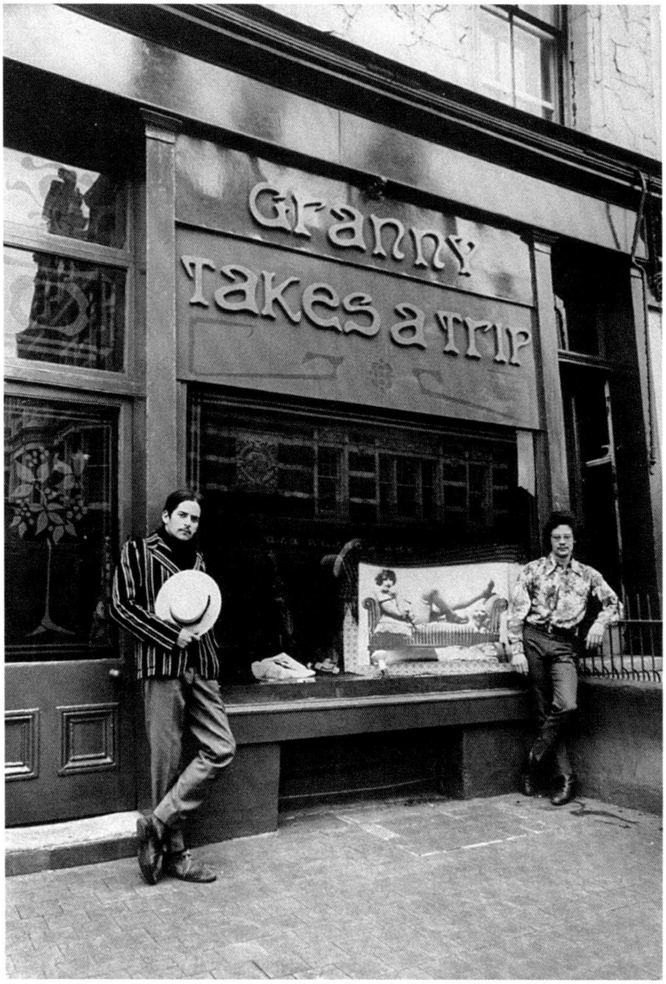

94 Michael Chaplin and Nigel Waymouth outside Granny Takes a Trip, 488 King's Road, London, photographed by Terence Spencer, 1966

society figure and married to another, Rainey represented the opening that such flamboyant shops offered to the young and well-born as financial backers, models, and customers. But he found himself driven from his own premises in 1966 by a more deep-pocketed aristocrat, Tara Browne, young heir to the Guinness fortune, whose unscrupulous partner in Dandies Fashions purloined both Rainey's designs and his suppliers. (The motor-racing Browne had only months to live, thereby becoming the subject of the Beatles "Day in the Life," that is, "the lucky man," who both "made the grade" and "blew his mind out in a car.") One of the recognized style leaders in the King's Road was an actual Polish prince, the half-forgotten Stanislaus (Stash) Klossowski de Rola.[5]

In shops of less strictly aristocratic pedigree, the proprietors tended to act as if they were, the charismatic boutique becoming, in effect, a shop about the concept of a shop – with some selling on the side. Granny Takes a Trip, the paradigm for such an enterprise, opened in February 1966 with a pile of vintage items gleaned by its co-owner Sheila Cohen from London flea markets. When that stock sold out in the first weekend, one of her partners, the trained tailor John Pearse, began to design and sew their own equivalents. The third principal, the graphic designer Nigel Waymouth, put himself to the fore, posing (flanked by the American actor Michael Chaplin in retro boating regalia) in front of an early iteration of the Granny's façade, Art Nouveau-style lettering and ornamental brackets heralding the link with the San Francisco psychedelic poster idiom (fig. 94). Waymouth applied his talents to making over the shop premises into an immersive sensory experience, which caught the attention of lifestyle commentators: as the *London Magazine* described its interior: "Plum colored walls, second-hand dresses, a black silk umbrella with tassels, coloured uniforms with their epaulettes and brass buttons, plants ... and bead curtains all make the texture of a picture that was intended, a picture seen through, so to speak, the fumes of Marijuana."[6]

The function of the talismanic shop as magnet and hub had thus altered significantly from its prior Mod permutations. In the hippie scene, experience was primary, profit a secondary consideration. Nor was the experience for everyone. The young Salman Rushdie, occasionally down from Cambridge with a friend whose mother lived above the shop, found himself among the excluded. "It was pitch dark," he wrote in a reminiscence that grumpily echoes the impressions of the *London Magazine*:

> *You went through a heavy bead curtain and were instantly blinded. The air was heavy with incense and patchouli oil and also with the aromas of what the police called Certain Substances. Psychedelic music, big on feedback, terrorized your eardrums. After a time you became aware of a low purple glow, in which you could make out a few motionless shapes. These were probably clothes, probably for sale. You didn't like to ask. Granny's was a pretty scary place.*[7]

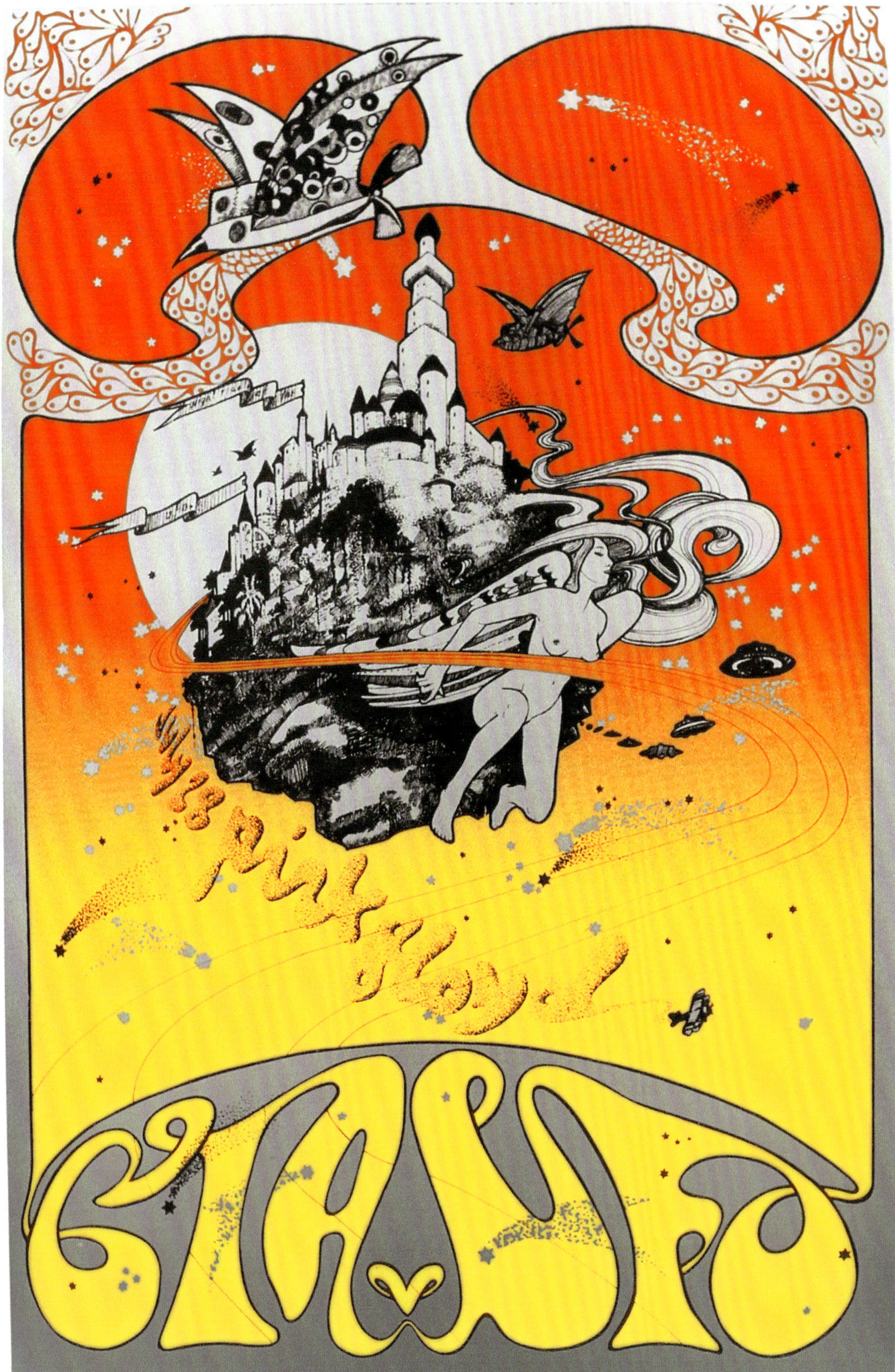

The Pink Floyd

95 Nigel Waymouth and Michael English (Hapshash and the Coloured Coat), poster for Pink Floyd at the UFO Club, Camden Town, London, 1967

Waymouth joined with Michael English in the graphic design partnership they called Hapshash and the Coloured Coat, their designs (fig. 95) marshaling the sinuously loopy shapes, eye-stinging contrasts, and fantasy/mystical motifs common to countercultural graphics from California to Poland (and perhaps paranoia, as attested by this example in which the letters CIA lie semi-hidden in a symmetrical arabesque with UFO, the name of the advertised venue). Following the comparatively restrained Art Nouveau on the street façade (see fig. 94), Waymouth subsequently transferred to the shop front as much as he could of the

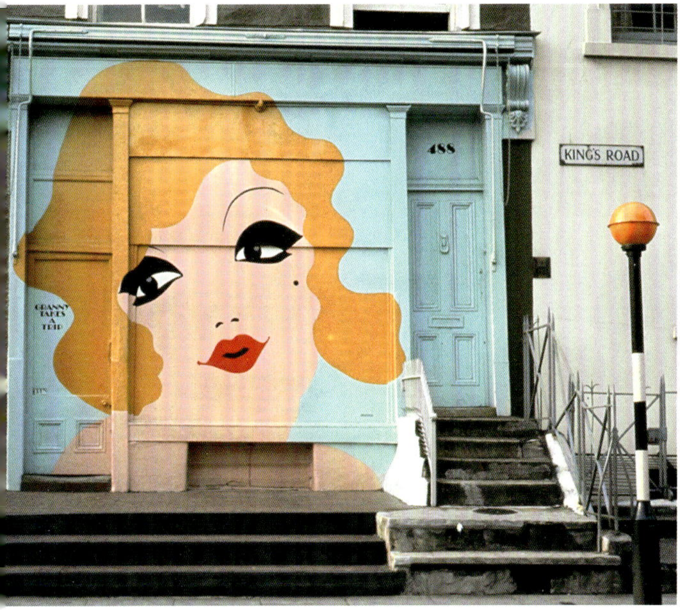

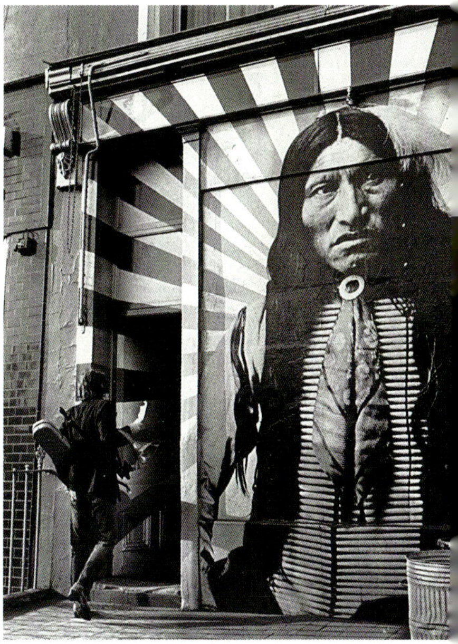

96 Granny Takes a Trip, 488 King's Road, London, photographed by David Graves, 1967

97 Granny Takes a Trip, 488 King's Road, London, photographed by Harold Chapman, 1967

extravagance he enjoyed on the printed page. In 1967 he covered the entire façade with an outsized Deco visage of the silent film star Jean Harlow (fig. 96); then, before the year was out, Harlow had given way to the apparition of the Lakota chieftain Kicking Bear (fig. 97), who had both joined in the defeat of Custer at Little Big Horn and later led the mystical, rebellious movement of the Ghost Dance. In August of the same year, *Bonnie and Clyde*, Arthur Penn's Depression-era updating of the American outlaw mythography, opened to approbation for its disabused humor and shock at its graphic mayhem. In London for the film's premiere, its breakout

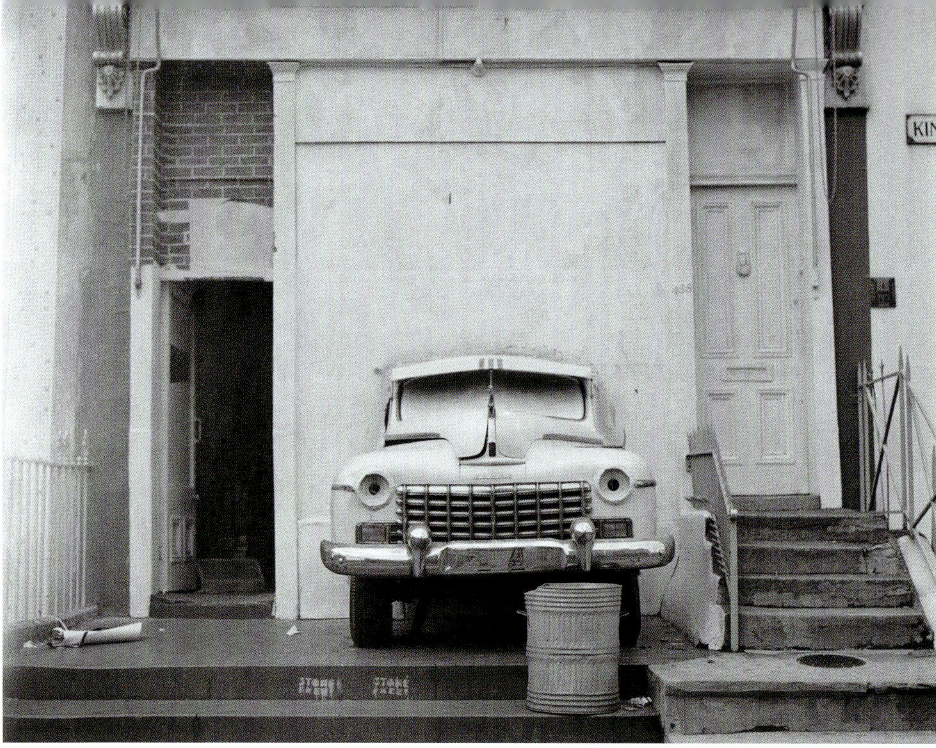

supporting star, Michael J. Pollard, posed on top of yet another transmutation of the Granny street exposure (fig. 98), a throwback American sedan, fortuitously congruent with the world of Bonnie and Clyde, projecting from the façade. And that piece of aggressive found sculpture, reminiscent of Ed Kienholz's 1964 *Backseat Dodge '38* (fig. 99) but emancipated from the confines of any gallery, went through various further

98 Granny Takes a Trip, 488 King's Road, London, photographed by Keith Morris, 1967

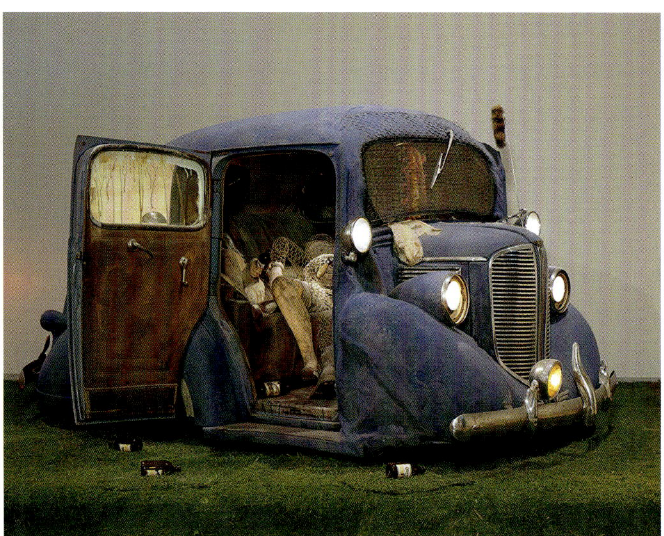

99 Ed Kienholz, *Backseat Dodge '38*, 1964
Time based mixed media, 167.6 × 304.8 × 396.2 cm
Los Angeles County Museum of Art

transformations, serving as a stage for undirected group gatherings and impromptu street theater. Over the course of this account, from Robyn Denny's Austin Reed Mural in 1959 (see fig. 17), fine art and youth style have stayed in at least precarious contact and exchange. But few among the clients and hangers-on at Granny's would have been cognizant of the Kienholz sexual tableau, which outraged the conservative forces of Los Angeles on its exhibition in 1966. Nor would the leading lights of London sculpture have had time for either incorrigible West-Coast funk art or the theatrical extravagance of the King's Road.

The reigning standard in fine-art quality and seriousness then rested with the sculpture course overseen by Anthony Caro at St. Martin's School of Art – directly adjacent to Soho but Modernist exclusively in the imported American sense of the term. As a condition of his teaching, Caro had secured freedom from the state requirements for the Advanced Diploma in Design, thereby enabling a seminar-like atmosphere in the regular group critiques, which plumbed what he and the group regarded as the most fundamental issues in the nature of sculpture per se.[8]

Bruce McLean, who joined the St. Martin's sculpture course as a young recruit in 1963, described the conduct of the Caro circle with a well known quip: "The St Martin's sculpture forum would avoid every broader issue, discussing for hours the position of one piece of metal in relation to another ... Twelve adult men with pipes would walk for hours around sculpture and mumble."[9] Something of a caricature, as McLean has admitted, but surely accurate as stylistic description, the pipes harking back to the slightly seedy aspect of the 1950s traditional jazz purists, in opposition to whom the sharply dressed, first-wave Mods had defined themselves. A photograph of McLean at age twenty (fig. 100), a year after his arrival in London from Glasgow, shows him standing in front of one student effort of his, mocked up in timber pieces. The date is 1964, and it would be fair, judging by the haircut and the layered, if slightly messy, outfit, to view McLean as responding to the younger style ethos of that moment. The lost piece of sculpture behind him offers a learner's lens onto

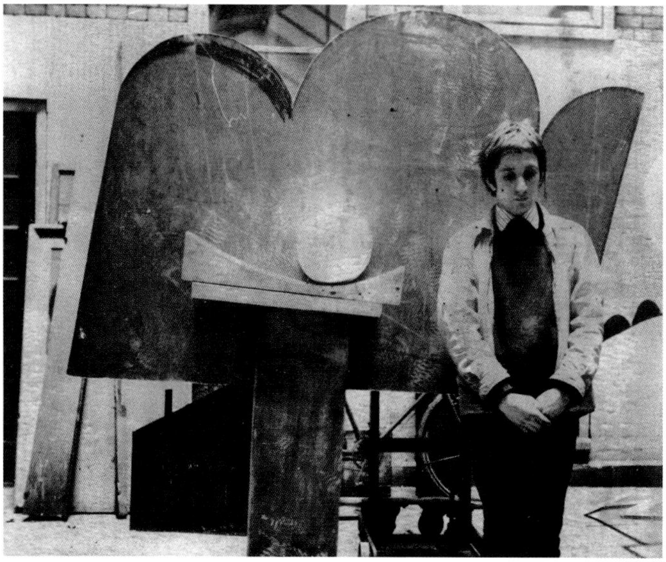

100 Bruce McLean with lost sculpture, St. Martin's School of Art, London, 1964

the characteristic outcomes encouraged on the St. Martin's course, which sought to exclude the local and topical as much as it rejected the organic analogies of the prewar generation.

The leading critic of the previous generation, Herbert Read, had laid down the dictum, consistent with the commanding example of Henry Moore, that sculpture "should by definition be imposing, enduring, and therefore compact."[10] McLean's juvenilia flouts all three requirements: it is provisional in conception as well as in execution; the built-in, spindly pedestal apes the instability of an upended pendulum, figuratively signaled by the implied rolling movement of the small circular element on a curving shelf. A disc takes the place of a ball, like all the surrounding forms reducing monumental volume to a layering of flattened planes. As a consequence, all the variety formerly provided by volumetric shape migrates to the emphatically inflected edges of the work's constituent planes.

By these traits, McLean was at one with his teachers and older fellow students at St. Martin's. To instance one of the most famous period examples: Philip King's fiberglass composite *Genghis Khan* from 1963 (fig. 101) stages a drama between volume and planarity, as its flat Rococo curves escape the large basal cone at the top, while curving horizontal shapes lap from beneath the base, as if revealing an internal flux that has escaped from the core and congealed into a frozen image of movement.

The fact that the title of the sculpture, *Genghis Khan*, means roughly the same thing as the artist's surname reinforces the implied regality of its deep purple hue, yet the splitting from which the tongues of matter emerge transforms the cone shape from a monumental solid into a parted robe or burst carapace, perhaps an organic petal-form recalling King's *Rosebud* from the year before.

Nearly all of these formal and technical choices can be seen to follow from American Modernist precepts intended to liberate the sculptural object from ponderous monumentality

101 Philip King, *Genghis Khan*, 1963
Fiberglass and plastic with steel supports, 213.4 × 274.3 cm
Tate

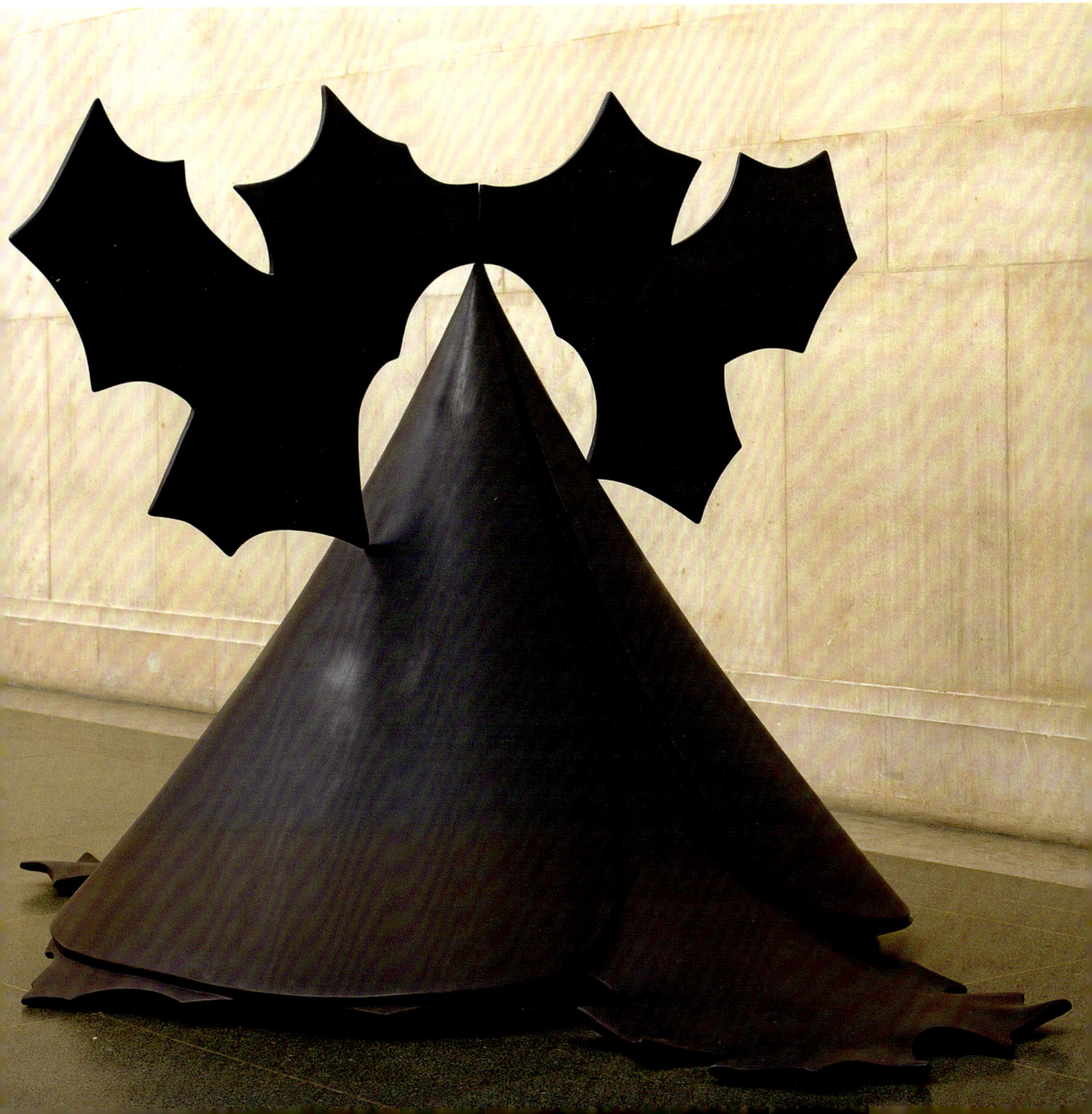

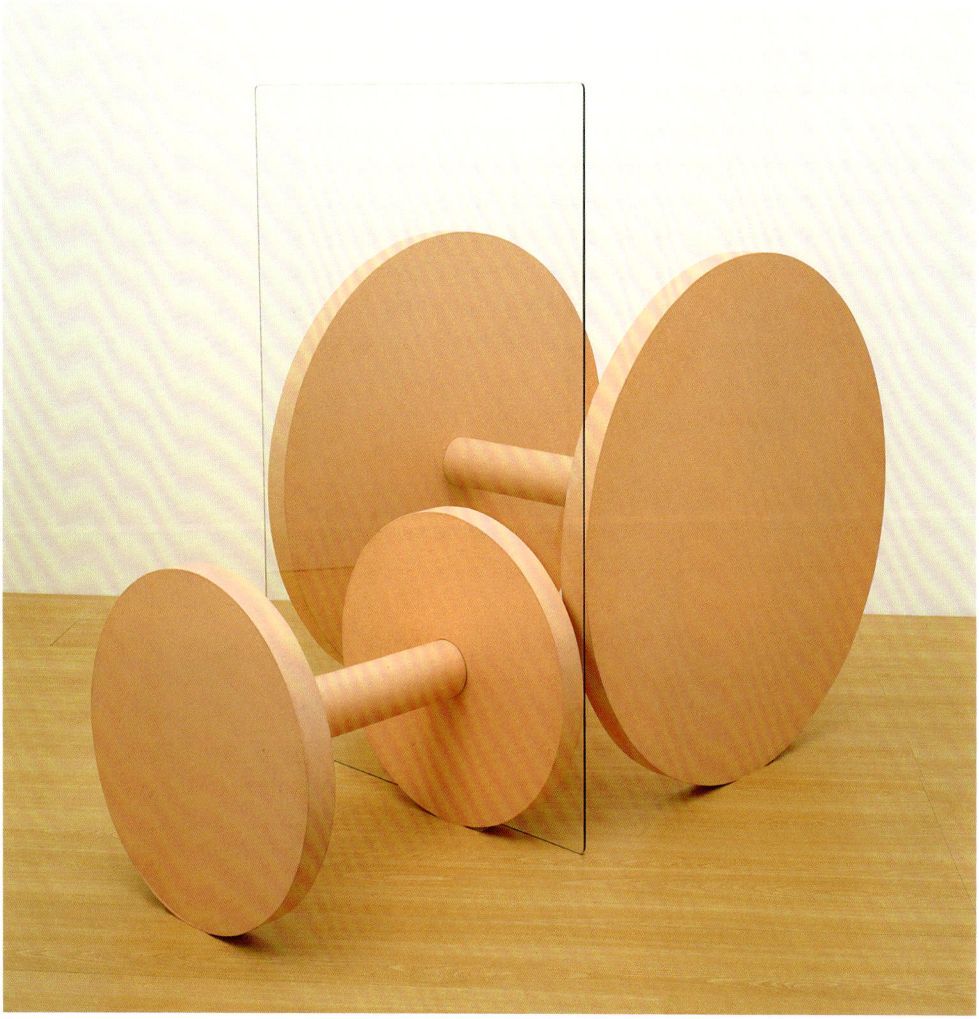

carved in marble or cast in bronze. The frankly synthetic colors and materials, the migration of complex incident to the outer contours of flattened planes, would both have followed from the imperative to make sculpture as free as possible from dependence on the inherited conventions of the medium. William Tucker, the main theorist among the St. Martin's group, defined the new sculpture as less a visual statement than a conditional proposition, in his words, "suppose such a thing should exist," which implies the regular give and take of informed discussion, testing the propositional cogency of each work, fine-tuning its syntax in the way that the impatient young McLean tuned out as interminable

102 Tim Scott, *Pink Wheels*, 1961–2

Painted wood and glass, 121.9 × 137.2 cm
Tate

mumbling.[11] But the self-estimation of Tucker as to the rigor and importance of the St. Martin's sculpture project commanded general assent. The *New Generation* exhibition at the Whitechapel in 1965 presented the group in its own chosen terms. Greenberg followed in 1968 with the approbation, "I think certain Englishmen are doing the best sculpture in the world today." Harking back to that visit to London subsidized by the St. Martin's crowd, he recalled, "I began to think of it as a possibility in the autumn of 1963 – that it may be up to the milieu formed by the new English sculptors to save the avant-garde."[12]

That judgment, however, would have resonated with greater authority three years earlier in 1965, when the Whitechapel exhibition effectively awarded the group title "New Generation" exclusively to the sculptors over and above the painters who had been exhibited under the same rubric in the same venue the year before. But this triumph obscured a weakness signaled in one of the rare dissenting responses to their moment of unchallenged ascendancy, a cruelly trivializing *Spectator* review by Neville Wallis: "The impression," he opined, "is of some gigantic artist's nursery cleaned up for the occasion, or open day in the school art department. Something too of a walk through Heal's [furniture store], or a well-set-out trade fair of glossy consumer goods."[13] The New Generation's paint-box colors, plasticky surfaces, and florid contours had all followed from seeking the fine-art Modernist's ideal of "radical unlikeness to nature," from working through its aversion to conventionally sculptural materials and surface effects. To viewers uninitiated into such protocols, however, it would have been difficult to see such objects as more than over-sized baubles or toys, despite their edifying genealogy: titles like Tim Scott's *Pink Wheels* (fig. 102) or Philip King's *Tra-La-La* (fig. 103) evince great confidence that the overriding seriousness of the enterprise behind the work will break through their facetious playfulness. Even an admirer like the young critic and editor Charles Harrison resorted to language like "brightly artificial confections."[14]

103 Philip King,
Tra-La-La, 1963
Plastic, 274.3 × 76.2 × 76.2 cm
Tate

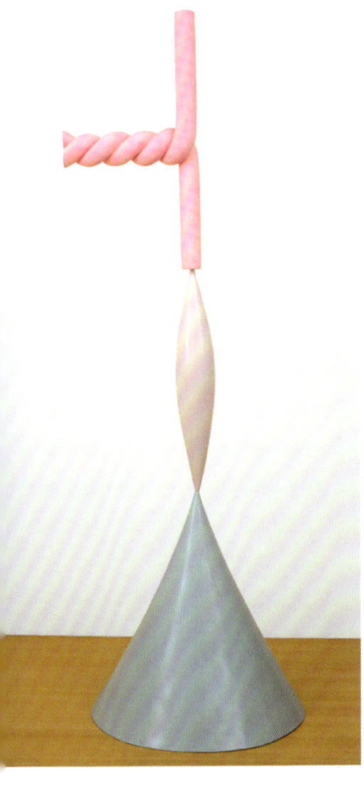

The year afterward, 1966, two lost sculptures by Bruce McLean owned up to the problem in a way his teachers could not. *Raspberry Ripple* (fig. 104), a lost exercise of carpentry in plywood, linked the St. Martin's ethos to a literal confection

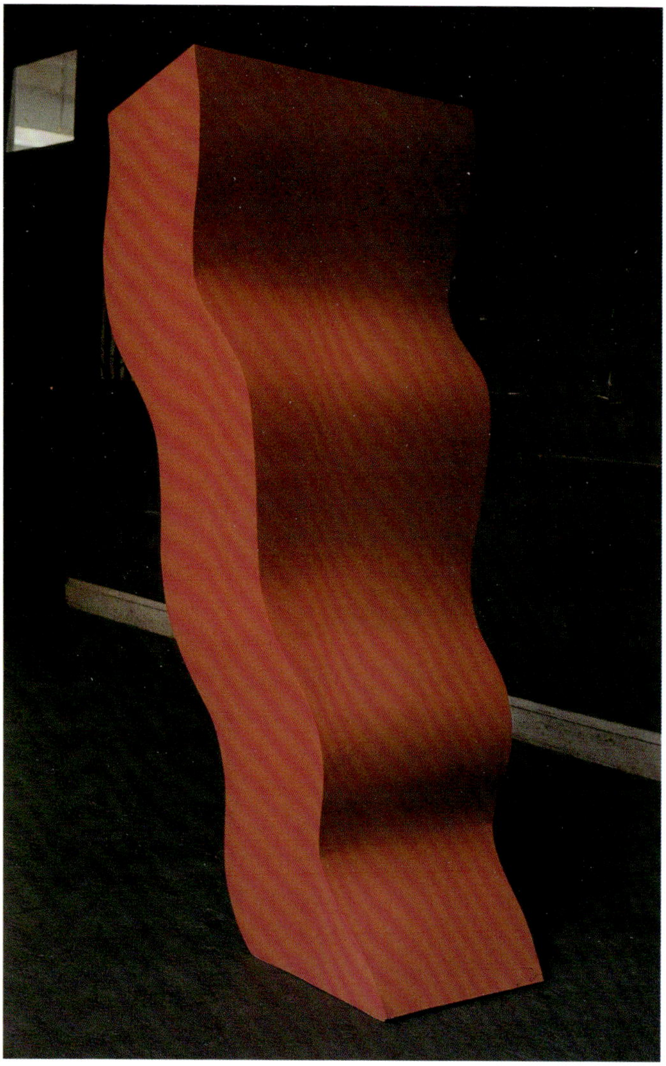

104 Bruce McLean,
Raspberry Ripple, 1966
Painted plywood, 198 × 107 cm
Destroyed

and to a child's appetite for the overly sweetened and artificially colored. *Big Rock Candy Mountain* (fig. 105) treated *Raspberry Ripple* as a module for a luridly pink and black ensemble that explodes sculptural compactness under the likewise confectionary rubric of the hobo's dream of heaven. That was the year of Pauline Boty's death, and there is a way in which McLean recognized in the vocabulary of New Generation sculpture a convergence with the fairground palette and florid lettering in her brand of London Pop. He was also anticipating the inadvertent convergence of New Generation sculpture, alongside its rival British Pop, with the favored visual vocabulary of the emergent international counterculture.

David Annesley was one St. Martin's artist who feared that a certain counterculture might crowd out their rigorous group project. Entertaining the term "assemblage" as applied to Caro's part-by-part method of composition from manufactured components, Annesley instantly rejected the term: "if you use a word like assemblage," he complains, "everyone immediately thinks of freaky West Coast shit ... so it has bad connotations."[15] One can suppose that he was thinking of Kienholz, Bruce Conner, or even George Herms (though he had probably seen little of their work in person), but one takes his point that Beat-style found-object accretions had to be kept at bay, lest they muddy the syntactical clarity of the New Generation's "propositional objects."

The trouble was that the freaky West Coast (whether shit or not) had been arriving in London in forms that ought to have given pause to the author of anything like the 1964 *Swing Low* (fig. 106). Annesley's undulating strip of parti-colored metal, which surmounts one bright yellow perspectival window while lifting another, found cognates by 1966 in the Art Nouveau revival that radiated across the world from the San Francisco hippie ballroom posters – to take an apposite

105 Bruce McLean, *Big Rock Candy Mountain*, 1966
Painted plywood, 366 × 366 × 366 cm
Destroyed

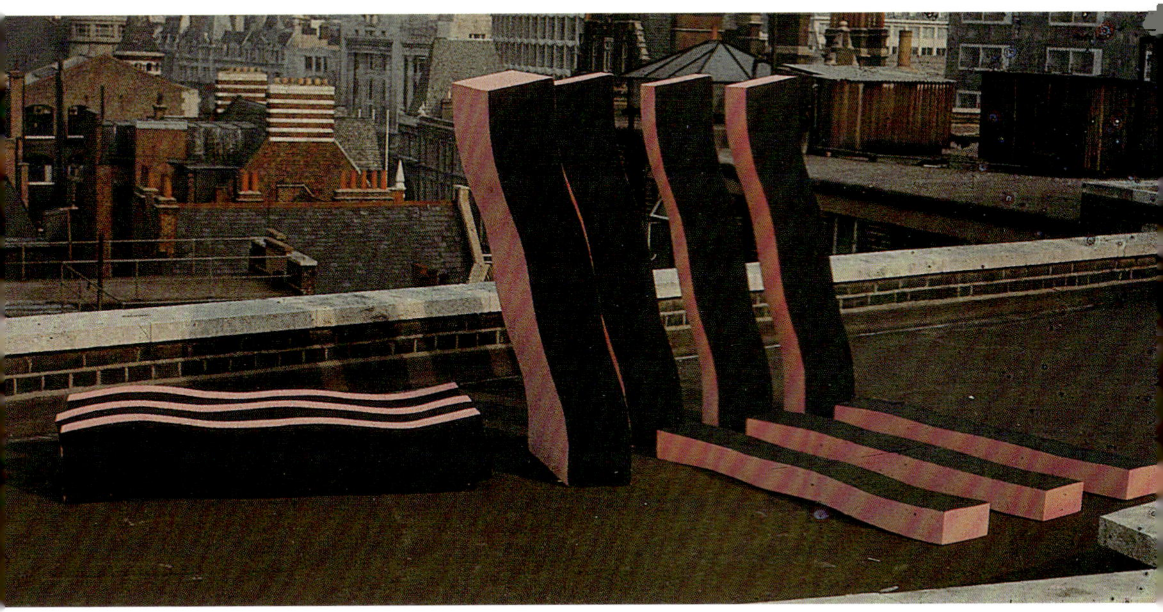

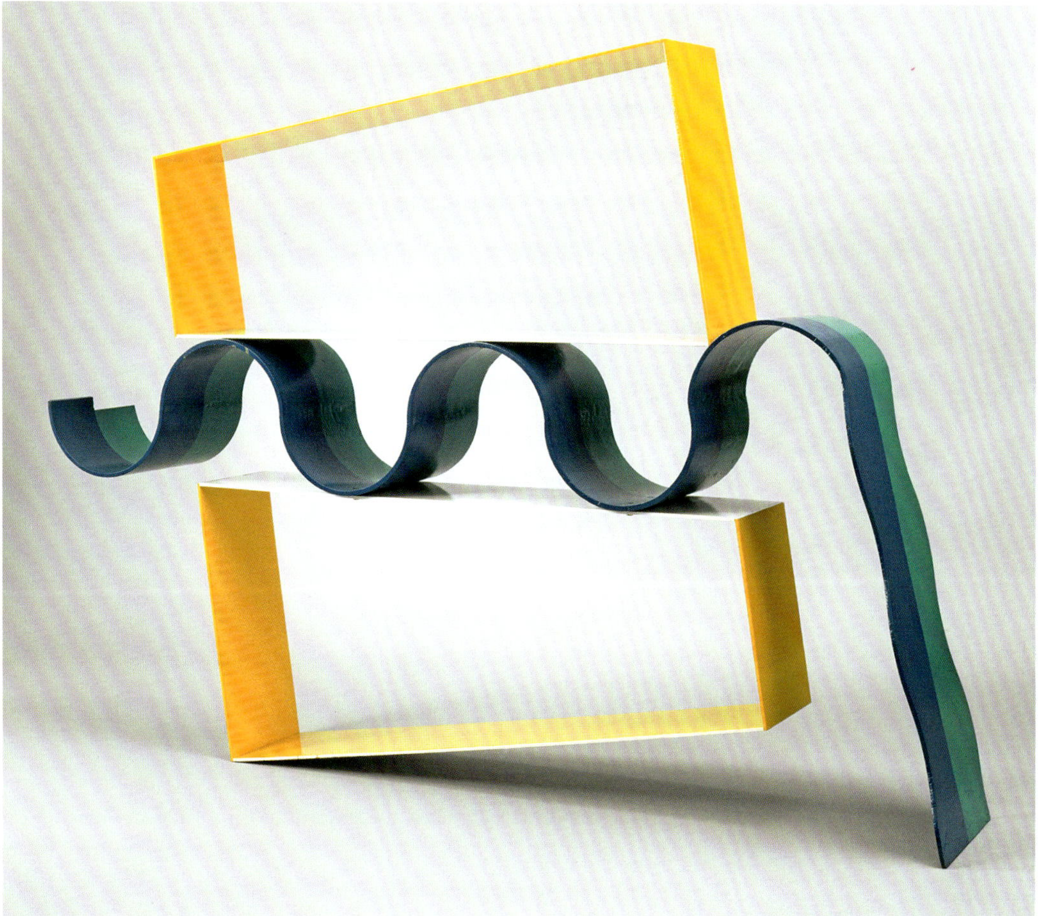

example by Wes Wilson (fig. 107), heralding a triple-bill of Chicago bluesman Otis Rush, the Grateful Dead, and Canned Heat. Imagine the flat component shapes of the Jean Harlow mural on the changing face of the boutique Granny Takes a Trip projected into three dimensions; the effect would not be far from works of sculpture like Annesley's 1965 *Orinoco* (fig. 108), just as a 1967 design by Michael English for an appearance by the band Soft Machine at Camden Town's UFO club (fig. 110) could be retroactively likened all too easily to one of the sculptor's rippling strips flattened into two dimensions. The second wave of Modernism imported into London, that is, American fine-art Modernism, may have begun to fade of its own accord as the decade wore on, but the hippie style in graphics and fashion had also come to stand in its way, commandeering all too cognate a repertoire (fig. 109) of bright ribbons, clouds, and rainbows – child-cultish whimsy

106 David Annesley, *Swing Low*, 1964
Painted steel, 128.3 × 175.9 × 36.8 cm
Tate

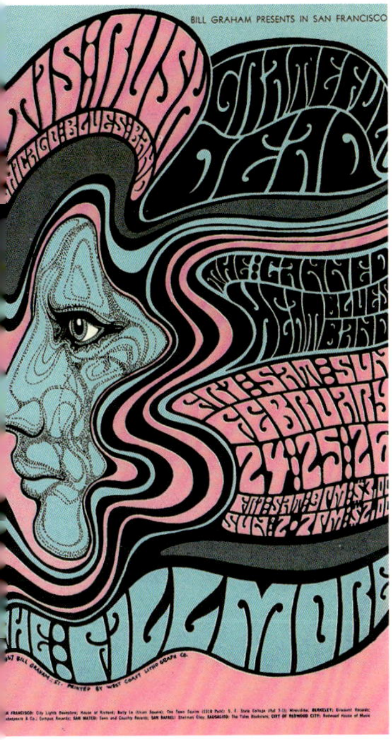

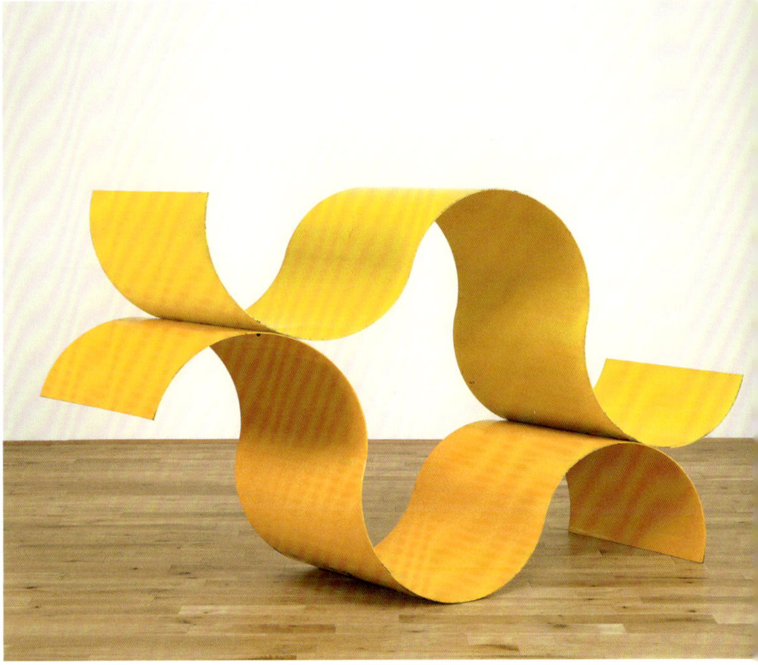

107 Wes Wilson, poster for Fillmore Auditorium, San Francisco, February 1966

108 David Annesley, *Orinoco*, 1965
Painted steel, 128.9 × 203.2 × 174 cm
Tate, London

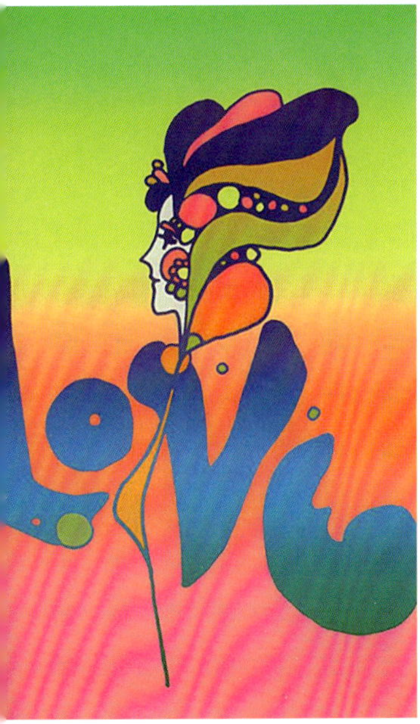

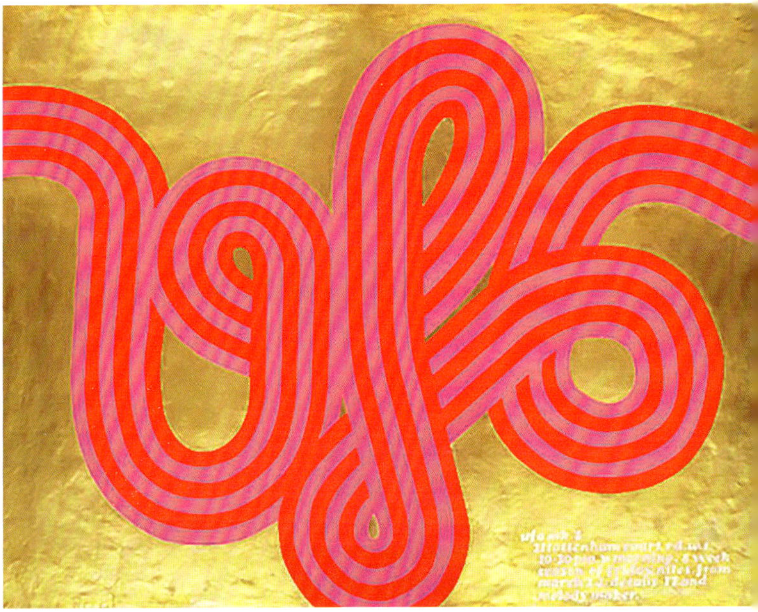

109 Peter Max, "Love" poster, 1967

110 Nigel Waymouth and Michael English (Hapshash and the Coloured Coat), poster for Soft Machine at the UFO club, Camden Town, London, 1967

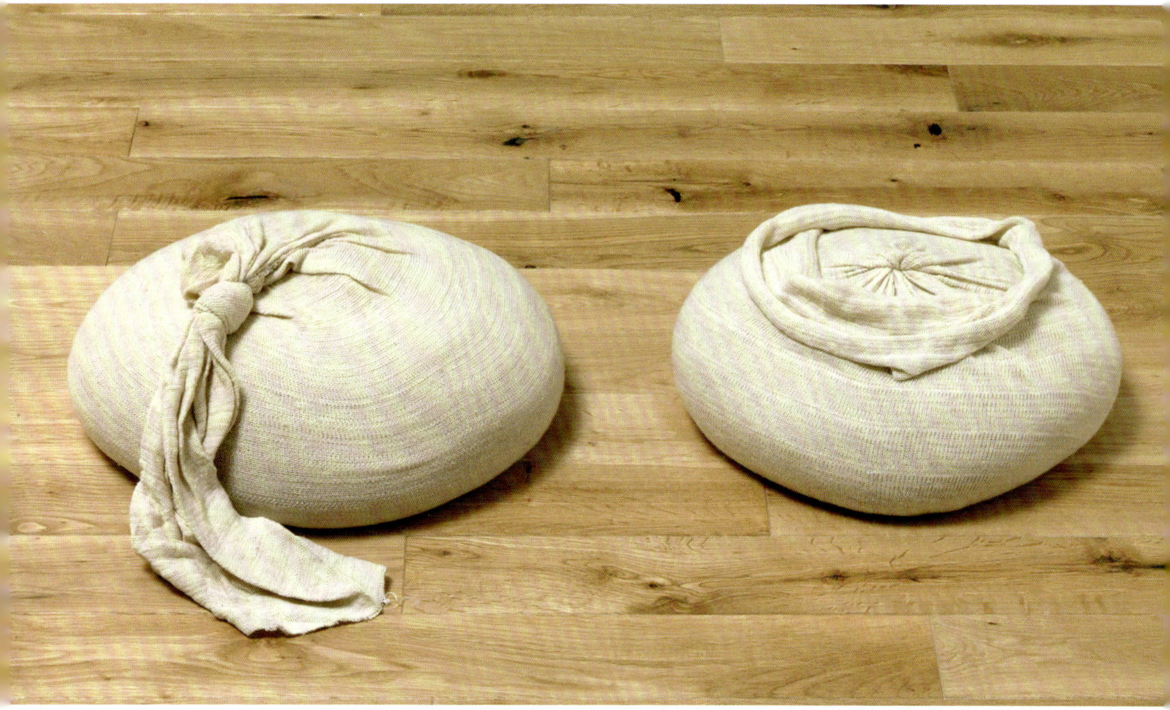

becoming a movement and then an industry – for the self-serious discoveries of the New Generation sculptors to stand out against it.

Even their champion Greenberg, renowned scourge of popular culture, could waver in face of pop culture's blandishments. Sometime in 1965, he sent a card to Kasmin concerning some service he had provided. "If you insist on compensating me," he wrote, "then I would appreciate your sending me two records (or discs) that are unobtainable over here: the Clayton Squares' *Come and Get It* and Marianne Faithfull singing *Yesterday*."[16] Besides the well-known Faithfull, he speaks of a now largely forgotten, Mod-friendly band from Liverpool, who enjoyed this one chart hit in that year.

111 Barry Flanagan, *sand muslin 2*, 1966
Sand and muslin, each object 18.1 × 30.2 × 30.2 cm
Tate

In multiple ways, the emergence of the counterculture created an impasse for British fine art, such that finding subsequent paths forward required discovering a counterculture of its own, one that would take an opposite tack to the dynamics of sensory flash and hip celebrity. As it happened, the first crucial steps in this development were also taken at St. Martin's, pursued in logical increments from the teaching and examples provided by the New Generation cohort. The emphasis in the work of Philip King on enveloping shells and upright cones probably served as one prompt to his student Barry Flanagan, but with outcomes a world away from slick pastel sheen. Beginning in 1965, Flanagan conceived a series of works in which the plainest flexible containers, like muslin sacks (fig. 111), assumed configurations when he filled them with frangible materials like grain, dry plaster, or sand. The rough outline of each shape could be anticipated, but its precise configuration, arising from the semi-autonomous interaction of materials and gravity, could not – the artist thus stepping back from over-attentive control.

A year later, for a 1966 private gallery exhibition, Flanagan simply scooped and poured sand into a low conical pyramid (fig. 112), which subtracted the residue of stability that the filled sack pieces retained; he later heaped a ton of earth into a gallery corner as a site-based work of sculpture (fig. 113), and would enlist a whole gallery as his sculptural envelope by entirely filling it to a certain depth of loose sand. Such trajectories may seem unremarkable and over-familiar to those steeped in the received art history of process and

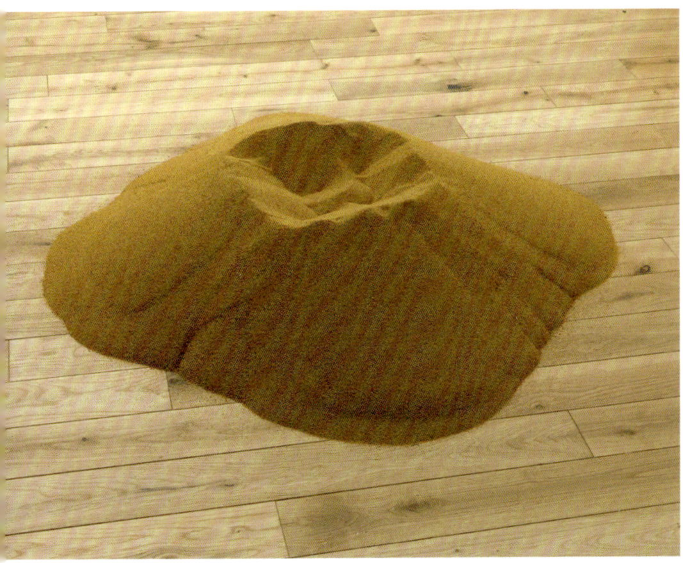

112 Barry Flanagan, *Ringn '66*, 1966
Sand, dimensions variable
Tate

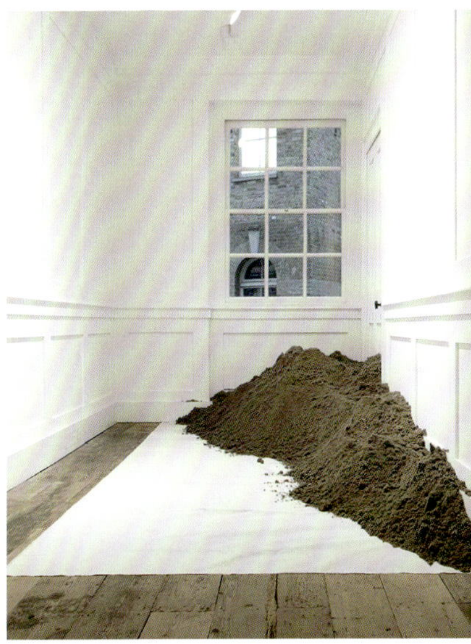

113 Barry Flanagan, *One Ton Corner*, 1967
Builder's sand and canvas, dimensions and location variable
Rowan Gallery, London

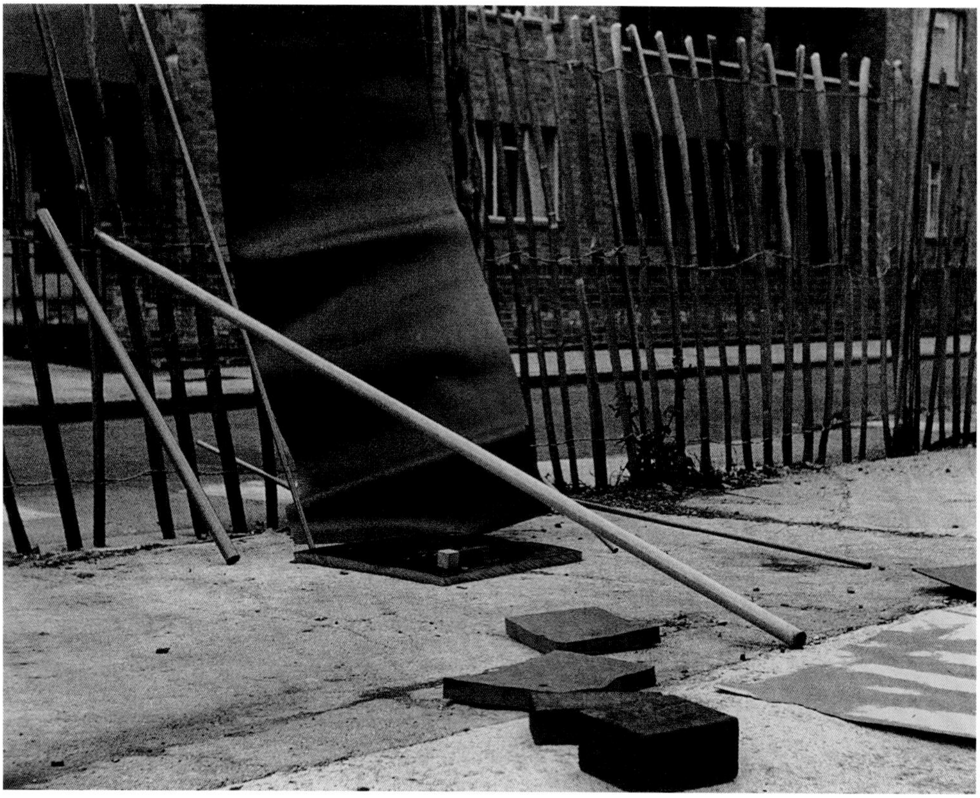

site-oriented sculpture, with its stress on the uninspiring pragmatics of basic materials in dull tones subjected to entropic processes like subsiding, settling, propping, seeping, congealing, melting, evaporating, smoldering, and decaying. So rapidly did these devices become pervasive across the terrain of advanced art in Europe and America that Flanagan felt moved to compile a photocopied book (never published) aimed at documenting British precedence in nearly all such innovations (a case in point, Flanagan's *One Ton Corner* preceding Walter de Maria's famous *Earth Room* by fully two years).

The restless McLean played his part as well. On leaving St. Martin's in 1967, he settled into nearly invisible suburban existence in Barnes, southwest London, while partially surfacing as a teacher at the Croyden School of Art. The work he then began making followed a parallel trajectory to Flanagan's, hovering at the bare edge of existence as objects susceptible to aesthetic apprehension (fig. 114). Charles

114 Bruce McLean, *Sculpture for Vacant Lot, Fence, and Street*, Stanton Road, Barnes, 1967
Lino, steel tube, foam rubber, and wood
Lost

Harrison supportively called attention to pieces that McLean had made in his local vicinity from debris found on various outdoor sites, works then abandoned to happenstance: "McLean," he said, "has set up a series of sculptural situations of determined originality, abandoning any arrangement or process once it begins to lose its particular identity and becomes identifiable as 'art'." Literally self-liquidating was a 1967 work that McLean titled *Floataway Sculpture* (fig. 115), which disintegrated at the instant of its manifestation in a moving stream and "survives," said Harrison, "as a positive affirmation of the mental reality of sculpture and as a forceful negative as regards its material reality."[17]

For everyone who rightly remembers Harrison as the rigorous voice of the Art & Language group, his assessments of 1960s British sculpture in the moment can come as something of a surprise. In keeping with the priority that Harrison placed on the mental rather than physical persistence of McLean's works in builders' debris, water, mud, and pond ice, his

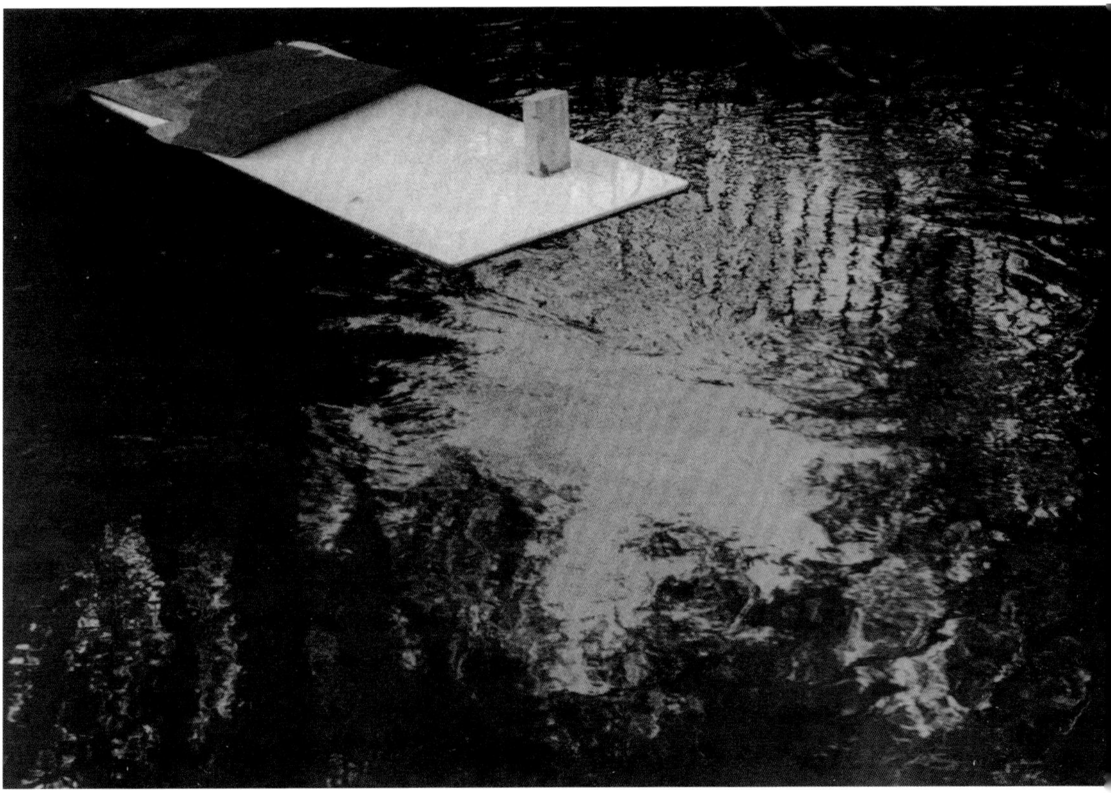

115 Bruce McLean, *Floataway Sculpture*, Beverley Brook, photographed by Dirk Buwalda, 1967
Hardwood, lino and woodblock
Lost

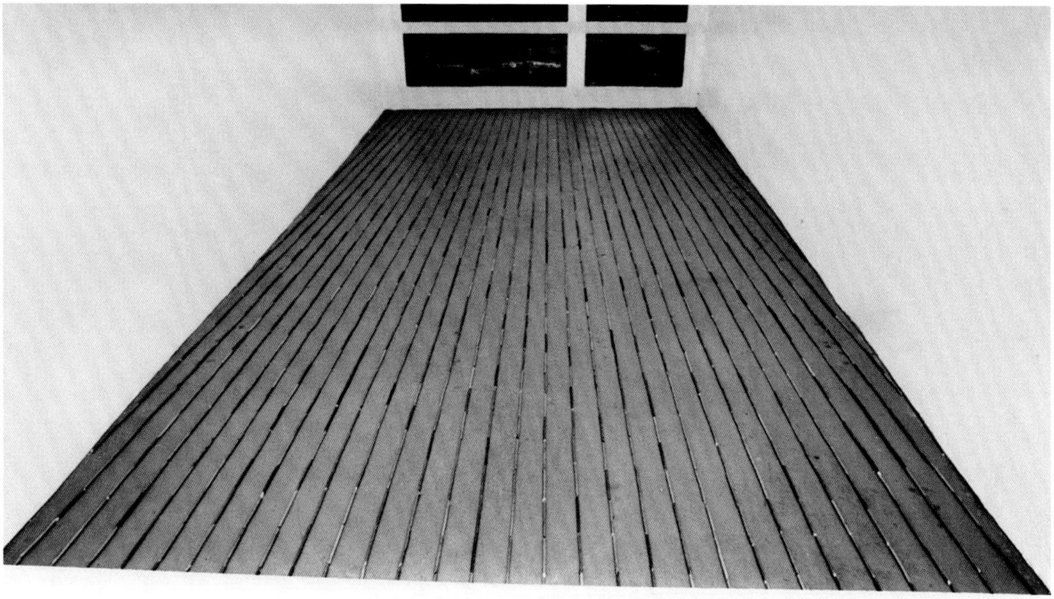

116 Richard Long, installation at Konrad Fischer Gallery, Düsseldorf, 1968

analysis of a 1968 installation by Richard Long, a St. Martin's contemporary of both Flanagan and McLean, offers another window into what posterity has forgotten about the import of such work at the moment of its first creation. The piece in question (fig. 116), installed at the Konrad Fischer Gallery in Düsseldorf, occupied the length of a narrow gallery in which Long laid straight twigs in seemingly parallel lines that actually converged toward the far end of the room. "The effect," Harrison observes, "was to make the real length of the gallery impossible to measure; the eye and mind wavered between yielding to the sense of exaggerated distance created by the illusion of perspective, and attempting by process of rational visual calculation to assess the real dimensions of the space."[18]

This double aspect of apperception, suspended between rationally calculable form and involuntary, unruly psychological effects, is cognate to the logic of a painting by Bridget Riley as explored in the previous chapter. But its more muted character and natural, unformed materials leads Harrison to a startling claim: "The intuitive realization that sustained illusion, or at least equivocation, acts as a means of undermining the physical and emphasizing the metaphysical ... In Long's gallery sculpture, the mind was liberated, as it were, to enhance the wide-ranging experience for which the gallery was made the equation."[19] Harrison's syntax is, as always, precise. But the connotations of metaphysical expansion of the mind are not; indeed they reveal how powerfully an alternative, counterculturally inflected idea of art could work on even this acute and highly skeptical observer.

That inflection lies in multiple aspects of Long's outwardly modest piece, not least in the fact that its materials have no intrinsic value whatsoever but speak of an earth that belongs to everyone; they could be thrown into a small suitcase to be reinstalled anywhere – or just discarded with any further reiterations of the artwork reconstituted on the spot. In a break from the pattern of London artists feeding off imported examples, the art of Flanagan, McLean, and Long became prime exports. As Long later reflected:

> *after doing the show with Konrad* [Fischer in Düsseldorf] *I began to meet people like Carl Andre and Josef Beuys. I fell into the international avant-garde and I did feel like I'd come home. I had to leave England to find my peer group and all my early exhibitions were abroad. When I first showed at the Lisson gallery in London it was a strange experience because everyone spoke English.*[20]

Underlying all of those traits lay the notion of a nomadic, primitive substratum recoverable from a corrupting modernity. It has little to do with the empyrean realm inhabited by the *Pepper*-era Beatles and much more to do with the hobo, thief, outlaw, and immigrant who populate the unadorned visions of Bob Dylan's comeback album, *John Wesley Harding*, released at the tail end of 1967 (with an admixture of the mystical/magical cult of nature and Celtic Britain that animated a large faction within the local counterculture).[21] It was in these years too that the Polish stage director and theatrical visionary Jerzy Grotowski emerged as a countercultural legend: in a way that seems mostly forgotten now, the 1968 translation of his essays and pronouncements, titled *Towards a Poor Theatre*, could be found on the brick-and-board bookshelves of countless students and young bohemians. Grotowski sought to strip away the machinery of his medium, but not so much to expose artifice in the manner of Bertolt Brecht and liberate his audience from its mystifying effects. Instead he was seeking to invest all the instruments and power of dramatic illusion into the body of the actor, who could henceforth carry the theater in his person, like a mendicant pilgrim moving from one makeshift shelter to another.

The artist guerrilla of this emerging international network would likewise need to travel light and use any material at hand. The critic and nomadic curator Germano Celant borrowed both Grotowski's term and ethos in gathering a group of Italian artists under the rubric Arte Povera. For this group, the naked apprehension of things-in-themselves, emancipated from the conventional protocols of art, stood for knowledge unfiltered and undistorted by parents, priests, teachers, policemen, generals, and politicians. As the Parisian uprising of May 1968 echoed across Western Europe and back to an America already roiling with racial rebellion and antiwar protests, Arte Povera could present itself as the closest artistic cognate to that spirit. Certainly, the Italian artists captured a quotient of the romantically anarchistic longing, the cult of direct experience and continual improvisation embodied in the revolts.

The international round-up that put the seal on this entire tendency appeared in its first iteration at a 1969 exhibition in Bern under the direction of Harald Szeemann. The young curator chose as his title *Live in Your Head: When Attitudes Become Form: Works – Concepts – Processes – Situations – Information*. That run-on string of words testifies to Szeemann's struggle to put a name to whatever it was that he had assembled, just as historians and critics still labor to summarize in words a constellation that nonetheless seems so intuitively coherent. The curator's short catalog introduction encapsulates the dilemma. When he attempts to stay within the boundaries of art, the radical core of the work dissolves into an open-ended and thoroughly eclectic litany:

> *the obvious opposition to form; the high degree of personal and emotional engagement; the pronouncement that certain objects are art, although they have not previously been identified as such; the shift of interest away from the result towards the artistic process; the use of mundane materials; the interaction of work and material; Mother Earth as medium, workplace, the desert as concept.*[22]

Szeemann then quite suddenly breaks it off and asks his reader to consider the inevitability that "hippie philosophy, the rockers and the use of drugs should eventually affect the position of a younger generation of artists." It remains an excellent question, which the discipline of art history has almost entirely ignored. The weightier German compounds used in his original Bern text, "Hippietum" and "Rockerexistenz," lend these countercultural references heightened status as conditions of life – from which, he posits, the art on view had emerged. In an interview for Swiss television at the time of the opening, part of a documentary on *Attitudes* that he had arranged, Szeemann repeats the same points with greater emphasis. He declares to his interviewer, speaking in French, that his desire is to transmit via the exhibition a certain "prise de conscience" (awakening or coming to awareness) born on the American West Coast: hippies, rockers, and drugs again, alongside Eastern thought and an "anti-société" (counterculture), all of which have formed, he maintains, an entire youth movement in need of new means of expression. States of mind heretofore diffused over this "existential expanse" now assume – he gestures implicitly toward the contents of the exhibition – condensed artistic "form."[23]

The countercultural tributary that Szeemann sought to represent in his exhibition took its distance, to say the least, from the peacock-boutique variety so visible in London. But the agrarian stream, the communes committed to voluntary poverty and plain self-sufficiency, provided an objective counterpart to the idealized nomad evoked in Grotowski's exalted rhetoric – and a guide as to how visual art could go round the blockade of psychedelic paraphernalia. Intensity of mental transformation, Szeemann was implicitly arguing, increases as the gap widens between inward vividness and outward modesty of means (figs. 117 and 118). On the side of the spectator, heightened perceptual acuity might transform the least prepossessing matter into a fascinating object of visual attention – that is, if one could really, REALLY see into that piece of felt or pile of sand.

Harrison's positing that the physical aspects of the new sculpture gave way to the metaphysical foreshadowed Szeemann's idea that unmediated apprehension of matter in its bare contingency left the clearest aesthetic impression on a mental plane of reality. And it was Harrison whom the Institute of Contemporary Arts commissioned to rejig and rehang Szeemann's *Live in Your Head* when it traveled to

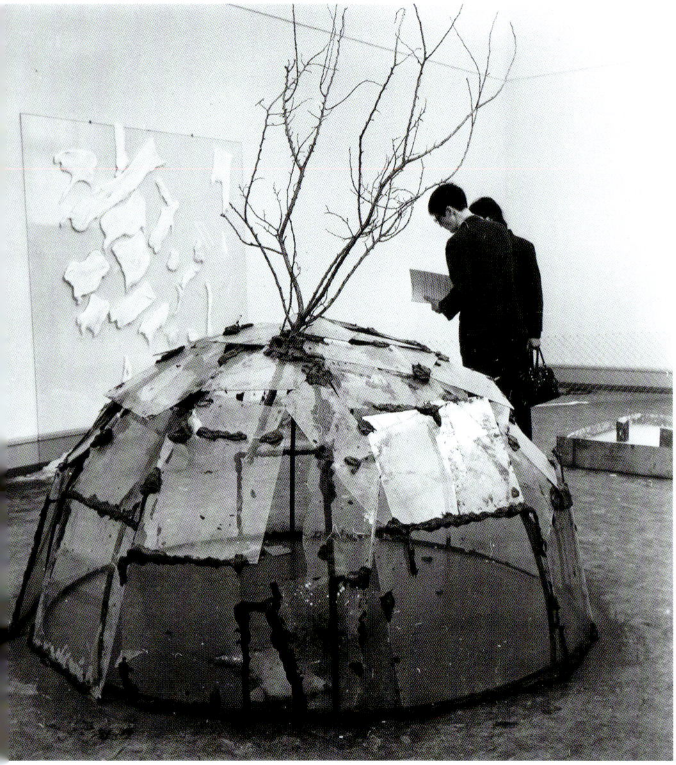

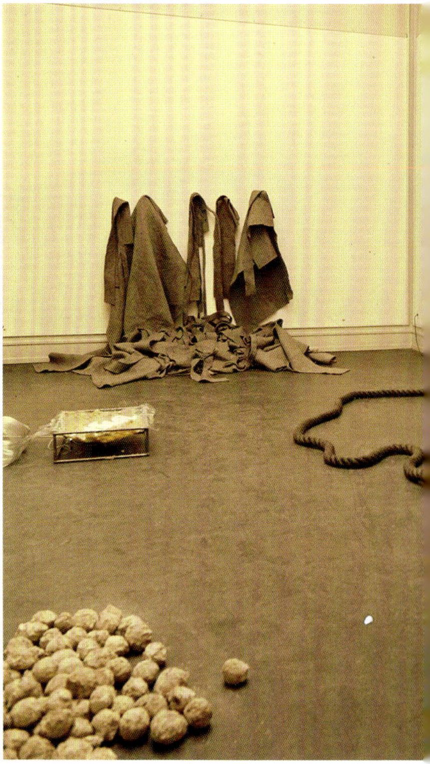

London for the third and last stop on its tour (fig. 119). So the transnational network that encompassed New York process artists, Joseph Beuys's shamanistic totems, and the unmediated materials of Arte Povera became a London phenomenon – indeed returning in significant respects to one of its strong, if underestimated points of origin.[24]

Harrison had little time for Szeemann and by all of his accounts next to no contact with him. He collected the crates from the shipping warehouse and made a show out of them, together with his own considered additions by British artists. Nor was "rocker-existence" or "hippie-dom" of any great interest to him. Yet his own introduction to the London version of the catalog sounds notes that make the same utopian points in a less flamboyant but more intense manner:

> *The effect of work like this is to stretch the range of our imagination and our conceptions. If we were not generally so terrified of devoting ourselves to what has not already been pronounced serious and socially acceptable, we might*

117 Mario Merz, *Water Slips Down (Glass Igloo)*, in *Live in Your Head: When Attitudes Become Form*, Kunsthalle, Bern, 1969

Getty Research Institute, Los Angeles, Harald Szeemann Papers, Special Collections

118 *Live in Your Head: When Attitudes Become Form*, Kunsthalle, Bern, 1969: works by Mario Merz, Robert Morris, Barry Flanagan, and Bruce Nauman

Getty Research Institute, Los Angeles, Harald Szeemann Papers, Special Collections

119 *Live in Your Head: When Attitudes Become Form*, Institute of Contemporary Art, London, 1969

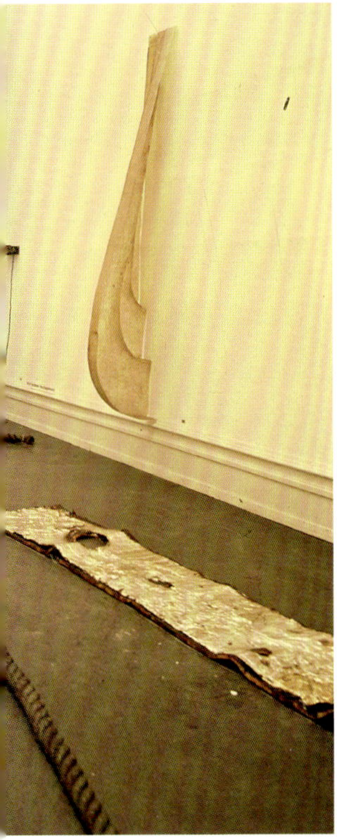

respond more easily to ... questions to which answers might come in a different language, suggesting a different grammar – a different system, a changed consciousness.[25]

The reigning retrospective art histories of this period have no time for this sort of language, advancing instead the idea that the contributors to Szeemann's and Harrison's show would belong to an early wave of postmodernism – an assumption that demonstrates little more than what kind of category follows from never leaving the frame of fine art. Art history, sadly, remains insistently incurious about the frame provided by the 1960s counterculture, which was demonstrably the most proximate and pertinent phenomenon to these developments in visual art. To be fair, artistic Modernism of the New Generation mold could not survive the encounter with the hippie realm, so that whatever followed would in the barest of senses be postmodernist. But there were other Modernists – that is, people who were called and called themselves Modernists – who continued to set themselves against the counterculture, and they will be a principal subject in the following and final chapter.

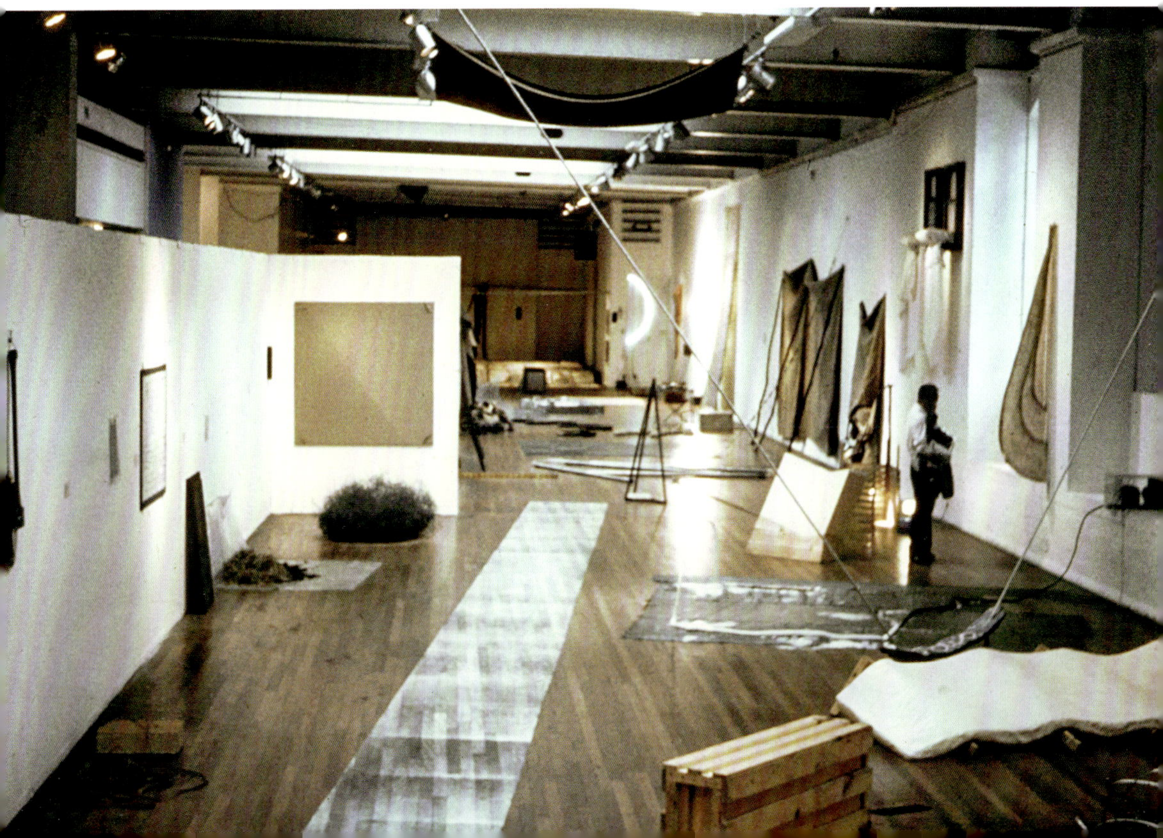

CHAPTER SIX
THE GREAT LOST LOOK: BEYOND CULTURAL STUDIES

THIS CONCLUDING CHAPTER REQUIRES AT ITS OUTSET a look back to an earlier moment in public perception of the London Modernist. In 1962, the esoteric sensibility captured by the novelists Colin MacInnes in *Absolute Beginners* and Terry Taylor in *Baron's Court, All Change*, as discussed at the outset of this account, began to emerge in the mass media. The ambitious publisher (and future Tory grandee) Michael Heseltine launched *Town* magazine as a flashy barometer of current London culture. In an early issue, its editor dispatched a writer alongside no less a photographer than Don McCullin (fresh from covering the 1961 Berlin crisis) to document the underground notoriety of three top Mods in northeast London (figs. 120 and 121).[1] By virtue of

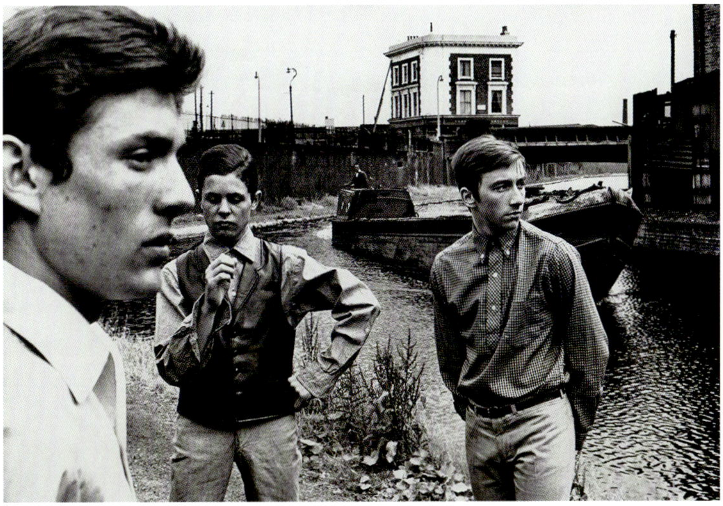

120 Young Mods (Peter Sugar, Mark Feld, Miki Simmonds), photographed by Sir Don McCullin, 1962

this assignment, McCullin, as had Ida Kar in her Soho portraits of Taylor from the previous year, brought an exceptional professional eye to Modernist existence.

One moody shot of the trio by the Regent's Canal in Hackney both exposes the leather waistcoat of their tacit leader, Mark Feld, the pride of his cultivated wardrobe, while inserting the young Mod style firmly in the downbeat London landscape to which the television films of Ken Loach shortly afterwards laid claim. In another, the best known of the set, the three stand in suits, expressions guarded, against a glimpse of fly-posted hoarding. The aspirational Feld, whose mother ran a market stall in Soho's Berwick Street, confided to a friend his expectation that "the *Town* article would make him famous."[2] He did some years later make good on that ambition by re-inventing himself as the Glam-Rock luminary Mark Bolan of T. Rex, but the *Town* feature achieved a certain enduring renown in the annals of academic interpretation on account of one Feld quotation, which has disproportionally colored the image of the Modernist ever since. Asked about the still-reigning Conservative Party, he replied, "They're for the rich, so I'm for them." The fact that Feld likewise extolled the Campaign for Nuclear Disarmament has not weighed in the balance, perhaps because he cited its "exhibitionist" character as the reason for his approbation. His Tory quip has anecdotally reinforced the condescending sociological scrutiny of the Mod phenomenon, as it has become a common reading of its working-class preoccupation with stylish suiting to declare it an aspirational imitation of the English professional classes by school leavers trapped in dead-end clerical or service jobs. But that persistent framework (to be examined further at the conclusion of this chapter) remains trapped in one-to-one mimetic correspondence of Modernist dress codes to an English stereotype of middle-class respectability. The Modernist templates were transatlantic and transracial before anything else, as its deep emotional urgency had come from the music of outsiders, from bebop, cool jazz, and the more propulsive hard bop that gained wider popularity among black audiences toward the end of the decade.

There was at least one exactly contemporaneous observer who made this case in impressively analytical terms. Richard Wollheim published his MacInnes-inspired essay, "Babylon/

121 Young Mods (Peter Sugar, Mark Feld, Miki Simmonds), photographed by Sir Don McCullin, 1962

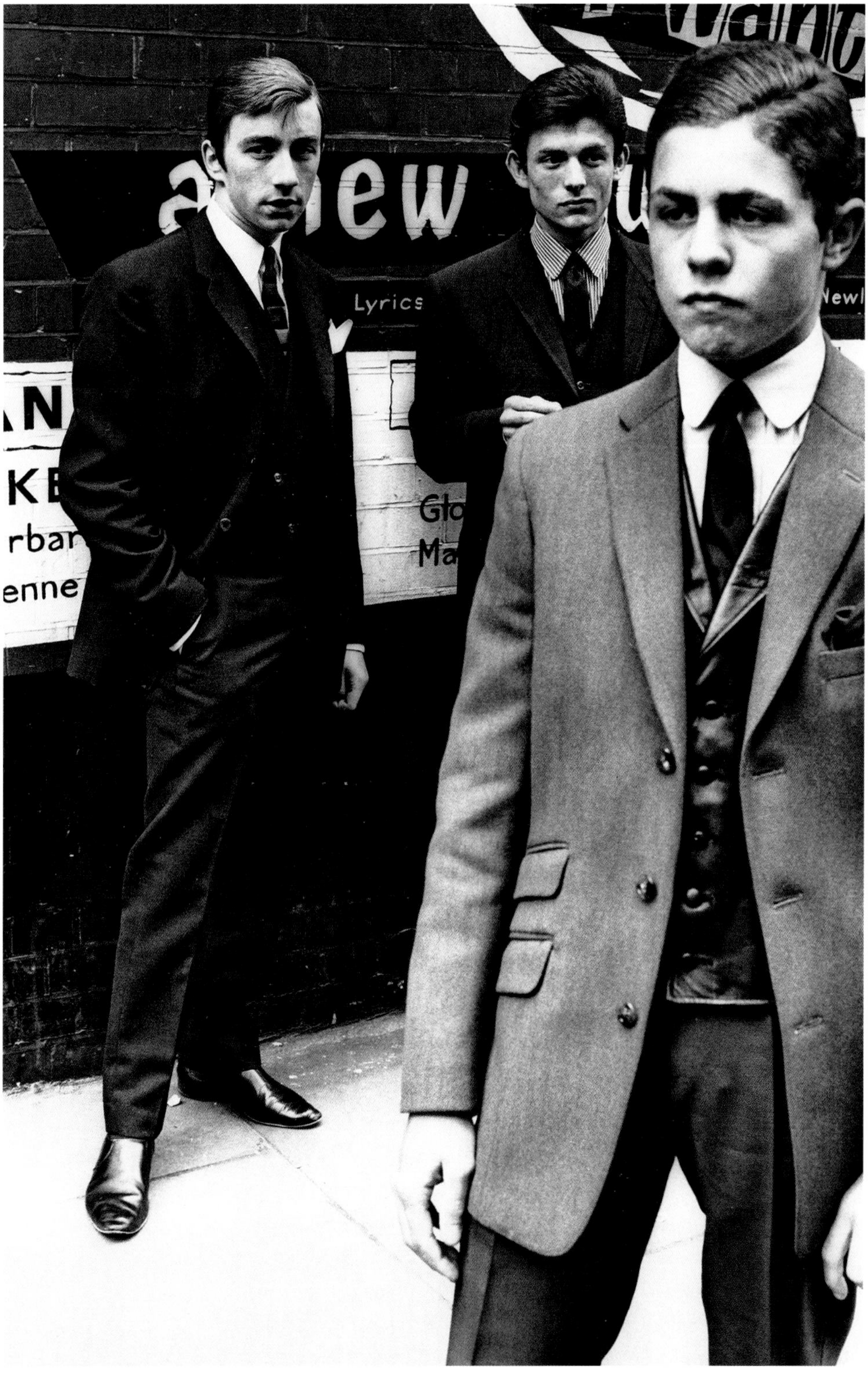
Lyrics

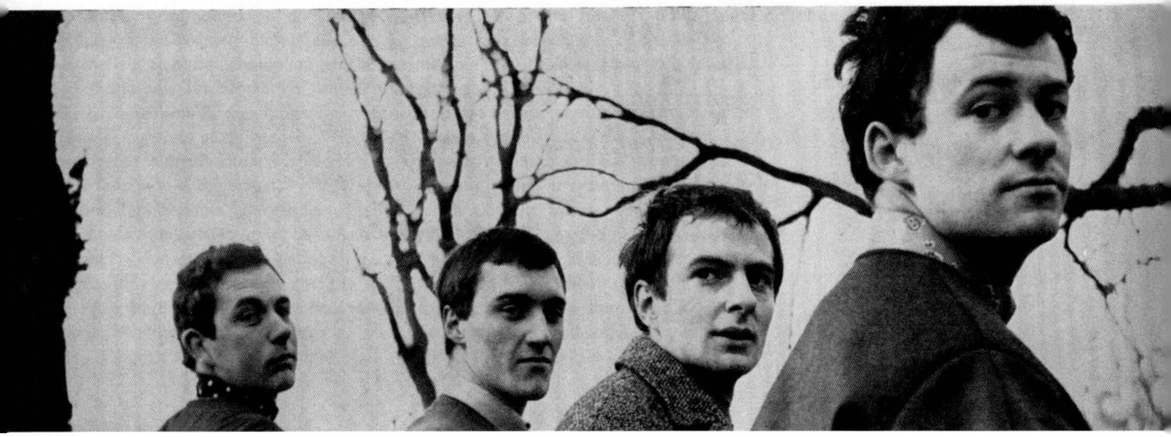

122 Fine-Artz Associates, "Fine-Artz? What or Who are the 'Fine-Artz'?" *Ark* 35, Journal of the Royal College of Art (Spring 1964), detail

Babylone," examined in the Prologue, during the same year that McCullin's photographs and Feld's quotations appeared in *Town*. But Wollheim's analysis has disappeared from intellectual memory, as has been the case with another perceptive and prescient analysis of period "style cults" that followed just a few years later. Between 1961 and 1963, four students at London's Slade School of Art – Terry Atkinson (observed in Chapter Two as an admirer of Hockney's American-style panache) with Roger Jeffs, Bernard Jennings, and John Bowstead – banded together as a collective entity they called Fine-Artz Associates (fig. 122), vowing to make and exhibit work under that name alone.[3] In their demotion of the unique creative personality as the prime artistic currency, they sought to prise apart the two meanings that Modernism had acquired in the London context, keeping the youthful style signifier and discarding the stale fine-art aesthetic that went under the same name.

They went about that task in two phases, both of them promulgated in the receptive pages of *Ark*. The first, launched early in 1964, featured a photograph of the group lined up in a uniformly over-the-shoulder address to the camera, cognate to a rock band's publicity image. Under the headline "What or Who are the 'Fine-Artz'?" Atkinson, Jeffs, Jennings, and Bowstead sustained a caustic jeremiad somewhat at odds with the coolly professional connotations of the term "Associates." "Our art schools," they declared, "are everyday

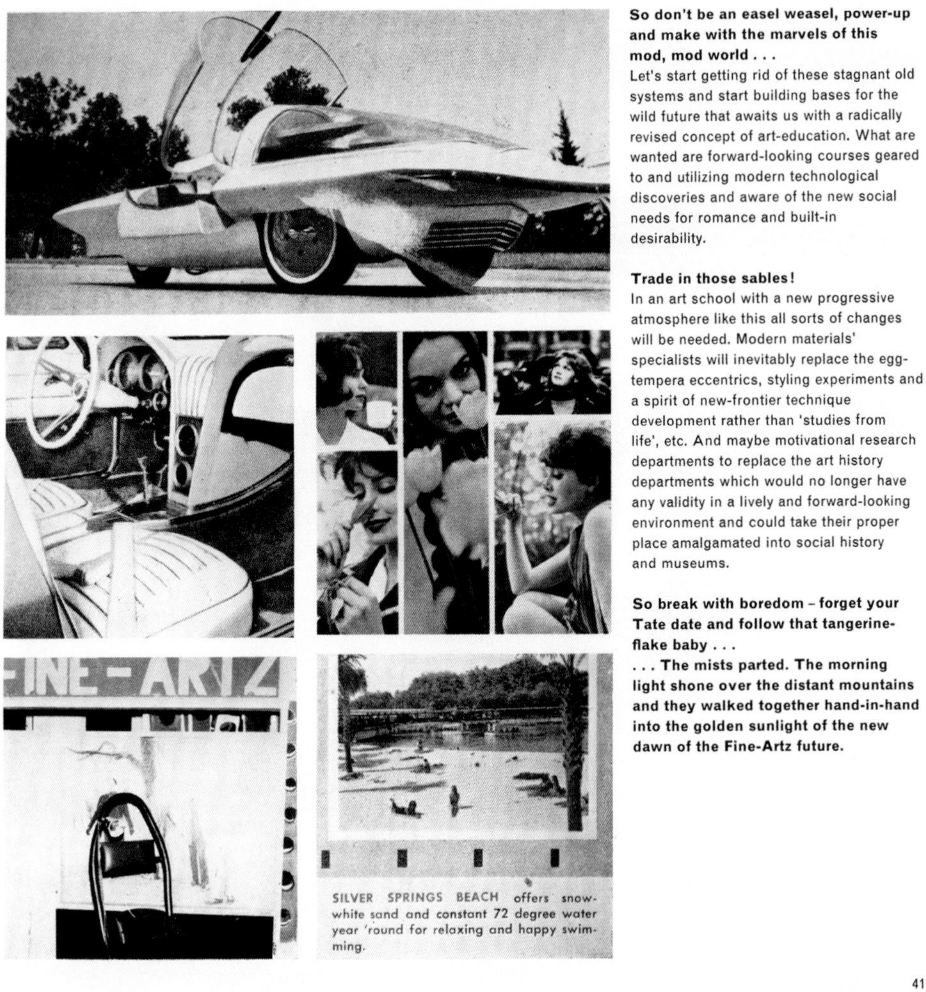

So don't be an easel weasel, power-up and make with the marvels of this mod, mod world . . .
Let's start getting rid of these stagnant old systems and start building bases for the wild future that awaits us with a radically revised concept of art-education. What are wanted are forward-looking courses geared to and utilizing modern technological discoveries and aware of the new social needs for romance and built-in desirability.

Trade in those sables!
In an art school with a new progressive atmosphere like this all sorts of changes will be needed. Modern materials' specialists will inevitably replace the egg-tempera eccentrics, styling experiments and a spirit of new-frontier technique development rather than 'studies from life', etc. And maybe motivational research departments to replace the art history departments which would no longer have any validity in a lively and forward-looking environment and could take their proper place amalgamated into social history and museums.

So break with boredom – forget your Tate date and follow that tangerine-flake baby . . .
. . . The mists parted. The morning light shone over the distant mountains and they walked together hand-in-hand into the golden sunlight of the new dawn of the Fine-Artz future.

41

123 Fine-Artz Associates, "Fine-Artz? What or Who are the 'Fine-Artz'?" *Ark* 35, Journal of the Royal College of Art (Spring 1964), detail

sapping our brightest and most creative young minds," led to "toy with their own subjective meanderings and reduce the impact-laden images and ideas of the outside world to worn-out tradition-bound media."[4] The photo-montage that sprawled over several pages sampled those "impact-laden images," harking back to the taxonomies of commercial imagery pioneered in those *Ark* issues edited by Roger Coleman in 1957 (see Chapter 1), but with an even more positive view of American vernacular modifications of manufactured products (fig. 123). Prominent among these are the space-themed hot-rods of the Los Angeles car customizer, Ed "Big Daddy" Roth, pointing directly to the group's most recent endeavor, the *Kandilac Kustomized Asterod Action Seat*, their manifesto of an "extrovert art." The meager surviving evidence offers little sense of what contemporaries describe as the imposing scale of the piece. Still less can one perceive its flashing, whirling sound-and-light components, the group's name rendered in jagged, billboard-scale lettering, which surmounted another black and white photograph of its members in the sort of staged motion popularized by the Beatles' *Hard Day's Night*. The seat itself (fig. 124), devised with friendly technical help from their allies, Harold Hurrell and David Bainbridge at St. Martin's School, could be moved via its electric-hydraulic substructure at the direction of the mounted aeronautical joystick. An unbeguiled Peter Blake, a juror on the panel for the 1964 *Young Contemporaries* exhibition, banished the apparatus from the painting section, where it had initially been entered.[5]

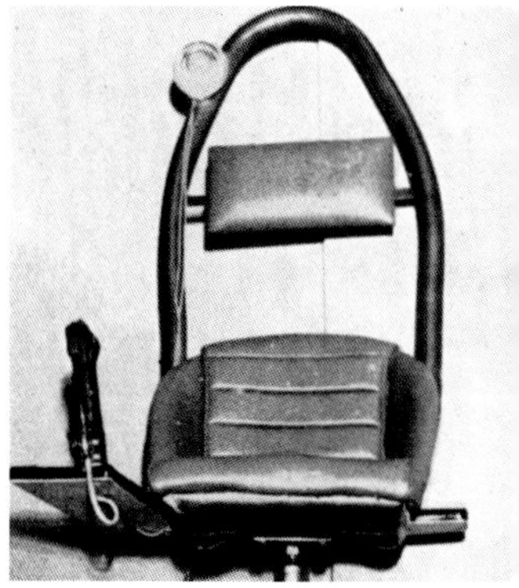

124 Fine-Artz Associates, *Kandilac Kustomized Asterod Action Seat*, 1964, detail (lost)

The accompanying text, channeling Tom Wolfe's famous article on California show cars, proclaims: "it's gonna be a fab kandy-colored, leisure-loving kustom-built for comfort, super-styled and slickline, bright new world," poised to upend once and for all "the eternal gilt-edged security of ... unique object-worship, as propagated by any connoisseur worth his Côtes-du-Rhône."[6] The success of the Kasmin Gallery in 1963, wedded as it was to American abstraction, would have firmly aligned fine-art Modernism with "unique object worship." For Fine Artz, the necessary alternative lay with the descendants of the Soho Modernists, whose appearance John Kasmin paradoxically emulated. The group made this alternative explicit in a second, even more graphically ambitious presentation (fig. 125) in the following issue of *Ark*: "The Fine-Artz View of Teenage Cults." Having initially identified themselves to *Ark* readers as four ex-painters, they had come to prefer the name "stylists," an intentionally anti-fine-art signifier aligned with this second (and last) of their fully achieved projects, one that did not then fall within any category of artwork at all, not even under the loosest available definition.[7] In its pages they recounted their various excursions into what they called "the teenage Netherworld," prefaced by a breakdown of the pertinent nomenclature: Mods, Rockers, Stylists, Mids, and Faces. Quickly dismissing Rockers as utterly past it and despised by all the others, they credit the up-to-date cults with "certain

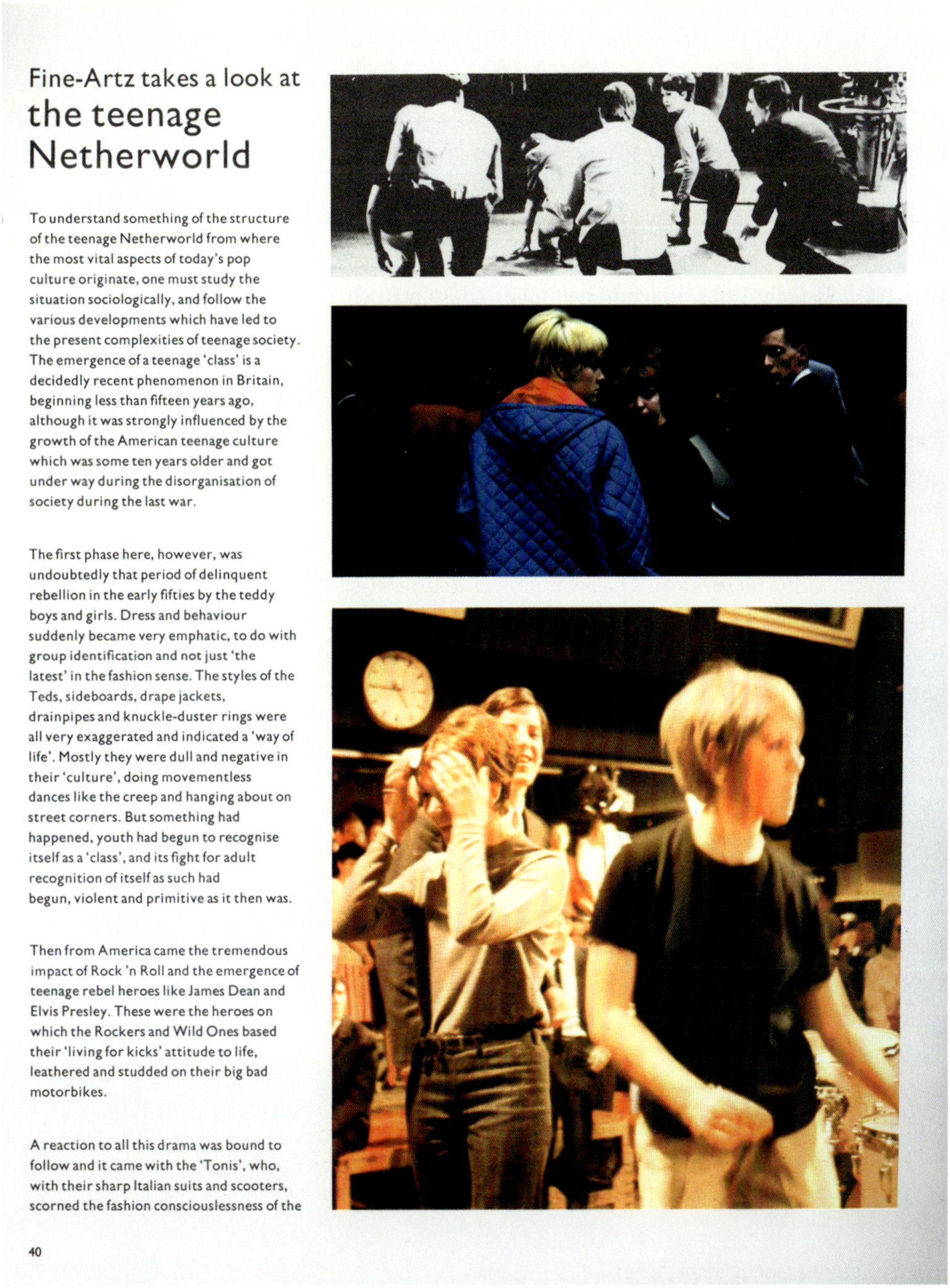

Fine-Artz takes a look at

the teenage Netherworld

To understand something of the structure of the teenage Netherworld from where the most vital aspects of today's pop culture originate, one must study the situation sociologically, and follow the various developments which have led to the present complexities of teenage society. The emergence of a teenage 'class' is a decidedly recent phenomenon in Britain, beginning less than fifteen years ago, although it was strongly influenced by the growth of the American teenage culture which was some ten years older and got under way during the disorganisation of society during the last war.

The first phase here, however, was undoubtedly that period of delinquent rebellion in the early fifties by the teddy boys and girls. Dress and behaviour suddenly became very emphatic, to do with group identification and not just 'the latest' in the fashion sense. The styles of the Teds, sideboards, drape jackets, drainpipes and knuckle-duster rings were all very exaggerated and indicated a 'way of life'. Mostly they were dull and negative in their 'culture', doing movementless dances like the creep and hanging about on street corners. But something had happened, youth had begun to recognise itself as a 'class', and its fight for adult recognition of itself as such had begun, violent and primitive as it then was.

Then from America came the tremendous impact of Rock 'n Roll and the emergence of teenage rebel heroes like James Dean and Elvis Presley. These were the heroes on which the Rockers and Wild Ones based their 'living for kicks' attitude to life, leathered and studded on their big bad motorbikes.

A reaction to all this drama was bound to follow and it came with the 'Tonis', who, with their sharp Italian suits and scooters, scorned the fashion consciouslessness of the

40

125 Fine-Artz Associates, "The Fine-Artz View of Teenage Cults," *Ark* 36, Journal of the Royal College of Art (Summer 1964), detail things in common; they are highly fashion-conscious, environment-conscious, and music-conscious; in all these respects they are extremely selective and sophisticated compared with their predecessors."[8]

Any use of the term Mod would have come into further disrepute by its diffusion among mainstream voices, conspicuous among them the prominent polymath Jonathan Miller. Reviewing the 1964 *New Generation* painting show at the Whitechapel Gallery, Miller actually proposed "Mod" Art ("cool, 'go' and very Purple Heart") as a terminological replacement for Pop. Having evoked an amphetamine rush ("Purple Heart"), Miller seemed to be trying to write as if he had dipped into his own physician's stash of pills: "There is now a curious cultural community, breathlessly à la mod, where Lord Snowdon and other desperadoes of grainy blow-ups and bled-off layout jostle with commercial-art-school Mersey stars, window-dressers and Carnaby street pants-peddlers. Style is the thing here – Taste 64 – a cool line and the witty insolence of youth." He even likens the contrast between "the pale arctic wit of this group" and "the loutish attack of the Abstract Expressionists" to the seaside rumbles between Mods and Rockers.[9]

Faced with a farrago of this order in as conspicuous an outlet as the *New Statesman*, it is no wonder that Fine-Artz would run a mile from Mod as any sort of useful descriptor or point of identification. The term they favored for themselves, "Stylists," had come to designate the habits and aspect of the mid-sixties cult closest to the original Soho Modernists. In the disparaging words of one young female informant they quote in "Fine-Artz View": "unlike the Stylists, the Mods dress alike," the latter group having evolved into a much larger and younger formation, with the Stylists being a smaller, trend-creating leadership, older than the newest Mods and thus closer to the artists themselves. Fine-Artz Associates took themselves to Stylist haunts like the East End scooter-customizing shop run by Eddy Grimstead. Their conversations with Grimstead revealed to them the volatility of purchasable consumer goods under pressure from a selective and sophisticated clientele: five years before, Grimstead had "noticed that sales were dropping and decided that the manufacturers were at fault, not having changed the styles of their

Fine-Artz takes a look at

kustomizing UK

Along with dress, dancing and beat music, the motor-scooter has become one of the prime objects in the teenagers' attempt to produce an environment of their own choosing and taste. Scooters first became popular in the late 50's, when the 'Italian' look came in as part of the first reaction to the primitives of teenage society, the 'Rockers', who were using their motorbikes as weapons in a violent stand against adult society. Recently scooters have arrived again, but with the more imaginative approach of the 'Mods' who, not satisfied in buying what was there, have personalized them and given them that distinctive baroque look that teenage culture forms so often seem to have. But in the East End of London more radical changes are coming in.

44

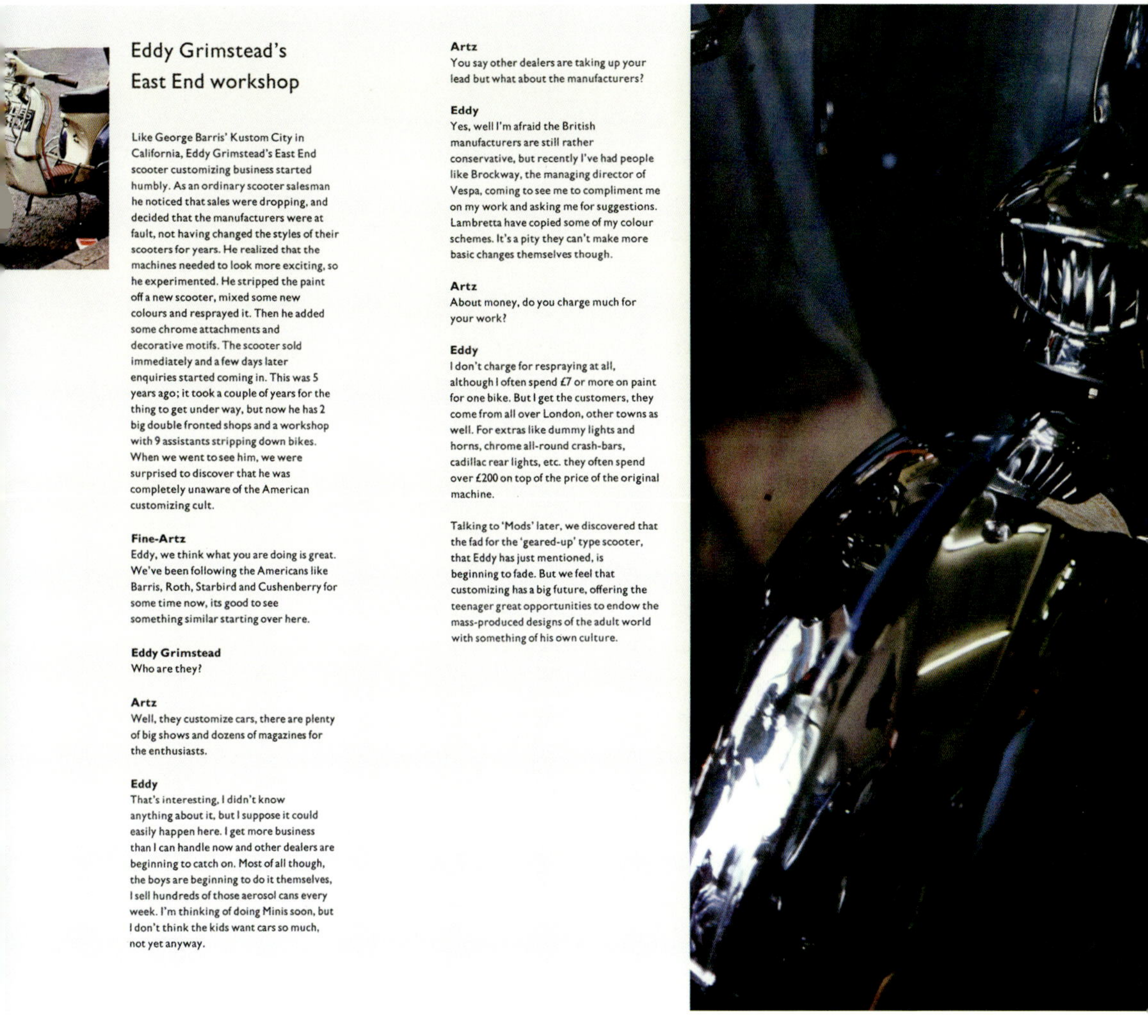

Eddy Grimstead's East End workshop

Like George Barris' Kustom City in California, Eddy Grimstead's East End scooter customizing business started humbly. As an ordinary scooter salesman he noticed that sales were dropping, and decided that the manufacturers were at fault, not having changed the styles of their scooters for years. He realized that the machines needed to look more exciting, so he experimented. He stripped the paint off a new scooter, mixed some new colours and resprayed it. Then he added some chrome attachments and decorative motifs. The scooter sold immediately and a few days later enquiries started coming in. This was 5 years ago; it took a couple of years for the thing to get under way, but now he has 2 big double fronted shops and a workshop with 9 assistants stripping down bikes. When we went to see him, we were surprised to discover that he was completely unaware of the American customizing cult.

Fine-Artz
Eddy, we think what you are doing is great. We've been following the Americans like Barris, Roth, Starbird and Cushenberry for some time now, its good to see something similar starting over here.

Eddy Grimstead
Who are they?

Artz
Well, they customize cars, there are plenty of big shows and dozens of magazines for the enthusiasts.

Eddy
That's interesting, I didn't know anything about it, but I suppose it could easily happen here. I get more business than I can handle now and other dealers are beginning to catch on. Most of all though, the boys are beginning to do it themselves, I sell hundreds of those aerosol cans every week. I'm thinking of doing Minis soon, but I don't think the kids want cars so much, not yet anyway.

Artz
You say other dealers are taking up your lead but what about the manufacturers?

Eddy
Yes, well I'm afraid the British manufacturers are still rather conservative, but recently I've had people like Brockway, the managing director of Vespa, coming to see me to compliment me on my work and asking me for suggestions. Lambretta have copied some of my colour schemes. It's a pity they can't make more basic changes themselves though.

Artz
About money, do you charge much for your work?

Eddy
I don't charge for respraying at all, although I often spend £7 or more on paint for one bike. But I get the customers, they come from all over London, other towns as well. For extras like dummy lights and horns, chrome all-round crash-bars, cadillac rear lights, etc. they often spend over £200 on top of the price of the original machine.

Talking to 'Mods' later, we discovered that the fad for the 'geared-up' type scooter, that Eddy has just mentioned, is beginning to fade. But we feel that customizing has a big future, offering the teenager great opportunities to endow the mass-produced designs of the adult world with something of his own culture.

126 Fine-Artz Associates, "The Fine-Artz View of Teenage Cults," *Ark* 36, Journal of the Royal College of Art (Summer 1964), detail

scooters for years."[10] So he began by stripping and repainting the bodywork of one scooter, then adding chrome accessories. The first one sold instantly, so alert was the Stylist network, with a flood of inquiries to follow. A representative from Vespa had been around, he said, and the Italian manufacturer had begun copying his colors for the UK market. A bold color close-up of chrome detailing (fig. 126) dominated one page of the *Ark* layout, an item of "mass art" in Lawrence Alloway's original sense of the term, inflected by Fine-Artz but originating in Grimstead's garage as a response to the demands and decisions of hundreds of self-aware young riders. In contrast to the outlook of the Independent Group cohort, Fine-Artz

Associates were fascinated less by material accessories and more by the people – like a club owner they interviewed, often prosaic actors who were making the most of the potential latent in such objects, fostering in the process a progression of charismatic identity formations, stemming from the first Soho Modernists.

But to call these groups "identity formations" sounds a bloodless, social-scientific note, against which the Fine-Artz terms "netherworld" and "cult" seem preferable – not in spite of their gothic and mystery-mongering connotations but because of them. Such terms acknowledge that there remained much to be learned from these phenomena, that there were enigmas needing to be puzzled out. A sense of mystery attended the experiences of those within the netherworld as well, where sightings of strangers possessed comparable significance to interactions among mates: a heretofore unknown Blue Note LP seen cradled under an arm, a new arrangement of pockets and vents on a bespoke suit, or a novel ornament on a Lambretta disappearing round the corner. Cults constituted themselves by shared predisposition to alert acuity and perpetual refinement of self-presentation in response to every input of new information.

Fine-Artz Associates thus felt themselves in no position to gainsay the enthusiasms that manifested themselves in the Netherworld, ceding sophisticated selectivity to the primary social actors. Never demeaning the individual participants they encountered, their project implicitly treated the cults as a network of distributed intelligence, a kind of organic computer for processing the yet unknown effects and possibilities for meaning latent in the economic machinery of consumer-product manufacture. Any given moment of style creation represents just a snapshot of a process typified by high aesthetic self-consciousness, concern for coherence and contained complexity, and an evolution driven by self-critique, that is, by the core qualities that one expects objects of fine art (or Fine-Artz) to exemplify.

There appears to have been an unspoken collective decision by the Stylists that anything marked as trendy be scrupulously avoided. "Carnaby Street," in the words of one, "was far too

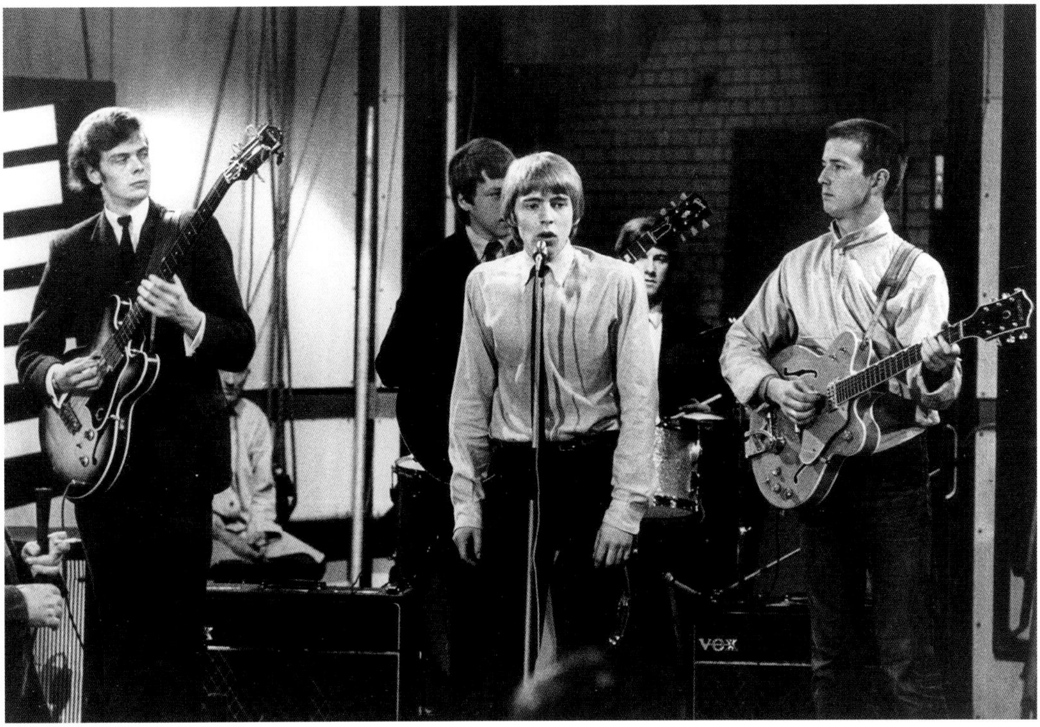

127 Eric Clapton (right) performing with the Yardbirds on Independent Television's *Ready Steady Go!*, 22 May 1965

commercial. I never bought anything out of there. I went off and created my own things ... Carnaby Street was a mass thing – the Beatles and those types went there."[11] If not custom-made, favored items were invariably of a style that went back decades in key instances and persist unchanged to the present day; how teenage does a pair of oxblood "Royal" brogues from the Loake shoe company appear, or a Fred Perry tennis shirt, and the Baracuta G9 "Harrington" jacket, as its design had persisted unchanged since 1937? That last item, worn by one exemplary figure, can help trace the fortunes of the Mod aesthetic life during its apparent eclipse in the later 1960s. That figure, the musician Eric Clapton, emerged in 1964 as the lead guitarist in the Yardbirds, a London band then devoted to the hard core of black American blues. In this phase, the Surrey-born Clapton had displayed impeccably Mod choices in both dress and coiffure. In period photographs of the band, Clapton wear what looks to be a nondescript waist-length jacket (fig. 127), which he insists on zipping to the throat and buttoning over the high collar. He combines the item with an even shorter version of the "college-boy" haircut favored by

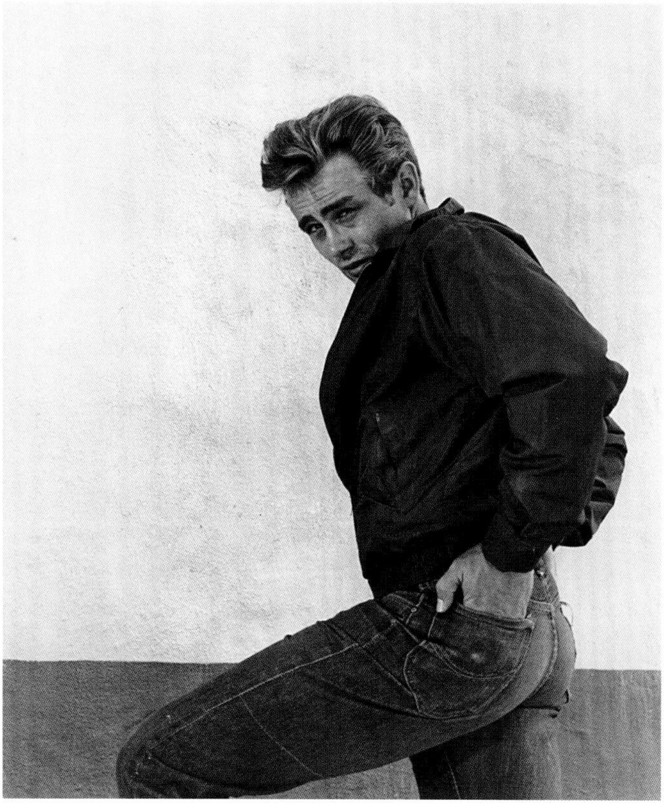

128 James Dean in *Rebel Without a Cause* (dir. Nicolas Ray), 1955

the early Modernists. Donned like a kind of armor in defiance of the heat in crowded venues, the jacket was not just any piece of outerwear. It went under a variety of names, the Ivy or after 1964 the Harrington, which referred to a television character played by Ryan O'Neal, who always wore one on the primetime soap *Peyton Place*. Officially a Baracuta G9, it was of English manufacture, even if its reputation had been made across the Atlantic by O'Neal and other style exemplars such as James Dean (fig. 128), Elvis Presley, and Steve McQueen. Along with Clapton's military-length hair, that particular Mod-identified garment signaled his hold-out position on the exclusive side of authentic black music: a Modernist affinity so fierce that it compelled him to leave the Yardbirds in mid-1965 on the day that their first chart hit, the pop tune "For Your Love," was released.

After a spell in the band of an older blues devotee, John Mayall's Bluesbreakers, Clapton was drawn by the heavy rock that had emerged as a powerful aesthetic and commercial option by 1966. The sheer musical prowess and literary inclination of Clapton's two partners in the power trio Cream, the bassist and singer Jack Bruce and the drummer Ginger Baker, drew him over the line from faithful emulation of African-American blues into both Baroque rock extravagance and the flamboyant hippie trappings that went with it (fig. 129). Gone was his old understatement. His hair now cascaded in permanent-waved ringlets, while the inflected outlines of his embroidered coats and flared velvet trousers came courtesy of one or another of the boutiques lately sprung up on the King's Road.

Out of this countercultural embrace came such supreme Pop objects as the Beatles' album *Sergeant Pepper's Lonely Hearts Club Band*, released in mid-1967. The bandmates dressed up in their satin military uniforms and turned over the production of its famous album sleeve to Robert Fraser, the old Etonian dealer in Pop Art.[12] Under that blanket of mass countercultural success, the continuation of the Modernist principles could be hard to discern. Paolo Hewitt writes of the years from about 1965 to 1968 as the phase that lacked a name, "but what this generation signified – consciously or not – was ... a true return to the Mod principles of exclusivity and

129 Eric Clapton, photographed by Robert Whitaker, 1967

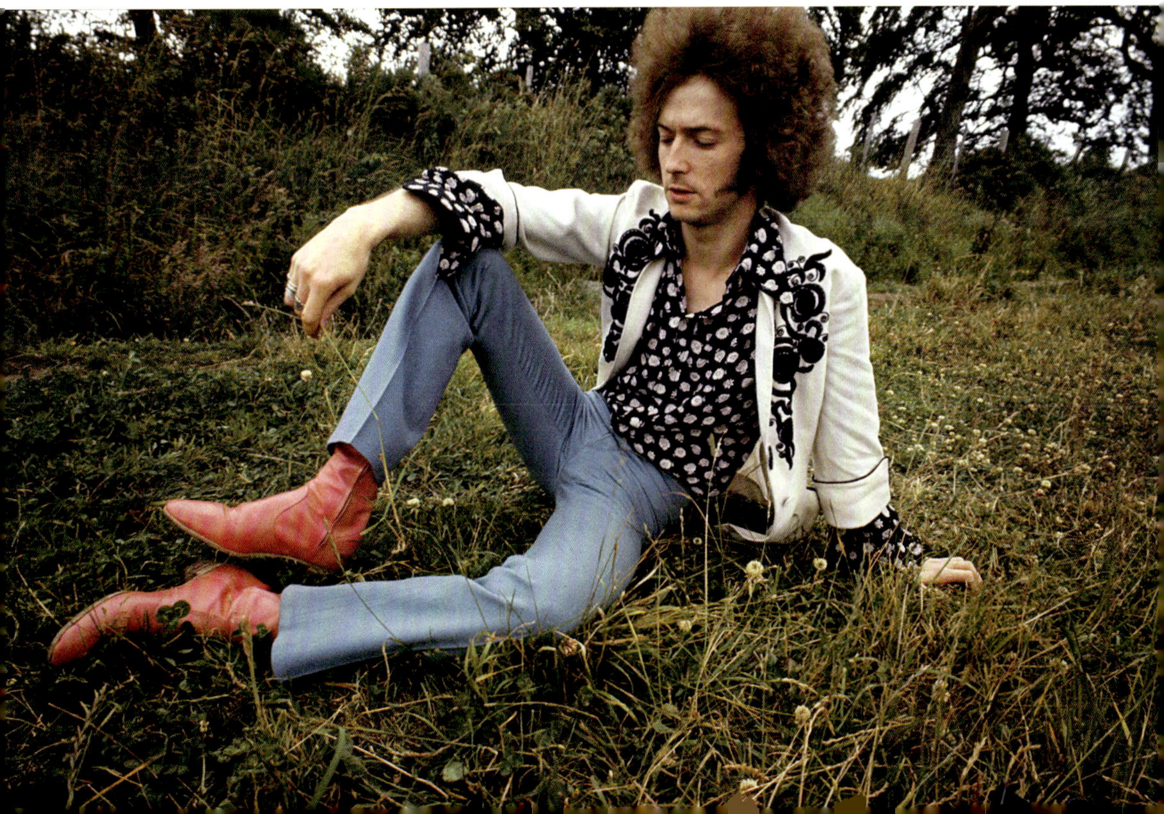

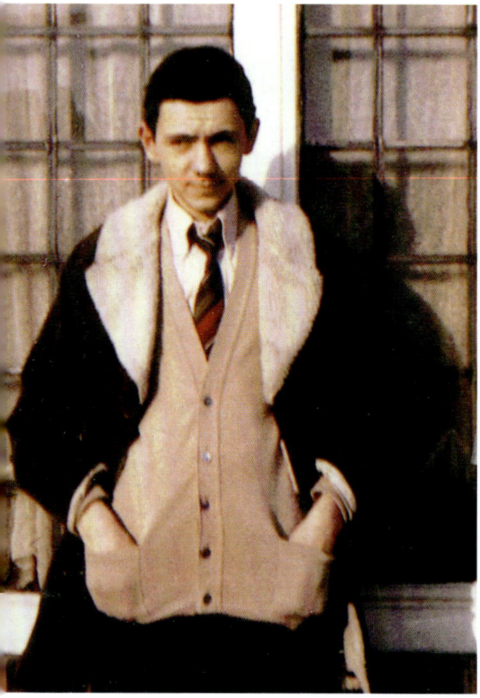

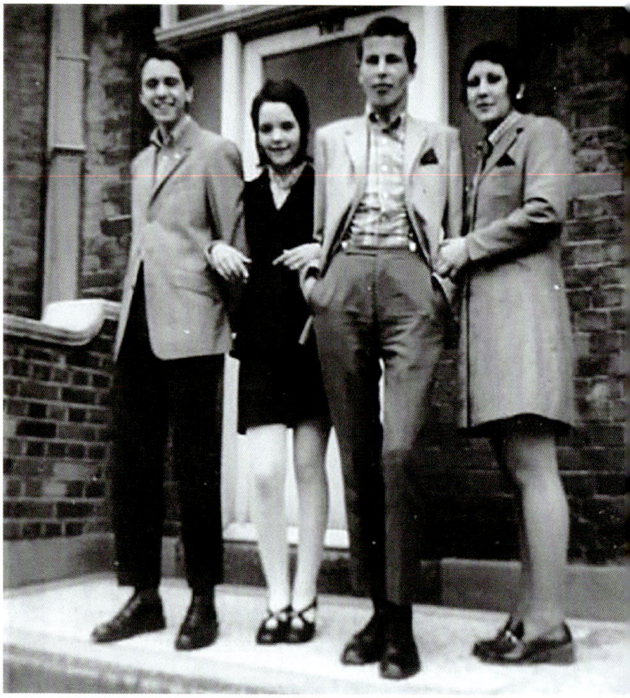

secrecy."[13] The buttoned-up aspect that Clapton abandoned for the rock-god style of Granny Takes a Trip had exemplified those Mod norms of extreme discretion and discrimination. If the guitarist had felt compelled to let them go, however, others were more than prepared to keep up and refine an increasingly contained and uninflected profile. One of Hewitt's informants recalls saying to his mates in July 1967, "Look at these Mods here, they've got their hair very short now," adding the observation that preferences in music were driving two factions apart: "You had the people that were Mods and grew their hair and turned into hippies. And the ones that didn't want to do that turned Skinhead and went into Reggae."[14]

130 Kevin Rowland, Harrow, London, 1968

131 Mods, Baron's Court, London, 1969

Such virtual invisibility to anyone outside their number harks back to the first Modernist principles of the late 1950s, that is, the defiant discretion in dress cultivated by American black musicians of the order of Miles Davis and Lee Morgan, whose coded defiance of racial subordination struck such a chord with their young British admirers. In keeping with this ethic, the contributors to these later Mod cults – even prime innovators – have remained unknown by name to the wider world. One exception is the musician Kevin Rowland (fig. 130), later of Dexy's Midnight Runners fame, who provides perhaps the richest written memoir of this period in the evolution of Mod, observed from the vantage point of far northwest London.

Rowland specifies October 1968 – at the crest of the hippie onslaught – as the moment when he first spotted, in his words, "the occasional guy who had this subtle American look." A few, by the next year, had their hair shaved off completely: "Against the background of London in 1969," he marvels, "it was completely and utterly outrageous." Rowland presents the summer of that year (fig. 131) as a brief, radiantly remembered moment of teenage bliss: "all the factors came together at the right time:" he declares, "the beautiful clothes, the explosion of all those great reggae records, which we listened to exclusively. That's when I felt alive, part of something. I was aware this was my time. We danced good – often all in a line, American-style shirts, Sta-Prest trousers with braces and brogues, loafers and Gibsons ... "[15]

But then the roof fell in. Late in the summer of 1969, the *Daily Mirror* travestied the scene under the subheading "What Is a Skinhead,"[16] indelibly impressing on public consciousness what Rowland rues as "the numbskull caricature ... a cartoon figure dressed in white T-shirt, braces, jeans, and big boots." In a mass-media-driven feedback loop, the cartoon (fig. 132) created by the press became real: as Rowland puts it, "A slightly younger version of ready-made skinheads – girls too appeared overnight, bless 'em (fig. 133). I hope they felt part of something." But he adds, "what really pissed me off" is that his own splendid, self-fashioned style current, the last to stem organically from the original Soho Modernists, "died before it had been given a chance to grow. *This was the great lost look* [emphasis in original]. The caricatures of skinhead had prevented natural development and destroyed all subtlety, so I guess the whole progression had to fizzle and die."[17]

While the progression fizzled and died, however, its corpse achieved another sort of shadow life by becoming an object of academic scrutiny as the centerpiece object of inquiry for the emerging discipline of Cultural Studies. Its signature term "subculture" has been avoided here for a number of reasons.

The simplest one is that the qualifying suffix "sub," in the sense of partial or dependent, implies that the entity so designated is a derivative artifact of something larger, prior, and determining, in this case, an unexamined mega-structure like "the working class" or the "parent culture." The music critic Ian Penman is more scathing on the subject where Mods are concerned: "Even the word 'subculture'," he complains, "suggests soil, shadow, dirt; airless oubliettes; greasy rungs leading down into a Harry Lime exile."[18] In its original, early-twentieth-century use by sociologists of the so-called Chicago School, the term signified the invidious attributes of deviance or delinquency. The initial moment of Culture Studies in the 1970s necessarily sought to remove such judgmental connotations, but substituted what was in the end ascription of rather pathetic dependency and self-deception. Only rarely captured by the academic observers of the evolving style cults is the possibility that they could surpass the "parent" culture and hold it up to skeptical scrutiny, thus too little of Wollheim's

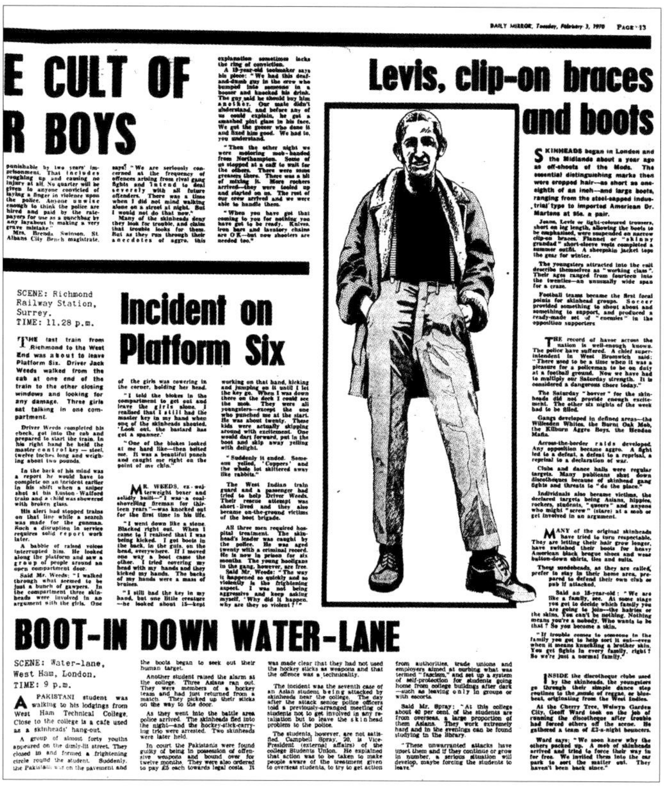

DAILY MIRROR, Tuesday, February 3, 1970 PAGE 13

E CULT OF R BOYS

punishable by two years' imprisonment. That includes roughing up and causing no injury at all. No quarter will be given to anyone convicted of laying a finger in violence upon the police. Anyone unwise enough to think the police are hired and paid by the ratepayers for use as a punchbag by any layabout is making a very grave mistake."

Mrs. Brenda Swinson, St Albans City Bench magistrate, says: "We are seriously concerned at the frequency of offences arising from rival gang fights and intend to deal severely with all future offenders. There was a time when I did not mind walking alone on a street at night. But I would not do that now."

Many of the skinheads deny they look for trouble, and claim that trouble looks for them. But as they run through their anecdotes of aggro, this explanation sometimes lacks the ring of conviction.

A 19-year-old toolmaker says his piece: "We had this deaf-and-dumb guy in the crew who bumped into someone in a boozer and knocked his drink. The guy said he should buy him another. Our mate didn't understand, and before any of us could explain, he got a smashed pint glass in his face. We got the greaser who done it and fixed him good. We had to, you understand.

"Then the other night we were motoring mob-handed from Northampton. Some of us stopped at a caff to wait for the others. There were some greasers there. There was a bit of mixing it. More rockers arrived—they were tooled up and started on us. The rest of our crew arrived and we were able to handle them.

"When you have got that coming to you for nothing you have got to be ready. Knives, iron bars and lavatory chains are O K—but now shooters are needed too."

SCENE: Richmond Railway Station, Surrey.
TIME: 11.28 p.m.

Incident on Platform Six

THE last train from Richmond to the West End was about to leave Platform Six. Driver Jack Weeds walked from the cab at one end of the train to the other closing windows and looking for any damage. Three girls sat talking in one compartment.

Driver Weeds completed his check, got into the cab and prepared to start the train. In his right hand he held the master control key — steel, twelve inches long and weighing about two pounds.

In the back of his mind was a report he would have to complete on an incident earlier in his shift when a sniper shot at his Euston-Watford train and a child was showered with broken glass.

His alert had stopped trains on that line while a search was made for the gunman. Such a disruption in service requires solid report work later.

A babble of raised voices interrupted him. He looked along the platform and saw a group of people around an open compartment door.

Said Mr. Weeds: "I walked through what seemed to be just a bunch of gawpers. In the compartment three skinheads were involved in an argument with the girls. One of the girls was cowering in the corner, holding her head.

"I told the blokes in the compartment to get out and leave the girls alone. I realised that I still had the master key in my hand when one of the skinheads shouted, 'Look out, the bastard has got a spanner.'

"One of the blokes looked at me hard like—then belted me. It was a beautiful punch and caught me right on the point of my chin."

MR. WEEDS, ex-welterweight boxer and solidly built—"I was a coal-shovelling fireman for thirteen years"—was knocked out for the first time in his life.

"I went down like a stone. Blacked right out. When I came to I realised that I was being kicked. I got boots in the back, in the guts, on the head, everywhere. If I moved one way a boot came the other. I tried covering my head with my hands and they kicked my hands. The backs of my hands were a mass of bruises.

"I still had the key in my hand, but one little creature—he looked about 15—kept working on that hand, kicking and jumping on it until I let the key go. When I was down there on the deck I could see the mob. They were all youngsters—except the one who punched me at the start. He was about twenty. These kids were actually skipping around with excitement. One would dart forward, put in the boot and skip away yelling with delight.

"Suddenly it ended. Someone yelled, 'Coppers' and the whole lot skittered away like rabbits."

The West Indian train guard and a passenger had tried to help Driver Weeds. Their rescue attempt was short-lived and they also became on-the-ground victims of the boot brigade.

All three men required hospital treatment. The skinhead's leader was caught by the police. He was aged twenty with a criminal record. He is now in prison for six months. The young hooligans in the gang, however, are free.

Said Mr. Weeds: "The way it happened so quickly and so violently is the frightening aspect. I was not being aggressive and keep asking myself, 'Why did it happen, why are they so violent?'"

Levis, clip-on braces and boots

SKINHEADS began in London and the Midlands about a year ago as off-shoots of the Mods. The essential distinguishing marks then were cropped hair—as short as one-eighth of an inch—and large boots, ranging from the steel-capped industrial type to imported American Dr. Martens at 85s. a pair.

Jeans, Levis or light-coloured trousers, short on leg length, allowing the boots to be emphasised, were suspended on narrow clip-on braces. Flannel or "skinny grandad" short-sleeve vests completed a summer outfit. A sheepskin jacket tops the gear for winter.

The youngsters attracted into the cult describe themselves as "working class". Their ages ranged from fourteen into the twenties—an unusually wide span for a craze.

Football teams became the first focal points for skinhead groups. Soccer provided something to shout about and something to support, and produced a ready-made set of "enemies" in the opposition supporters.

THE record of havoc across the nation is well-enough known. The police have suffered. A chief superintendent in West Bromwich said: "There used to be a time when it was a pleasure for a policeman to be on duty at a football ground. Now we have had to multiply our Saturday strength. It is considered a dangerous chore today."

The Saturday "bovver" for the skinheads did not provide enough excitement. The other six nights of the week had to be filled.

Gangs developed in defined areas—the Willesden Whites, the Burnt Oak Mob, the Kilburn Aggro Boys, the Hendon Mafia.

Across-the-border raids developed. Any opposition became aggro. A fight led to a defeat, a defeat to a reprisal, a reprisal to a declaration of war.

Clubs and dance halls were regular targets. Many publicans shut down discotheques because of skinhead gang fights and threats to "do the place."

Individuals also became victims, the declared targets being Asians, hippies, rockers, students, "queers" and anyone who might "screw" (stare) at a mob or get involved in an argument.

MANY of the original skinheads have tried to turn respectable. They are letting their hair grow longer, have switched their boots for heavy American black brogue shoes and wear button-down shirts, ties and suits.

These suedeheads, as they are called, prefer to stay in their home area, prepared to defend their own club or pub if attacked.

Said an 18-year-old: "We are like a family, see. At some stage you got to decide which family you are going to join—the hairies or the skins. You can't be nothing. Nothing means you're a nobody. Who wants to be that? So you become a skin.

"If trouble comes to someone in the family you got to help sort it out—even when it means knuckling a brother skin. You get fights in every family, right? So we're just a normal family."

INSIDE the discotheque clubs used by the skinheads, the youngsters go through their simple dance step routines to the music of reggae, or bluebeat, originating from the West Indies.

At the Cherry Tree, Welwyn Garden City, Geoff Ward took on the job of running the discotheque after trouble had forced others off the scene. He gathered a team of £3-a-night bouncers.

Ward says: "We soon knew why the others packed up. A mob of skinheads arrived and tried to force their way in for free. We invited them into the car park to sort the matter out. They haven't been back since."

BOOT-IN DOWN WATER-LANE

SCENE: Water-lane, West Ham, London.
TIME: 9 p.m.

A PAKISTANI student was walking to his lodgings from West Ham Technical College. Close to the college is a cafe used as a skinheads' hang-out.

A group of almost forty youths appeared on the dimly-lit street. They closed in and formed a frightening circle round the student. Suddenly, the Pakistani was on the pavement and the boots began to seek out their human target.

Another student raised the alarm at the college. Three Asians ran out. They were members of a hockey team and had just returned from a match. They picked up their sticks on the way to the door.

As they went into the battle area police arrived. The skinheads fled into the night—and the hockey-stick-carrying trio were arrested. Two skinheads were later held.

In court the Pakistanis were found guilty of being in possession of offensive weapons and bound over for twelve months. They were also ordered to pay £5 each towards legal costs. It was made clear that they had not used the hockey sticks as weapons and that the offence was a technicality.

The incident was the seventh case of an Asian student being attacked by skinheads near the college. The day after the attack senior police officers told a previously-arranged meeting of students not to get involved in any retaliation but to leave the skinhead problem to the police.

The students, however, are not satisfied. Campbell Spray, 20, is Vice-President (external affairs) of the college Students Union. He explained that action was to be taken to make people aware of the treatment given to overseas students, to try to get action from authorities, trade unions and employers aimed at curbing what was termed "fascism," and set up a system of self-protection for students going home from college buildings after dark—such as leaving only in groups or with escorts.

Said Mr. Spray: "At this college about 40 per cent. of the students are from overseas, a large proportion of them Asians. They work extremely hard and in the evenings can be found studying in the library.

"These unwarranted attacks have upset them and if they continue or grow in number, a serious situation will develop, maybe forcing the students to leave."

132 *Daily Mirror*, 3 February 1970

133 Two young people wearing skinhead fashions (Glenda Peake and Tony Hughes), photographed by Doreen Spooner, Finchley, 7th October 1969

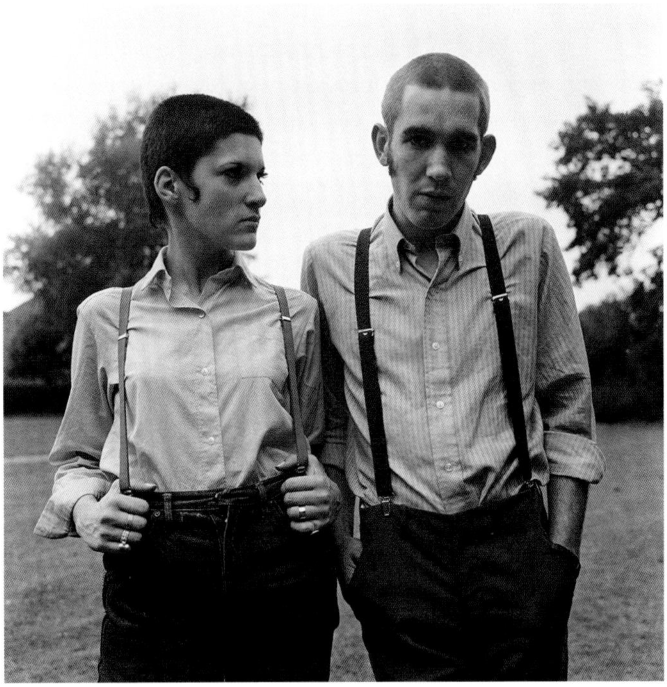

admiration for the proto-Mod hero created by his friend Colin MacInnes: "The Absolute Beginner," as he put it, "bids fair to be the hero not only of the Non-starter but also of the High Flyer."[19]

The social analyst who put this model on the map was the somewhat unheralded educational scholar Phil Cohen, then doing social work in the East End of London, who delivered a landmark presentation in 1972 to the seminar of the Centre for Contemporary Cultural Studies at Birmingham University, the cradle of this emerging field. Cohen had put together an analytical paper in an effort to comprehend the behavior of the young Skinhead males around him. Others have become more famously linked to the concept, but the essentials of the subcultural model were already articulated in Cohen's presentation, though he says he thought little more about it after leaving the Birmingham session and returning to London.[20]

Titling his presentation "Subcultural Conflict and Working-Class Community," Cohen influentially characterized the earlier Mod styles "as an attempt to realize, but in an imaginary relation, the conditions of existence of the socially mobile white-collar worker."[21] This bare formulation, in keeping with Mark Feld's pro-Tory quip, remained more influential over the years than the contemporaneous work carried out at the Centre by Dick Hebdige. The latter indeed addressed the point: "The mods are often described as exploring the upward option, but it seems probable that this has been deduced incorrectly from the mod's fanatical devotion to appearance and the tendency to boast when in a blocked or amphetamine-induced state."[22] At moments, Hebdige can be counted among the few in the Cultural Studies milieu to carry on (knowingly or unknowingly) where Wollheim had left off, as when he observes, "The mod's adoption of a sharp but neat and visually understated style can be explained ... by his desire to do justice to the mysterious complexity of the metropolis in his personal demeanour ... "[23]

No theoretical framework, however sophisticated, can be mapped without remainder onto such elusive, essentially literary apperceptions. Cohen's model presented his colleagues with a decisive advance in the ways that the discriminations of the style cultists could be understood. Taking advantage of French-derived semiotic theory, he had extracted the whole subject area from the trivializing category of juvenile fads, regarding with commensurable seriousness every identifiable element in a vernacular stylistic formation, each of which counted toward its production of meaning and message. What was more, reality appeared to be cooperating via the roughly contemporaneous emergence of a post-Mod formation pared down in its stylistic attributes so as to match almost exactly the inherent, inevitable schematism of the model. Others besides Kevin Rowland have described the boots-and-braces Skinhead figure as a numbskull travesty of its complex antecedents, which had flourished under necessary conditions of Mod discretion. The previous exploitative panic promoted by the tabloids – egging on the Mod–Rocker dust-ups of the mid-1960s – had driven the later Stylists underground; the 1969 Skinhead affair in the press then weakened the more fragile remaining network to the point of extinction.

The reduced form that remained met the needs of the Cultural Studies template for reductive simplification and for subjects who could safely be anatomized with analytical condescension. The comparatively miniaturized style and ritual syndrome of adolescent Skinheads thus offered itself as a bridge entity, one that condensed a larger pattern of social behavior into a pattern of vivid if impoverished stylistic coherence. From that foundation, Cohen and others built such abstracted definitions of subculture as "a compromise (imaginary) solution to two contradictory needs: the need to create and express *autonomy and difference* [emphasis in original] from parents and, by extension, their culture, and the need to maintain the security of existing ego defences and the parental identifications which support them."[24] There are a lot of parents in that formula – an emphasis on childish dependency that follows logically from the sub- prefix. In the title of Cohen's seminal paper, it is revealing that the adjective "subcultural" modifies the disturbing term "conflict;" while "working class" is attached to the reassuring "community." One wonders what Rowland, in his golden summer of 1969, would have made of these clinical paradigms; Cohen, though, parries the question in advance by reminding his readers "that subcultures are symbolic structures and must not be confused with the actual young people who are its bearers and supports."[25] Would Rowland have found this relegation any more palatable? Bearers and supports? The language of subordination again, along with investing a provisional, abstract model with a god-like power to direct actual human behavior.

Contributing to this elevation of the model over the agency of its objects (that is, the Mods/Stylists themselves) lies the almost compulsory attitude of suspicion and critique that prevails as a badge of seriousness in the academic humanities. The core contention of Theodor Adorno, aesthetic mainstay of the Western-Marxist Frankfurt School, was that the post-war "culture industry" floods the consumer marketplace with superficially distinctive offerings that are all equally meretricious and empty in the final analysis. In his influential thinking (as in Clement Greenberg's conception of Modernism), the achieved coherence and self-sufficiency of the singular work of art served as a last refuge against this onslaught. Having witnessed their cherished Germanic culture descend to the depths of barbarism, followed by the ignominy of being rescued by the crass North American giant, Adorno, along with his collaborator Max Horkheimer and their followers, found consolation in pointing scolding fingers at an alternative villain: Americanized culture as the source, in their blinkered view, of far too many seductive consumer goods and far too few recondite and demanding aesthetic challenges.

By contrast, Terry Atkinson and his Fine-Artz partners opposed the Teenage Netherworld, in its shared inventiveness, to the regime of the singular art object and to all the hierarchical assumptions that went with it, as quoted earlier in this chapter: "the eternal gilt-edged security of ... unique object-worship, as propagated by any connoisseur worth his Côtes-du-Rhône."[26] The cults (as they preferred to call them) could not be described as unwittingly acting out in miniature larger social phenomena beyond their ken; their "sophisticated and selective" leaders were about mastery, perpetually processing, by their own lights, the possible furnishing of life and definitions of self. As everyone needs clothes and shoes and transport, choices can be perfunctory, conformist, or considered as meaningful aspects of a public life proudly aloof from the commercial dictates of the fashion cycle. And the same can be said of the Reggae music that both served as preferred dancing material in the later 1960s for Mods shading to Skins, faithful to the tradition of refined taste in imported black music.[27] Indeed, the most sought-after prize was music so far from commodity status that it was not even for sale: as Nick Knight observes, " Reggae music was not organized like popular commercial music of the big groups and their imitators ... Recordings were put out by small companies [and] white-label, i.e. pre-release, copies of records were the mark of a skin who knew his music."[28]

The initiators of Cultural Studies, careful to preserve their Marxist credentials, effectively dismissed the wisdom and inventiveness of their youth-culture subjects, endorsing ideas at the furthest remove from theirs (did Adorno, for example, bear his vindictive animus toward jazz in spite of its African-American origins or because of them?). While such absence of sympathy may be concomitant to some necessary analytical insights, it comes at significant cost in the sort of fresh information and observation that the non-academic literature of enthusiasm provides.[29] Thus the authors most frequently cited over the course of the present account – Fine-Artz Associates, Paul "Smiler" Anderson, Paolo Hewitt, Paul

Gorman – unabashedly see Mods and their progeny as a good thing, as the creators of a vital but elusive legacy in need of assiduous curating. Through their efforts, there are avenues (with due allowance for the historian's comparative weighing of sources) by which the Absolute Beginners may still be heard.

The writer and curator Lawrence Alloway receives significant credit for having either invented or made current the term Pop Art in the mid-1950s. He had of course figured prominently in the discussions at the Institute of Contemporary Arts held by the so-called Independent Group, where artists, architects, and designers first addressed with curiosity and sympathy the products of postwar, American-driven consumer culture. Unlike the rest of them, as noted in Chapter One, he also adopted and kept up with the trim Modernist's style right into the early 1960s. Reflecting in 1956 on the pedigree of his own contemporary investigations, however, Alloway reached back centuries to reflect that "persistence of visual themes across lines of taste is well known to scholars of the Warburg Institute, of course."[30] The namesake founder of that London library and research institute had looked to the gesticulating mummers of Florentine street processions in the later fifteenth century as lying behind some of the most august rediscoveries of classical prototypes in art. For Aby Warburg, the figure in motion, derived from the direct experience of performers in the guise of ancient deities, constituted the true subject of advanced Florentine mimesis in the 1480s. The core Warburgian idea was that the elusive rituals and props of local cults carried a vernacular charge necessary to the achievements of the most distinguished Renaissance art, a potency that lay beyond any merely bookish catalog of mythological stories and aesthetic canons. To have transferred the word cult to London in the 1960s, as Fine-Artz Associates proposed, made possible a parallel project that seems barely advanced since their disbanding in 1966. For everyone who feels that the British art of the 1960s merits greater stature in relation to its American and continental counterparts, this could be the further quotient of Pop genius essential to the argument.

NOTES

PROLOGUE · THE HIDDEN MOD IN THE NEW ART HISTORY PAGES 1–15

1. For a summary with bibliographic references, see Thomas Crow, "The Practice of Art History in America," *Daedalus* (Spring 2006), 80–3. As will be further addressed below, one study in particular, T. J. Clark, *The Painting of Modern Life: Paris in the Art of Manet and His Followers* (1984), rev. edn (Princeton: Princeton University Press, 1989), became a primary focus of this development. But there were of course some deep antecedents and complex strands to the perceived phenomenon of a New Art History or Social History of Art as it emerged over the 1970s into the 1980s, by no means all of which concerned French modern-life painting. Michael Baxandall's *Painting and Experience in Italy* (Oxford: Oxford University Press, 1972), though brief, broached some crucial modes of empirical analysis by which the habits and decisions of artists might be correlated to various mental skills cultivated by their patrons out of financial or bureaucratic necessity. But it could be argued that his example had more impact on scholars working in later periods than his own. It is sometimes forgotten that the serious specialized study of the nineteenth century was still relatively new in the discipline, so there was less weight of convention to inhibit fresher approaches. This period in France juxtaposed admired innovations in painting with a history of repeated social revolutions, the advent of democracy after 1871, the constant drumbeat of political ferment from below, accelerated urbanization, along with the rapid modernization of industrial technology, mass communication, and the intellectual disciplines. The intellectual and political allure of these phenomena drew into art history scholars with critical social attitudes formed in the 1960s New Left and in the emergent feminist movement. These recruits brought with them much greater skepticism toward the traditional claims of singular artistic genius and enlightened patronage that had been the unstated assumptions of most art-historical inquiry. Linda Nochlin's 1971 essay "Why Have There Been No Great Women Artists?" preceded John Berger's 1972 BBC television series *Ways of Seeing*, with its accompanying book, in synthesizing these tendencies. Griselda Pollock's recent essay, "A Muscular Defence," *Journal of Visual Culture* (August 2012), 127–31, pays tribute to Berger in these terms, while also highlighting the watershed importance of Carol Duncan's "Virility and Domination in Early Twentieth-Century Vanguard Art," which appeared in *Artforum* at the end of 1973. Reinforcing these directions for the discipline were the contributions and examples provided by, again, Nochlin and by Robert Herbert in particular, whose prominence created a path dependence for social art history along their joint trajectory from Gustave Courbet at mid-century to the Impressionist and Neo-Impressionists of the 1870s and 1880s (Meyer Schapiro having provided key precedents for both). Courbet, with whom T. J. Clark also began in his earlier research, was known for his politically radical tendencies. Turning a similar lens on the Impressionists took advantage of the intriguing paradox entailed in addressing scenes of relaxation and pleasure with the arsenal of critical historical analysis attuned to themes of class exploitation and revolt. Thus the moment of coalescence around Parisian modern-life painting as an early focus (but not exclusive arena) for these tendencies.

2. Edmond and Jules de Goncourt, *Mémoires de la vie littéraire*, 18 November 1860, vol. 1 (Paris: Fasquelle, Flammarion, 1956), 835, trans. and quoted in Clark, *Painting of Modern Life*, 34–5.

3. E. Drumont, *Mon vieux Paris* (1897), trans. and quoted in Clark, *Painting of Modern Life*, 213; for an illuminating account of the most popular singers and their music, see Carol Gouspy, "La Représentation des chanteuses au café-concert: les genres de la romancière comique et de la diseuse," *Volume! La Revue des musiques populaires* (2003), http://journals.openedition.org/volume/2218; DOI: 10.4000/volume.2218, accessed 18 January 2020.

4. Richard Wollheim, "Babylon, Babylone," *Encounter*, 8:5 (1962), 29, 25; for a discussion, see Tony Gould, *Inside Outsider: The Life and Times of Colin MacInnes* (London: Allison & Busby, 1983), 140–4.

5. Wollheim, "Babylon," 25.

6. Meyer Schapiro, "The Social Bases of Art," *Proceedings of the First American Artists Congress against War and Fascism* (1936), 31–7.

7. Wollheim, "Babylon," 28.

8. Ibid., 29.

9. Clark, *Painting of Modern Life*, 237.

10. Wollheim and Schapiro had been well acquainted since the mid-1950s; see Wollheim, "Bardic," *London Review of Books* (22 June 1995), 16; on his friendship with MacInnes, along with a rare discussion of "Babylon, Babylone," see Gould, *Inside Outsider*, 141–4.

11. Wollheim, "Babylon," 29.

12. Ibid., 32.

13. Ibid., 30.

14. Miles Davis with Quincy Troupe, *Miles: The Autobiography* (New York: Simon & Schuster, 1989), 238–9; as he reflects: "I would have expected this kind of bullshit about resisting arrest and all back in East St. Louis (before the city went all-black), but not here in New York City, which is supposed to be the slickest, hippest city in the world. But then, again, I was surrounded by white folks and I have learned that when that happens, if you're black, there is no justice. None."

15. Paolo Hewitt and Mark Baxter, *The Fashion of Football: From Best to Beckham, from Mod to Label Slave* (London: Mainstream, 2004), 33.

16. Richard Barnes, *Mods!* (London: Plexus, 1979), 8.

17. On Morgan's style and that of the younger jazz musicians around 1960, see Alphonso D. McClendon, *Fashion and Jazz: Dress, Identity and Subcultural Improvisation* (London: Bloomsbury Academic, 2015), 39, 139–40.

18. Alyn Shipton, *A New History of Jazz* (London: Bloomsbury, 2002), 501. For more on Morgan, see David H. Rosenthal, *Hard Bop: Jazz and Black Music 1955–1965* (Oxford and New York: Oxford University Press, 1992), 7–8, 118–26. The club was the avant-garde venue Slug's, where Sun Ra played on a regular basis.

19. On the myriad complexities of Soho's twentieth-century character and history, see Frank Mort, *Capital Affairs: London and the Making of the Permissive Society* (New Haven and London: Yale University Press, 2010), 197–281 and *passim*.

20. MacInnes, *Absolute Beginners*, 62.

21. Paul "Smiler" Anderson, *Mods: The New Religion* (London: Omnibus, 2013), 19.

22. For an extended discussion of Cultural Studies and the academic study of London youth style, see Ch. 6 below.

23. Clark, *Painting of Modern Life*, 237.

24. See Susan Hiner, "Monsieur Calicot: French Masculinity between Commerce and Honor," *West 86th* (Spring–Summer 2012), 32–60.

25. Clark, *Painting of Modern Life*, 236, 310.

26. Wollheim, "Babylon," 34–5.

27. Wollheim's antennae may have failed him slightly here, as "jiving" would not have been in the Mod vocabulary, and the "Manor House" would probably have been the Wood Green Jazz Club; my thanks to the anonymous reviewer for the Paul Mellon Centre for these corrections.

28. Wollheim, "Babylon," 33.

29. Ibid.

1 · MODERNIST FACES: HARD BOP AND CLEAN DESIGN PAGES 17–43

1. Nik Cohn, *Today There Are No Gentlemen* (1971), repr. in Cohn, *Ball the Wall* (London: Picador, 1989), 28; see also Richard Lester, *Boutique London, A History: King's Road to Carnaby Street* (London: ACC Editions, 2010), 10–13; Jeremy Reed, *The King of Carnaby Street: The Life of John Stephen* (London: Haus Publishing, 2010), 7–12, 18.

2. Cohn, *Ball the Wall*, 28.

3. Malcolm McLaren quoted in Paul Gorman, *The Look: Adventures in Pop and Rock Fashion* (London: Sanctuary Publishing, 2001), 49.

4. See Alex Seago, *Burning the Box of Beautiful Things* (Oxford: Oxford University Press, 1995), 157, 174.

5. Ibid., 183.

6. Gordon House quoted at http://thetown-outside.tumblr.com/post/18749715989/gordon-house-painter-designer-modernist, accessed June 2017, now expired; on Gordon House and the style preferences of the Alloway circle, see David Mellor, *The Sixties Art Scene in London* (London: Phaidon, 1993), who first made this observation about the characteristic dress sense of the Place/Situation principals.

7. Jeff Dexter, quoted in Paul "Smiler" Anderson, *Mods: The New Religion: The Style and Music of the 1960s* (London: Omnibus, 2013), 28–9.

8. On the Beatles' reputation as "untrustworthy and unmanageable," see Jon Savage, *1966: The Year the Decade Exploded* (London: Faber & Faber, 2016), 296.

9. John Lennon, interviewed by Leonard Gross, "A Shorn Beatle Tries It on His Own," *Look* (13 December 1966).

10. Michael Chalk, "Arcade Fever," *Ark*, 20 (Autumn 1957), 8.

11. Lawrence Alloway, "The Arts and the Mass Media," *Architectural Design and Construction* (February 1958), 84–5.

12. See Nigel Whitely, *Lawrence Alloway: Art and Pluralism* (Liverpool: Liverpool University Press, 2012) 14–15, 62–71; also Victoria Walsh, "Lawrence Alloway: Pedagogy, Practice, and the Recognition of Audiences," in Courtney J. Martin et al., eds., *Lawrence Alloway: Critic and Curator* (Los Angeles: Getty Research Institute, 2015), 11–24.

13. Reyner Banham, "Alloway and After," *Architect's Journal* (26 December 1957), 941.

14. Lawrence Alloway, "English and International Art," *Art International* 1: 9–10 (1957), 72.

15. See Whitely, *Alloway*, 115–17.

16. Coleman described the principle of the installation in the ephemeral leaflet that served as a guide for visitors, reproduced at https://situationnisteblog.com/2016/01/21/ralph-rumney-ica-place-guide-to-place-1958–59, accessed January 2020: "24 canvases were fixed back to back to make 12 double-sided pictures which were on the gallery floor at 45 degrees to the walls and at

90° to each other ... This gave four directions in which the pictures faced, three of which taken, one by each painter, with the fourth side shared." See Mellor, *Sixties Art Scene*, 62–5; Eric de Chassey, "Place: A Constructed Abstract Situation in the Urban Cultural Continuum of the 1960s," *October* (Spring 2007), 24–52; Whitely, *Alloway*, 138–40.

17. Ralph Rumney, *The Consul: Conversations with Gérard Berréby*, trans. Malcom Imrie (San Francisco: City Lights, 2002), 63–5; Jean-Michel Mension, *The Tribe*, trans. Donald Nicholson-Smith (San Francisco: City Lights, 2001) offers the most detailed insider's account; see also for first-hand testimony Gianni Menichetti, *Vali Meyers: A Memoir* (Fresno, CA: Golda Foundation, 2006), 18–32. In the extensive literature on the Situationists, two synthetic interpretations pay particular attention to the "tribe," the Letttrists, and their perpetual state of intoxication: McKenzie Wark, *The Beach beneath the Street: The Everyday Life and Glorious Times of the Situationist International* (London: Verso, 2011), 9–12; Lori Waxman, *Keep Walking Intently: The Ambulatory Art of the Surrealists, the Situationist International, and Fluxus* (Berlin: Sternberg, 2017), 118–23.

18. Patti Smith, "Photos: Revisiting Love on the Left Bank," *Vanity Fair* (April 2011), www.vanityfair.com/culture/2011/04/love-on-the-left-bank-patti-smith-201104, accessed July 2018.

19. Mension, *The Tribe*, 43.

20. Ibid., 89–91.

21. See Guy Atkins, *Asger Jorn 1954–1964: The Crucial Years* (London: Lund Humphries, 1977), 56–9.

22. For Rumney's account of the creation of the Situationist International, see Rumney, *The Consul*, 36–9.

23. See *Internationale Situationiste*, 1 (June 1958), 28.

24. Guy Debord, "Definitions," in ibid., trans. in Ken Knabb, ed., *Situationist International Anthology* (Berkeley, CA: Bureau of Public Secrets, 2006), 114.

25. It is likely that Rumney had been tapped to fill out the trio for more reasons than his Situationist pedigree alone. He had long been active around the ICA, even venturing at the age of eighteen to lecture the IG on the destructive effects of modernist architectural precepts on the rebuilding of bomb-ravaged London ("No one listened to me," he recalled: *The Consul*, 18–19, 30). By the later 1950s, already selling paintings in Mayfair, he enjoyed a good relationship with the ICA president Roland Penrose, so his inclusion would have made sense on an institutional level. He had even displayed a certain Mod inclination when living and showing in Milan, habitually wearing a dark raincoat and bowler hat, carrying a rolled umbrella: as he explained, "this seemed to me more intelligent than going around in rags with long hair" (ibid., 43).

26. Alloway, "Making a Scene," *Art News and Review* (26 September 1959), 2–3.

27. Ibid., 3; Alloway had reason to be sensitive on the subject, given how much the esoteric concept of "constructed situation," along with a Debordian suspicion of individuated works of art, had guided the brief for *Place*. He had gone further and joined Rumney in Venice during the summer of 1958 just at the time the latter was realizing his investigation into the "psychogeography" of Venice, photographing the movements of a friend, the Beat poet Alan Ansen (called "A"), through the less traveled parts of the city, then setting the images alongside his comments in a graphic parody of the romantic *fotoromanzo* popular in Italy. The interpolated texts begin with Debord's definition of the term ("the study of the exact effects of geographic environment, controlled or otherwise, on the affective behaviour of individuals": quoted in "The Leaning Tower of Venice," *Ark* 24 [1959], double-page foldout). In a panel near the conclusion, there appears a full-length portrait of Alloway in Venice, captioned "Dover Street playboy," after the address of the ICA. Robyn Denny also turned up in Venice that summer and offered to arrange for its publication in *Ark* in three successive issues (ibid., nos. 24–6) in 1959 and 1960. See Royal College of Art, Critical Writing in Art & Design Programme, *Ark: Words and Images from the Royal College of Art Magazine 1950–1978* (London: Royal College of Art, 2014), 104–9.

28. Coleman, *Place* program (1959).

29. As is well known, Clark later became a member of the Situationists, *c.*1966, then like Rumney suffered exclusion after a relatively short period. He similarly remained an exponent of Debord's ideas and invokes the latter's concept of the Spectacle at the outset of his *The Painting of Modern Life: Paris in the Art of Manet and His Followers*, rev. edn (Princeton: Princeton University Press, 1984), 9–10.

30. Rumney, quoted in Robert Kudielka, ed., *Robyn Denny*, exh. cat. (London: Tate Gallery, 1973), 27.

31. Review of *Place* in *The Observer*, September 1959, quoted in Seago, *Burning the Box*, 121.

32. Wollheim, "Babylon," 26.

33. Ibid., 31.

2 · GALLERY ONE AND THE ABSOLUTE BEGINNER PAGES 45–63

1. John Kasmin, personal communication (January 2017); I am grateful to John Kasmin for his generous conversation; Kasmin, unpublished extract of oral history, 2016, *Voices of Art*, British Library, courtesy of Cathy Courtney.

2. Kasmin, oral history, *Voices of Art*.

3. Kasmin, quoted in Val Williams, *Ida Kar Photographer 1908–1974* (London: Virago, 1989), 28.

4. Robyn Denny, "On showing at Victor Musgrave's Gallery One," 2014, *Voices of Art*, British Library, https://www.bl.uk/collection-items/robyn-denny-on-showing-at-victor-musgraves-gallery-one, accessed June 2019.

5. Kasmin, oral history, *Voices of Art*.

6. Ibid.

7. Colin MacInnes, "City after Dark," *Twentieth Century* (December 1957), quoted in Tony Gould, *Inside Outsider: The Life and Times of Colin MacInnes* (London: Allison & Busby, 1983), 113.

8. Kasmin, oral history, *Voices of Art*.

9. Ibid.

10. Terry Taylor, *Baron's Court, All Change: Beats, Bums and Bohemians* (London: New London Editions, 1961; 2011), 76, 135, 62: "I'm sure half of them can't tell the difference between a trumpet and a trombone, and go there for a change from the Palais. There are exceptions, of course, and some of the cats do go there to listen to the music, but we're definitely in the minority. The others congregate at the Kradle just to show each other how sharp they dress, it's a sort of weekly Easter Parade."

11. Richard Wollheim, "Babylon, Babylone," *Encounter*, 8:5 (1962), 30; the Casino cinema in Old Compton Street then specialized in extended runs of American Cinerama spectaculars; the film on display in the background is *Search for Paradise*, a scenic Himalayan documentary that played between March and November 1961: http://www.incinerama.com/ctcasino.htm, accessed June 2019.

12. Kasmin quoted in Christopher Simon Sykes, *David Hockney: A Rake's Progress: The Biography, 1937–1975* (New York and London: Doubleday, 2011), 88.

13. For comment on the character of the Fabulous Hoplite, see Richard Hornsey, *The Spiv and the Architect: Unruly Life in Postwar London* (Minneapolis and London: University of Minnesota Press, 2010), 255–8.

14. Kasmin, quoted in Sykes, *David Hockney*, 89.

15. "Top Drawer: Design by Music," *Print Review*, 15:11 (March–April 1961), 14.

16. For the definitive biographical account of Barrie Bates/Billy Apple, see Christina

Barton, *Billy Apple: Life/Work* (Auckland University Press, forthcoming); I have drawn the details of his exhibiting career, here and in the following chapter, from Barton's exemplary research and synthesis; and I owe a great debt of thanks to Billy Apple and Mary Morrison for their generous conversation in Auckland (March 2017).

17. For this quotation from Bates and much insight, see Anthony Byrt, *RCA '62: Sex, Self, and the Year that Transformed British Art* (Auckland University Press, forthcoming 2020).

18. Terry Atkinson, unpublished typescript, n.d., courtesy of the author.

3 · APPLE ARRIVES AS HOCKNEY TAKES OFF PAGES 65–85

1. Alastair Sooke, "'David Hockney was usually in emotional turmoil', John Kasmin, the dealer who discovered the artist David Hockney in the Sixties, tells Alastair Sooke about their adventures," *Daily Telegraph* (31 August 2013).

2. See Lisa Tickner, "The Kasmin Gallery," *Oxford Art Journal* (June 2007), 233–68; also "Playing it by Ear: Kasmin in the 1960s," 2018, *Voices of Art*, British Library, www.bl.uk/voices-of-art/articles/lisa-tickner-playing-it-by-ear-kasmin-in-the-1960s, accessed June 2019.

3. Lawrence Rubin to John Kasmin, 4 June 1962, John Kasmin papers, Getty Research Institute, Los Angeles, Special Collections, box 24 f3.

4. Kasmin to Kenneth Noland, n.d., Kasmin papers, box 24 f3.

5. Kasmin, typescript list and undated letter [1962–3] to Lawrence Rubin, Kasmin papers, box 26 f1.

6. See Clement Greenberg, "Modernist Painting" (1960), in *Clement Greenberg: The Collected Essays and Criticism*, ed. John O'Brian (Chicago: University of Chicago Press, 1993), vol. 4, 86–9. See also "After Abstract Expressionism," in ibid., 131.

7. Clement Greenberg, *Art and Culture: Critical Essays* (Boston, MA: Beacon Press, 1961).

8. Nikos Stangos, ed., *Hockney by Hockney: My Early Years* (London and New York: Thames and Hudson, 1988), 100.

9. See Sykes, *David Hockney*, 74–5; also Richard Meyer, "'Los Angeles Meant Boys': David Hockney, Bob Mizer, and the Lure of Physique Photography," in Andrew Perchuk et al., eds., *Pacific Standard Time: Los Angeles Art 1945–1980* (Los Angeles: Getty Research Institute, 2011), 183–5. Meyer points out that the details of the apron and bucket are actually derived from a particular 1963 *Physique Pictorial* spread of still photographs from a short film titled *Cruel Stepbrothers*, in which one put-upon character is made to do all the domestic chores in an all-male household. Dian Hanson, *Bob's World: The Life and Boys of AMG's Bob Mizer* (Cologne: Taschen, 2009), includes an extensive range of photographs, many in color, too explicit for publication in *Physique Pictorial*; see also Cécile Whiting, *Pop L.A.: Art and the City in the 1960s* (Berkeley and Los Angeles: University of California Press, 2008), 120–33.

10. See Elaine Woo, "Betty Freeman dies at 87; Art Philanthropist and Photographer," *Los Angeles Times* (6 January 2009).

11. Betty Freeman, interview with Hunter Drohojowska-Philp (4 July 2006), quoted in Drohojowska-Philp, *Rebels in Paradise: The Los Angeles Art Scene and the 1960s* (New York: Henry Holt, 2011), 122.

12. Hockney, 2 letters to Kasmin, n.d. [1967], Kasmin papers, box 24 f3.

13. On Hockney's subsequent use of fluid paint application, see Ian Alteveer, "Flatness, Fullness, Wetness: Water and Abstraction in Hockney's First Decade," in Chris Stevens and Andrew Wilson, eds., *David Hockney*, exh. cat. (London: Tate, 2017), 222–9.

14. Hockney's statement appears as the epigraph to Hanson, *Bob's World*, 5.

15. Hockney to Kasmin, 26 March 1968, Kasmin papers, box 24 f3.

16. For a detailed, illuminating account of Billy Apple's New York career, see Christina Barton, *Billy Apple: Life/Work* (Auckland University Press, forthcoming).

4 · PAINTING SENSATIONS: PAULINE BOTY AND BRIDGET RILEY PAGES 87–113

1. I am profoundly grateful to both Sue Tate and Kalliopi Minioudaki for their deep research and insight into Boty's career; see Sue Tate, *Pauline Boty: Pop Artist and Woman*, exh. cat. (Wolverhampton Art Gallery, 2013); Minioudaki's research is sketched in "Pop's Ladies and Bad Girls," in Sid Sachs and Kalliopi Minioudaki, eds., *Seductive Subversion: Women Pop Artists 1958–1968* (New York and London: Abbeville Press, 2010), 113–21. David Alan Mellor's pioneering exposition can be found in his *The Sixties Art Scene in London* (London: Phaidon, 1993), 136.

2. See Ali Smith, *Autumn* (London: Hamish Hamilton, 2016), 72–6: "The background is rich dark blue, Daniel said. A blue much darker than sky. On top of the dark blue, in the middle of the picture, there's a shape made of pale paper that looks like a round full moon. On top of the moon, bigger than the moon, there's a cut-out black and white lady wearing a swimsuit, cut from a newspaper or a fashion magazine. And next to her, as if she's leaning against it, there's a giant human hand. And the giant hand is holding inside it a tiny hand, a baby's hand. More truthfully, the baby's hand is also holding the big hand, holding it by its thumb. Below all this, there's a stylized picture of a woman's face, the same face repeated several times, but with a different coloured curl of real hair hanging over its nose each time ... "; the listening child grows into an art-history postgraduate who undertakes, against the condescending contempt of her male supervisor, a dissertation on Boty.

3. On Terry Taylor's role in the emergent British counterculture, see Stewart Home, "Introduction," in Terry Taylor, *Baron's Court, All Change: Beats, Bums and Bohemians* (London: New London Editions, 1961; 2011), 8–10.

4. See Tate, *Pauline Boty*, 55–6, 70.

5. Pauline Boty, "Teenage Heroes," *The Public Ear* (BBC, recorded 11 November, transmitted 17 November 1963); quoted in the unpublished study and biography by Adam Smith, "Pauline Boty – First Lady of British Pop" (downloadable pdf at www.writing-room.com, accessed September 2012).

6. Tate, *Pauline Boty*, 72.

7. Vicki Wickham quoted in Jon Savage, *1966: The Year the Decade Exploded* (London: Faber and Faber, 2015), 156.

8. For an illuminating discussion of the collage-based set design for *Ready Steady Go!*, see Paul "Smiler" Anderson, *Mod Art: Music and Graphics, Fashion and Art, Mod Design from the 1950s to 1990s* (London: Omnibus Press, 2018), 50–61.

9. Richard Mabey, *The Pop Process* (London: Hutchinson Educational, 1969), 93.

10. Barbara Hulanicki, *From A to Biba: The Autobiography of Barbara Hulanicki* (London: V&A Publications, 2007), 79.

11. See Mabey's illuminating, post-MacInnes reflection on 1960s Mod fashion, *Pop Process*, 80–5; also Angela McRobbie and Jenny Garber, "Girls and Subcultures: An Exploration," in Stuart Hall and Tony Jefferson, eds., *Resistance through Rituals: Youth Subcultures in Post-War Britain* (London: Hutchinson, 1976), 217–18.

12. Hulanicki, *From A to Biba*, 79.

13. See Smith, "Pauline Boty": "In January or February 1963 Joseph Janni and John Schlesinger shortlisted Pauline to play Liz in the film version of *Billy Liar*. Tom Courtenay ... became a frequent visitor to Addison Road to coach Pauline for her big break ... Topsy

Jane landed the part, but fell ill when shooting began in March. Janni and Schlesinger replaced her with Julie Christie, sealing Pauline's might-have-been. Christie's eleven minutes in *Billy Liar* which start with Schlesinger's unforgettable zoom-tracking shot led to an Oscar for best actress in Janni and Schlesinger's next film *Darling* and the role in *Dr Zhivago* which made Christie an international star. Pauline's friends could only share her disappointment. They all thought it rather a cheek the way Christie dressed as Pauline in *Billy Liar*." Smith (91–106) also provides a thorough account of *Pop Goes the Easel!*

14. *The Guardian*, 1965, quoted in the valuable study by Frances Follin, *Embodied Vision: Bridget Riley, Op Art and the Sixties* (London: Thames & Hudson, 2004), 119.

15. See Paul Moorehouse, *Bridget Riley, A Very Very Person: The Early Years* (London: Ridinghouse, 2019), 219–28.

16. For a paraphrase of Riley's account of the process, see ibid., 210–14.

17. Lawrence Alloway, *West Coast Hard-Edge*, exh. cat. (London: Institute of Contemporary Arts, 1960), n.p.

18. See Simon Rycroft, *Swinging City: A Cultural Geography of London 1950–1974* (Farnham: Ashgate, 2011), 58–60.

19. David Sylvester, "Fences," *New Statesman* (25 May 1962), 770.

20. See Moorehouse, *Bridget Riley*, 227–8.

21. "Painters who explore the mechanics of vision," *The Times* (1 October 1963), quoted in Follin, *Embodied Visions*, 153.

22. Norbert Lynton, "Ups and Downs," *New Statesman* (1 July 1963), 370.

23. Bridget Riley quoted in Robert Kudielka, ed., *The Eye's Mind: Bridget Riley Collected Writings 1965–1999* (London: Thames & Hudson, 1999), 30; for further serious discussion of this issue in the Riley literature, see Follin, *Embodied Vision*, 70–83.

24. Rycroft, *Swinging City*, 60.

25. Bridget Riley, 1967 interview with David Sylvester, reprinted in Sylvester, *London Recordings* (London: Chatto and Windus, 2003), 86.

5 · HIPPY HIPPY SHAKE: SCULPTURE THROUGH THE COUNTERCULTURE
PAGES 115–141

1. Magazine poll, 1967, cited in Frances Follin, *Embodied Visions: Bridget Riley, Op Art and the Sixties* (London: Thames & Hudson, 2004), 121.

2. The chief problem with the term "counterculture," as introduced here, is that it did not come into wide use until the 1969 publication of Theodore Roszak's *The Making of a Counter Culture: Reflections on the Technocratic Society and Its Youthful Opposition* (Garden City, NY: Anchor Books). The term "hippie," coincident with the phenomena in question, comes in handy but carries more restrictive connotations.

3. The polemic of Warren Hinckle, the editor of *Ramparts*, encapsulated the argument at the moment: "The Hippie: A Social History," *Ramparts* (March 1967), 5–26. Synthetic historical literature on the counterculture is curiously thin, where one might expect a half-dozen large tomes to exist, given the time that has passed and the evident historical importance of the phenomenon. The numerous art historians specializing in the 1960s appear, for the most part, to have a pronounced aversion to the topic. Historians and sociologists have been prolific on the New Left and the anti-war movement, but almost as incurious about the mystical, psychedelic, aesthetic, and hedonistic pursuits of the same period. Tom Wolfe's *Electric Kool Aid Acid Test* (New York: Farrar Straus and Giroux, 1968), despite its restricted focus on Ken Kesey's Merry Prankster entourage and lack of documentary apparatus detailing his sources, remains the best-researched overview. It is particularly insightful on the tensions and limited overlap between hippie culture and the New Left. Simon Rycroft's approach to alternative postwar London, *Swinging City: A Cultural Geography of London 1950–1974* (Farnham: Ashgate, 2011) takes a different tack from the present account. His concentration on the underground press, both in London and internationally, has the effect of amalgamating the two strands, as editors of the period sought to address both varieties of dissidence (for reasons of enhanced circulation, if nothing else). As he observes (134–5), even *Oz* under its editor Richard Neville, the journal most committed to the ethos of ecstatic personal liberation, found room for regular reports from Left activists. Rycroft notes, however, that the design of the pages, intended to confound legibility with unpredictably free-form layouts and strident color contrasts, frustrated leftist writers concerned with effective communication.

4. See Richard Lester, *Boutique London, A History: King's Road to Carnaby Street* (Woodbridge, Suffolk: ACC Editions, 2010), 52–9, 79–81; Paul Howard, *I Read the News Today, Oh Boy* (London: Picador, 2016), 279–83.

5. See the Klossowski entry on the invaluable site *Dandy in Aspic*, http://dandyinaspic.blogspot.com/2012/03/prince-stash-klossowski-de-rola-1960s.html, accessed November 2018.

6. Stephen Gardiner, *London Magazine* (October 1966), quoted in Lester, *Boutique London*, 64.

7. Salman Rushdie, quoted in Paul Gorman, *The Look: Adventures in Pop & Rock Fashion* (London: Sanctuary, 2001), 72–4; Gorman, 64–74, provides the most complete history of Granny's boutique.

8. See Mel Gooding, *Bruce McLean* (London: Phaidon Press, 1990), 12–14; Charles Harrison, "Sculpture's Recent Past," in Harrison, *Since 1950: Art and Its Criticism* (New Haven and London: Yale University Press, 2009), 7–24.

9. Bruce McLean quoted in Harrison, "Sculpture's Recent Past," 17.

10. Herbert Read, "Introduction," *Sculpture: Open-Air Exhibition of Contemporary British and American Works* (London County Council, Battersea Park, 1963); cited in Harrison, "Sculpture's Recent Past," 4.

11. See "Reflections on Sculpture: A commentary by Tim Scott on notes by William Tucker," *Tim Scott: Sculpture 1961–67*, Whitechapel Gallery, 1967, n.p.

12. Edward Lucie-Smith, "An Interview with Clement Greenberg," *Studio International* (January 1968), 117.

13. Neville Wallis, "The New Generation," *The Spectator* (19 March 1965), 9.

14. Charles Harrison, "Some Recent Sculpture in Britain," *Studio International* (January 1969), 20.

15. David Annesley, "Anthony Caro's Work: A Symposium by Four Sculptors," *Studio International* (January 1969), 18.

16. Clement Greenberg to John Kasmin, 1965, John Kasmin papers, Getty Research Institute, Los Angeles, Special Collections, box 26 f3.

17. Harrison, "Some Recent Sculpture in Britain," 30; see also Jo Applin, "*There's a Sculpture on My Shoulder*: Bruce McLean and the Anxiety of Influence," *Sculpture Journal* 17:2 (Winter 2008), 102–15.

18. Harrison, "Some Recent Sculpture in Britain," 28.

19. Ibid.

20. Richard Long, quoted in Nicholas Wroe, "No Stone Unturned," *The Guardian* (28 June 2003).

21. British and London-based artists were quickest in responding to the 14-song acetate of Dylan demo songs (from the so-called Basement Tapes) distributed by his publisher, Dwarf Music, in January 1968. British cover versions included *Quinn the Eskimo* by Manfred Mann, *This Wheel's on Fire* by Julie Driscoll with Brian Auger and the Trinity, *Tears of Rage* by the expatriate Londoner Jimi Hendrix, *I Shall be Released* by Joe Cocker, and *Million Dollar Bash* by Fairport Convention. The last group also had strong affinities to the romance of ancient and medieval Britain analyzed by Rycroft, *Swinging City*, 139.

22. See Harald Szeemann, "Zur Austellung," in Szeemann, ed., *Live in Your Head: When Attitudes Become Form, Works – Concepts – Processes – Situations – Information*, exh. cat. (Bern: Kunsthalle Bern, 1969), n.p.; repr. in English as "About the Exhibition," in Christian Rattemeyer, ed., *Exhibiting the New Art: "Op Losse Schroeven" and "When Attitudes Become Form" 1969* (London: Afterall, 2010), 192–3.

23. Harald Szeemann interviewed by Marlène Bélos and André Gazut, *L'Attitude de l'Artiste*, https://www.rts.ch/archives/tv/culture/en-marge/3436012-l-attitude-de-l-artiste.html, last accessed June 2020; quoted remarks occur between 15'40" and 16'50".

24. For a thorough, important discussion of McLean's contributions to *Live in Your Head*, see Applin, "*There's a Sculpture on My Shoulder*," 102–15.

25. Harrison, "Against Precedents," Introduction to *Live in Your Head: When Attitudes Become Form* (London: Institute of Contemporary Arts, 1969), repr. in Rattemeyer, *Exhibiting the New Art*, 195.

6 · THE GREAT LOST LOOK: BEYOND CULTURAL STUDIES PAGES 143–163

1. Peter Barnsley and Don McCullin, "Faces without Shadows," *Town* (September 1962).

2. Mark Feld to Jeff Dexter, quoted in Paul "Smiler" Anderson, *Mods: The New Religion: The Style and Music of the 1960s* (London: Omnibus, 2013), 25–6.

3. See Oliver Peterson Gilbert, "Pop Art Redefined: British Pop Arts of the 1960s: Towards a Social and Institutional History," D.Phil. diss., University of Southampton (2015), 196; Peterson Gilbert's account is based in part on his interviews with Roger Jeffs and John Bowstead.

4. Fine-Artz Associates, "Fine-Artz?: What or Who are the 'Fine-Artz'?" *Ark* 35 (Spring 1964), 40; the importance of the Fine-Artz contributions to *Ark* was signaled by Alex Seago, *Burning the Box of Beautiful Things: The Development of a Postmodern Sensibility* (Oxford: Oxford University Press, 1995), 18, 45, 207–8.

5. On this episode, see Peterson Gilbert, "Pop Art Redefined," 203–7.

6. Fine-Artz Associates, "What or Who are the 'Fine Artz'?" 39.

7. Fine-Artz Associates effectively disbanded in disagreements over a 1966 multimedia, time-based piece performed at Aston University, Birmingham, under the title *Miss Misty and the Tri-cool Data*, mounted with assistance from the Hornsey College Light/ Sound Workshop. Atkinson, the most disaffected by this direction, accused the work of having "ossified into a statuesque fetish of a projected populist technoprogress." Moving to a teaching position at Coventry College of Art, he joined the student Michael Baldwin and his old St. Martin's allies Hurrell and Bainbridge to found a new and enduring collective, Art & Language; see Peterson Gilbert, "Pop Art Redefined," 207.

8. Fine-Artz Associates, "The Fine-Artz View of Teenage Cults," *Ark* 36 (Summer 1964), 40.

9. Jonathan Miller, "à la Mod," *New Statesman* (29 May 1964), 853.

10. Fine-Artz Associates, "Fine-Artz View of Teenage Cults," 44; for a more extended, well-illustrated account of Grimstead, see Paul "Smiler" Anderson, *Mod Art: Music and Graphics, Fashion and Art, Mod Design from the 1950s to 1990s* (London: Omnibus Press, 2018), 62–73.

11. Mickey Tenner, quoted in Anderson, *Mods: The New Religion*, 31.

12. Peter Blake, who designed the cover with his wife, Jann Haworth, showed in Fraser's gallery.

13. Paolo Hewitt, *The Soul Stylists: Six Decades of Modernism – from Mods to Casuals* (London: Mainstream, 2000), 75.

14. Ibid., 77.

15. Kevin Rowland quoted in Paul Gorman, *The Look: Adventures in Rock and Pop Fashion* (London: Adelita, 2006), 92.

16. "No Love from Johnny," *Daily Mirror* (3 September 1969).

17. Rowland in Gorman, *The Look*, 93.

18. Ian Penman, "Even If You Have to Starve (review of Richard Weight, *Mods*)," *London Review of Books* (29 August 2014), https://www.lrb.co.uk/the-paper/v35/n16/ian-penman/even-if-you-have-to-starve, accessed December 2019.

19. Richard Wollheim, "Babylon, Babylone," *Encounter*, 8:5 (1962), 33.

20. See Thomas Crow, "Substance over Style: Phil Cohen's Rethinking the Youth Question," *ArtForum* (October 1997), 15–16.

21. Phil Cohen, "Subcultural Conflict and Working Class Community," in Cohen, *Rethinking the Youth Question* (Durham, NC: Duke University Press, 1999), 58.

22. Dick Hebdige, "The Meaning of Mod," in Stuart Hall and Tony Jefferson, eds., *Resistance through Rituals: Youth Subcultures in Post-War Britain* (London: Hutchinson, 1976), 91.

23. Ibid., 89.

24. Cohen, "Subcultural Conflict," 59.

25. Ibid., 57.

26. Fine-Artz Associates, "What or Who are 'Fine Artz'?," 39.

27. For an early recognition of this affinity, see Dick Hebdige, "Reggae, Rastas & Rudies," in Hall and Jefferson, *Resistance through Rituals*, 148–50.

28. Nick Knight, *Skinhead* (London: Omnibus, 1982), 14.

29. One of the founding cohort at the Birmingham Centre in the 1970s, John Clarke, later offered (*New Times and Old Enemies: Essays on Cultural Studies and America* [London: HarperCollins, 1991, 77–86]) a thorough examination of the difficulties entailed in Frankfurt-School-style pessimism over the cultural dominance of the commodity form in the face of the relative autonomy of the "subcultural" articulation of contrary identities via discriminating consumer choices. But he concludes by pulling back from the self-elected style cults, firstly on the grounds that they affirm "that view of capitalism which capitalism would most like us to see: the richness of the marketplace and the freely choosing consumer," and secondly that ascribing to them any exceptional value entails a romantic failure to acknowledge and include the mass of consumers, "pushing prams trying to keep to the week's budget," who are thereby excluded from most meaningful choices. He thus maintains his analysis on an almost global level, from which the style cultists become effectively invisible.

Angela McRobbie, another Birmingham Centre pioneer, has pointed out a more recent indignity visited on the model of subcultural semiotics (*Be Creative* [Cambridge: Polity, 2006], 7–8): "One additional and unanticipated consequence of the idea of 'cultural studies' has been the immense commercial value emerging out of 'subcultural theory'. The pathway here could be traced through the idea of bricolage, 'cut ups' and the subversion of style, as theorized by Hebdige, finding its way out of the classroom or seminar room of the art school into the hands of the fashion designers, the graphic designers and communications graduates able to translate the ideas of the street and of 'authentic' working-class culture or even of revolt into the very stuff of collections, or for the 'edgy' visual image of global labels such as Dior or YSL."

30. Lawrence Alloway, "The Robot and the Arts," *Art News and Review* (1 September 1956), 1.

PHOTOGRAPH CREDITS

Musée des Beaux-Arts, Lyon / Bridgeman Images: 1; National Gallery of Art, Washington, Ailsa Mellon Bruce Collection: 2; Metropolitan Museum of Art, New York, Mr. and Mrs. Henry Ittleson Jr. Purchase Fund, 1959: 3; The Art Institute of Chicago, Bequest of Brooks McCormick: 4; A. F. Archive / Alamy Stock Photo: 5; Records / Alamy Stock Photo: 6; Francis Wolff: 7; Metropolitan Museum of Art, New York, Rogers Fund, 1970: 8; Terence Spencer / The LIFE Images Collection / Getty Images: 9, 94; Gordon Moore / The Royal College of Art: 10; Trinity Mirror / Mirrorpix / Alamy Stock Photo: 12a, 77; Mirrorpix / Mirrorpix via Getty Images: 12b; Daily Mirror / Mirrorpix / Getty Images: 12c, 133; Ken Harding / Stringer / Getty Images: 15; The Estate of Robyn Denny. All Rights Reserved, DACS 2020: 17, 23; Mark and Colleen Hayward / Redferns / Getty Images: 18; Royal College of Art, London: 19, 43, 122, 123, 124, 125, 126; Richard Smith Foundation. All Rights Reserved, DACS 2020: 20, 21; Barratt's Photo Press Ltd: 22; John Deakin / John Deakin Archive / Bridgeman Images: 26; Nederlands Fotomuseum / Ed van der Elsken: 27, 28; Photo by David McLane / NY Daily News Archive via Getty Images: 29; National Portrait Gallery, London: 32, 35, 36, 37, 38, 39, 89, 90; Yves Klein c/o ADAGP, Paris: 33; British Film Institute Archive, London / Burt Hyams: 34; David Hockney. Photo: Paul Oszvald. Collection Hamburger Kunsthalle: 40; Billy Apple: 41, 42, 44, 46, 49, 50, 51, 52; Haspel, New Orleans: 45; Tony Evans / Timelapse Library Ltd: 47; Armstrong Jones: 48, 53; David Hockney. Photo: Fabrice Gibert: 55, 57; David Hockney / Photo: Yale Center for British Art, Paul Mellon Fund: 56; David Hockney. Photo: Richard Schmidt: 58, 59, 65; Courtesy of John Kasmin: 60; J. Paul Getty Trust. Getty Research Institute, Los Angeles: 61, 62, 63, 117, 118; Jim Bartsch: 64; David Hockney / Photo: Tate: 66; BBC TV: 67; Courtesy of the Pauline Boty Estate, courtesy of Whitford Fine Art: 68, 69, 70, 71, 72; Lewis Morley Archive: 73; Pictorial Press Ltd Photo Tony Gale: 75; David Redfern / Getty Images: 76; Pictorial Press Ltd / Alamy Stock Photo: 78; PictureLux / The Hollywood Archive / Alamy Stock Photo: 79; Smithsonian Institution, Washington DC, Samuel J. Wagstaff papers 1932–1985, Archives of American Art: 81; Bridget Riley 2020. All rights reserved. Courtesy the artist and David Zwirner: 82, 85, 86, 88; Ellsworth Kelly: 84; The Bert Stern Trust: 91; The Irving Penn Foundation: 92; George Freston / Stringer / Getty Images: 93; Hapshash and the Coloured Coat / Bridgeman Images: 95, 109; David Graves / Shutterstock: 96; Harold Chapman / TopFoto: 97; Estate of Keith Morris / Redferns / Getty Images: 98; Los Angeles County Museum of Art: 99; Bruce McLean. All rights reserved, DACS 2020: 100, 104, 105, 114, 115; Philip King. All rights reserved, DACS / Photo: Tate: 101, 103; Tim Scott / Photo: Tate: 102; David Annesley / Photo: Tate: 106, 108; Peter Max: 110; The Estate of Barry Flanagan, courtesy Plubronze / Photo: Tate: 111, 112; The Estate of Barry Flanagan, courtesy Plubronze / Photo: Bridgeman Images: 113; Richard Long. All rights reserved, DACS, 2020: 116; Tate: 119; Don McCullin / Contact Press Images: 120, 121; Val Wilmer / Redferns / Getty Images: 127; ScreenProd / Photononstop / Alamy Stock Photo: 128; Robert Whitaker / Getty Images: 129; MGN Limited: 132

INDEX

NOTE: Page numbers in **bold** refer to illustrations; page numbers followed by *n* and a number refer to information in a note.